The Archaeological and Linguistic
Reconstruction of African History

The Archaeological and Linguistic Reconstruction of African History

Edited by
Christopher Ehret and
Merrick Posnansky

UNIVERSITY OF CALIFORNIA PRESS
Berkeley   Los Angeles   London

UNIVERSITY OF CALIFORNIA PRESS
Berkeley and Los Angeles, California

UNIVERSITY OF CALIFORNIA PRESS, LTD.
London, England

Library of Congress Cataloging in Publication Data
Main entry under title:

The Archaeological and linguistic reconstruction of
   African History.

   Includes revised papers presented at a conference at
the University of California, Los Angeles, held
in June 1979.
   Includes bibliographical references and index.
   1. Linguistic paleontology—Africa—Congresses.
2. Man, Prehistoric—Africa—Congresses.   3. Africa—
Antiquities—Congresses.   4. African languages—History—
Congresses.   I. Ehret, Christopher.   II. Posnansky, Merrick.
P35.5.A35A7   1983   417'.7'096   82-8431
ISBN 0-520-04593-9   AACR2

PRINTED IN THE UNITED STATES OF AMERICA

1   2   3   4   5   6   7   8   9

Contents

MAPS

Acknowledgments

WE WISH TO EXPRESS our deep thanks to the African Studies Center of the University of California, Los Angeles, and to its director, Professor Michael Lofchie, whose support made this volume possible. The funding for an initial conference on the archaeological and linguistic reconstruction of African history, held at UCLA in June 1979, was provided by the center, and center personnel handled the arrangements and took care of the clerical needs of the conference. We are especially grateful to Maxine Driggers, presently the graduate adviser of the center, who was a flawless overseer of these activities. The papers presented at the conference constitute in their revised forms the core portions of this book. We also want to thank all the contributors for their responsiveness to the requirements of the editorial process; they helped to make the task a rewarding one.

C. E.
M. P.

Los Angeles, December 1981

Contributors

William Y. Adams, Department of Anthropology, University of Kentucky

Stanley H. Ambrose, Department of Anthropology, University of California, Berkeley

D. P. Collett, Cambridge University

Nicholas David, Department of Archaeology, University of Calgary

Christopher Ehret, Department of History, University of California, Los Angeles

M. E. Kropp Dakubu, Institute of African Studies, University of Ghana

Derek Nurse, Institute of Swahili Research, University of Dar es Salaam

Merrick Posnansky, Department of History, University of California, Los Angeles

Douglas E. Saxon, Department of History, University of California, Los Angeles

Robert Soper, Institute of African Studies, University of Nairobi

Robin Thelwall, Department of Linguistics, New University of Ulster

1 | Introduction

THIS BOOK IS CONCERNED with two different sources of historical evidence, archaeology and linguistics—essential and primary resources where written and oral documents fail but valuable even when those sources exist. They are complementary approaches. Archaeology opens a window into the material life of the past and, by inference, into many other aspects of earlier societies. Its evidence can be quantified and given relative and absolute dating, and its assemblages of artifacts can be identified as the work of previous human communities, traced back in time and mapped according to occurrence and spread. Linguistics allows reconstruction of intangible in addition to tangible elements of past cultures and identifies former societies and cultures by the language affiliations of their makers. The techniques of linguistic reconstruction of history also allow very rough locating of earlier societies in time and space, although much more imprecisely and provisionally than archaeology. It is such areas of parallel inference which make possible the correlation of archaeological and linguistic documentation. From that correlation a fuller and more satisfying early history of Africa can begin to be built.

Neither linguistics nor archaeology has yet yielded up more than a tiny fraction of what these two disciplines will eventually reveal to us of Africa's history. Archaeology's problem is that the workers are relatively few, the continent is vast, and the forces of decay are especially pervasive. Linguistical historians and history-minded linguists are even fewer in number than archaeologists; moreover, they have to overcome the barriers that academic compartmentalization imposes on the imagination.

Yet the signs of progress are unmistakable, and they augur well for the marriage of the two kinds of evidence. Over the past decade archaeologists have finally begun, for instance, to push back the beginnings of the agricultural revolution in Africa toward the early dates that linguistic evidence seemed to require (see Greenberg 1964). They have begun to consider carefully much more than monuments and pottery. At the same time the use of linguistic evidence has changed from a pious expectation of historians, often expressed but seldom acted on, to a significant line of research. The full-time practitioners of this cross-disciplinary art still number less than the fingers of one hand, but a number of linguists and a few archaeologists contribute from time to time, and a journal devoted largely to this approach, *Sprache und Geschichte in Afrika*, has been established.

What is needed now is a standpoint from which to judge current progress and measure the inadequacies and the unevenness of present knowledge and thus to stimulate the next generation of linguistic-cum-archaeological efforts at historical reconstruction in Africa. It is that need, of determining exactly where the work of correlating the two sources presently stands, which this book aims at fulfilling.

In pursuance of that aim the contributors to the volume, carefully matched for regional interests, were asked to speak to the same, some-times broad, topics, from the perspective of their particular expertise. Their papers, all except two presented in joint sessions at a conference held at the University of California, Los Angeles, in June 1979, fall into four regional divisions: Nubia and the northern Sudan, equatorial Africa, eastern Africa, and the area of present-day Ghana. The partici-pants in the conference naturally learned from one another, and their papers presented here in revised form benefited accordingly. The discus-sion and exchange of information helped to strengthen some hypotheses and eliminate others and to better coordinate the contributions belonging to each geographical division.

Each section of the book is prefaced with a wider regional overview of archaeological and linguistic correlation. In part the overview serves to introduce the papers and themes that make up the section. But, more important, each overview situates the section's offerings within a longer time frame of historical change. It summarizes the situations antecedent to those directly covered by a set of articles, explains the gaps in coverage, and considers the complementary and supplementary correlative pro-posals of other scholars.

The opening section, on northeastern Africa, focuses on Nubian history, where many of the issues of correlation are as near settled as they ever will be. For that reason it offers an eminently suitable starting point for the volume. On the other hand, the focus on Nubians and their predecessors and antecedents neglects most of the vast expanse of north-ern and northeastern Africa within which the northern Sudan, the setting of Nubian history, is embedded. Several recent articles published else-where speak directly to this problem, however, and argue for some broad, earlier linkages, not inconsistent with one another, between archaeolog-ical and linguistic evidence in the eastern Sudan, the Horn, and North

Africa. The overview to the northeastern African section thus has a special importance in that it provides a synthetic review of the proposed correlations of the two sources of evidence and extends the reach of the section beyond the northern Sudan of the past 3,000 years.

The second set of papers turns our attention southward toward equatorial Africa, comprising the areas extending from the savannas of the southern Republic of Sudan and the Central African Republic through the equatorial rain-forest belt to the southern savanna zone. It is a region in which the linguistic portion of the enterprise is further advanced than the archaeological, but one for which nevertheless an archaeological synthesis, showing striking correspondences with the linguistically attested history, can be proposed.

The articles in the third section deal with the eastern regions of the continent lying between equatorial Africa as defined here and the Indian Ocean. Like the equatorial regions to the west, eastern and southern Africa were affected by Bantu expansion, but at a later period when alternative styles of food production had already become widely established, at least in the northern parts. The balance of articles is opposite to that of the preceding section, with three contributions being archaeological and two linguistic.

The final section takes us to West Africa. It is, perhaps surprisingly, a necessarily shorter section than those on eastern and equatorial Africa. West Africa has been the subject of good archaeological work in recent years, but frequently in disparate areas and for disparate time periods. The publication record is, also, much weaker than in other areas. Archaeology in West Africa, with a few exceptions, began rather later than in eastern Africa and was for a long time dominated in Nigeria, the country with the most archaeologists, by the search for new art historical materials in areas such as the Jos Plateau, Ife, Benin, and Igbo Ukwu. The archaeological successions of the past several thousand years, those eras susceptible to linguistic and archaeological correlation, have rarely been fully established even over relatively limited areas. The places where these have been constructed do not necessarily coincide with the areas for which a historical patterning of linguistic data is as yet available. Hence West Africa is represented here by the territorially rather restricted example of Ghana and some immediately adjoining districts in neighboring countries. As in the northeastern Africa section, the introductory overview provides the only look at the wide regional context, West Africa as a whole, into which the particular area discussed in detail fits.

The unevenness of historical coverage of the continent is, then, at least in some part a function of the unevenness of the work done. West Africa is a particularly glaring problem area.

From the contributions that follow, the immense potential of archaeological-linguistic approaches for African history, and for history in many other parts of the world, becomes quickly evident. The detailed application of the two resources all across the continent, however, will not come quickly or easily, as much of the basic evidence remains to be collected. But even at this point broad syntheses are possible for many parts of Africa, as this volume demonstrates. The twelve articles in their own right expand our knowledge of early African history. They form the basis as well for the raising of new problems and issues on which to found future research and so further advance understanding.

Part I

Northeastern Africa

OVERVIEW

The pair of articles that form this section focus on identifying the peoples involved in the developments, in the last millennium B.C. and the first millennium A.D., to which archaeology and the written notices of the middle Nile region attest. W. Y. Adams's contribution also has implications for archaeological correlation with Meroitic speech along the river in the immediately preceding times. And Robin Thelwall's chapter, by showing that Nubian's nearest relationships are to the Tama language group of Darfur and Wadai, indicates that before the riverine settlement the plains between the Nile, the Nuba Mountains, and Darfur had long been the Nubian homeland.

For a considerably longer period than that covered, even implicitly, by the two articles, however, the areas of the Nile River in the northern half of the Sudan have lain at major crossroads of historical change, whose repercussions could reach large areas of the Sudan belt or of northern and northeastern Africa. In recent years three sweeping proposals of archaeological and linguistic correlation in the northern and northeastern African region, of which the northern Sudan is a part, have been offered. None has yet been put to the test of extended scholarly criticism, and none is predicated on so large a base of detailed study as are Thelwall's and Adams's papers. Nevertheless, all three are plausible interpretations of the evidence presently available, and they help to put the lesser reach of the pair of Nubian articles into better perspective.

The two schemes of longest reach back into the past are those of Patrick Munson (1978) and Christopher Ehret (1979). Munson argues for the emergence of two widespread groupings of related stone-tool industries, one by about 18,000 years ago which eventually extended from the Horn across North Africa, and the other before 10,000 years ago which extended across the Sudan and the southern Sahara. Munson suggests linking the first with the speakers of early Afroasiatic languages and the second with the early Nilo-Saharans. Ehret independently arrived at the first of these propositions through an investigation of the internal relationships of the Afroasiatic (Hamito-Semitic) family and by suggesting possible reconstructions of proto-Afroasiatic subsistence vocabulary. Upholding the conclusion that the Afroasiatic homeland was somewhere along the Red Sea hinterland of Africa, he suggests that Afroasiatic speakers were the innovators of the practices of wild-grain collection visible in the archaeology of Nubia and other northern African regions, often from before 15,000 years ago.

Previous hypotheses about Afroasiatic's archaeological correlates, such as that of McBurney (1975), tended to look for links to early spreads of food production. But the time depth of relationships within Afroasiatic is much greater than has generally been realized, surely on the order of 15,000 years or even more at the deepest (Fleming 1976; Ehret 1979); and the only known archaeological parallel that comes close in time is that separately proposed by Munson and Ehret.

Munson links the second grouping of industries to Nilo-Saharan speakers. His views mirror those of J. E. G. Sutton (1974), who sees the spread of the Aquatic way of life as the manifestation of Nilo-Saharan expansion. The Aquatic tradition, a highly developed specialization exploiting the food resources of lakes and rivers, turns up all across the Sudanic belt from Lake Turkana to the bend of the Niger by the eighth millennium B.C., during a long era of markedly wetter climate and higher stream and lake levels than prevail today. Before 6000 B.C. the Aquatic peoples had invented pottery. It is probable, as Sutton proposes, that communities following the Aquatic way spoke Nilo-Saharan languages; the correlation of Aquatic and later Nilo-Saharan distributions is too close to dismiss. But it also seems probable that the spread of the Aquatic adaptation does not wholly account for Nilo-Saharan locations. The reason is that the Nilo-Saharan family has deep internal divisions, probably reflecting a time depth of original divergence on the same order as that of Afroasiatic. The Aquatic tradition may thus, as Phillipson (1977*b*: 45–46) suggests from the archaeology, have been an adaptation that in some areas diffused to already established Nilo-Saharan peoples.

The third proposal is of the partial correlation of the development and spread of food production in the eastern Sudan belt, particularly a more fully pastoral version of food production, with the expansion of peoples of the Eastern Sudanic branch of Nilo-Saharan (Ehret 1974*b*: chap. 5). Pastoralism had come into being by at least the fifth millennium B.C. in the northern Sudan, and that is not unduly out of line with the linguistic indications for the spread of the Eastern Sudanic societies. The pre-Nubians, ancestral to the Nubian settlers dealt with by Thelwall and Adams, would in that event have been the descendants, along with the Tama farther west, of the particular early eastern Sudanic people who settled the plains between Darfur and the Nile in those eras (see chap. 2, below, for Nilo-Saharan classifications).

Robin Thelwall, a scholar of the languages of Sudan, and W. Y.

Adams, the leading archaeologist of historical Nubia, provide from their separate perspectives convincingly parallel reconstructions of ethnic and language shifts in Nubia and the rest of northern Sudan during the period of the last millennium B.C. and the first half of the first millennium A.D. The first few centuries A.D. are, of course, a watershed of primary importance in Sudan history, for they saw the end of the long Meroitic dominance and the emergence of the Nubians, whose preeminence was to last in some areas down to recent centuries. The two contributors show not only developments narrowly affecting the riverine zone, but the shifting ethnic composition of steppe areas away from the rivers; they also explain how these changes spilled over into the more favored areas of the Nile.

Adams's contribution is useful for the ideas of wider applicability which emerge from his discussion. In particular, his work calls attention to the point that rarely in history do abrupt and complete breaks with the past occur. Most often language shift takes place because of the entrance onto the scene of a newly dominant ethnic group. A gradual shift in ethnic identification of the bulk of the population, rather than replacement of people, then occurs, and many specific cultural features may continue to exist through the ethnic transition and become embedded eventually in the new culture. The linguistic manifestation of this effect is word-borrowing, the movement of words from the old into the new language of the area. The proportion and kinds of word-borrowing help in the correlation with archaeology by suggesting to what extent continuities may be expected in the corresponding archaeological record of ethnic shift. The presence of Meroitic loanwords in Nubian is clear, and so it is not surprising that the transition between the Nubian period and the preceding Meroitic era is neither complete nor entirely abrupt in the material record.

Adams's contribution has the specific additional feature that it is in itself a skillful correlation of different kinds of evidence, of archaeology with the contemporary written documentation of the region. It thus illustrates the potential that archaeology has for enriching our understanding of even the most recent centuries of African history, where heretofore reliance has been placed on written and oral sources.

Thelwall's article, which closes the section, makes several fundamental points about the application of lexical evidence in the historical classification of languages, points that need to be kept in mind when reading later linguistic offerings in the volume. Thelwall also presents in succinct fashion the current classifications of the Nilo-Saharan languages.

The charting of Nilo-Saharan (or, to use M. L. Bender's term, Nilo-Sahelian) relationships is important not only to Thelwall's and Adams's articles, but as a guide to the overview on the northeastern African past (above) and for putting in perspective the Nilo-Saharan peoples, such as Nilotes and Central Sudanians, who figure in equatorial and eastern African developments.

2 | The Coming of Nubian Speakers to the Nile Valley

WILLIAM Y. ADAMS

I FEAR THAT, FROM the vantage point of archaeology, I can address only a fraction of the total range of problems suggested in Dr. Thelwall's companion paper (chap. 3, below). The reason for this limitation is quite simple: in the whole vast expanse of the western Sudan—presumed homeland of the Nubian language family—there has been no archaeology worthy of the name. Hence I can say nothing on the relationships among Birgid, Meidob, and Hill Nubian, or on the equally important question of the external relationships of the Nubian family as a whole. It is only in the Nile Valley, occupied in the recent past by speakers of the Nobiin and Dongolawi languages, that archaeology and linguistics offer a meaningful conjunction.

Thanks to the succession of dams built at Aswan since 1902, the region between the First and Third cataracts of the Nile has witnessed more systematic archaeology in this century than has any other part of Africa, and perhaps of the world. Archaeology, moreover, is not our only source of historical information. This region, unlike most of the continent, has lain on the fringes of the literate world almost since the dawn of history, and it has figured from time to time in descriptive and historical accounts written by ancient Egyptians, classical Greeks, and medieval Arabs. There is in addition an internal record of sorts left by the Nubians themselves. Although texts in the indigenous Meroitic and Old Nubian languages are not very informative from a historical point of view, they are of course invaluable as evidence of the languages spoken by the Nubian peoples. Modern place-names can also furnish a clue to the ethnic makeup of the Nile Valley population in earlier times.

In this paper, then, I consider in the light of archaeological, historical, and philosophical evidence the questions of how and when the Nubian speakers came originally to settle in the Nile Valley, and how they came to be distributed as they are currently found.[1] I traverse some of the

[1]Throughout this paper, for the sake of simplicity, I ignore the wholesale resettlement of the Nubians which was necessitated by the building of the Aswan High Dam; I speak of the different groups as though they were still settled in the territories they occupied before 1960.

same ground that Thelwall has already covered, with the difference that I am considering linguistic evidence in conjunction with archaeology and history.

The Setting of the Problem

In Nubia, as in most of the world, archaeologists at one time were prone to attribute nearly all prehistoric cultural change to the movement of peoples. The lifeways of preliterate societies, it was assumed, evolved only with a glacial slowness; any indications of very rapid change must be evidence of the coming of new peoples bringing new cultures with them. This type of explanatory approach is fully exemplified in the work of George A. Reisner, the pioneer archaeologist who first discovered and named nearly all the Nubian cultural periods, and who attributed each of them to the arrival of a new people in the Nile Valley (Adams 1968, 1978; Adams et al. 1978).

More recently it has been recognized that there are many threads of cultural continuity running through the whole of Nubian history. Migration theories, by ignoring these continuities, are apt to raise more problems than they solve. In my recent work of synthesis, *Nubia: Corridor to Africa*, I suggest that the whole of Nubian history may be viewed as "a continuous narrative of the cultural development of a single people, in which . . . comings and goings . . . have been unimportant" (Adams 1977:5). This view seems to be finding acceptance at least among my fellow anthropologists; indeed it is congruent with the general reaction against migrationist and diffusionist explanations which is apparent in historical anthropology today (Adams et al. 1978).

It must be acknowledged, nevertheless, that a simple evolutionary view of Nubian history leaves unexplained a number of linguistic anomalies. Most significantly, it appears that the inhabitants of the middle Nile Valley 2,000 years ago did not speak a language ancestral to, or even closely related to, the Nubian dialects of today. We must therefore either envision a movement of Nubian speakers into the Nile Valley, or we must account for the change of language on some other basis. This problem of linguistic discontinuity between ancient and medieval times furnishes a point of departure for considering the more general question of when and how the Nubian speakers first came to the Nile Valley.

I take it as generally accepted that the surviving Nubian languages of today are remnants of what was once a continuous distribution, extending from the Nile Valley westward across the steppelands of Kordofan and Darfur. I also accept the principle of least moves, which suggests that the original homeland of any language family is to be sought in that area where the various member languages show the widest diversity. Application of this principle in the Nubian case quite clearly establishes the ancestral home of the family somewhere in Kordofan or Darfur, as Thelwall indicates (chap. 3 below). From thence the speakers of the Nile Nubian languages (Nobiin and Dongolawi) presumably moved eastward into the Nile Valley at some undetermined time in history. My problem is to consider when that movement, or those movements, took place, and what is the relationship between the two Nile Nubian languages of modern times.

A Note on Geographical Terminology

Conventional usage distinguishes between Lower Nubia, between the First and Second cataracts of the Nile, and Upper Nubia, to the south of the Second Cataract. Although this distinction coincides approximately with the modern political boundary between Egypt and the Sudan, it is not very useful historically. Insofar as we can recognize political, cultural, or ethnic differences between the northern and southern parts of Nubia, the dividing line seems much more often to have been around the Third Cataract than around the Second (see map 1).

As a toponym the name Nubia is itself ambiguous, since modern parlance applies it only to that area, extending today from Debba to Aswan, which is occupied by speakers of the two surviving Nile Nubian languages. But we know that until the recent past Nubian speakers were much more widely distributed; they extended up the Nile at least as far as modern Khartoum, and probably over much of the Gezira as well. We are therefore obliged to think of "Nubia" as an area having fluctuating boundaries, a circumstance that limits the geographical utility of the term.

In an effort to reduce ambiguity I employ in this paper a series of unfamiliar, but I hope unambiguous, toponyms, whose parameters remain constant at all periods.

Northern Nubia refers to the Nile Valley between the First and Third cataracts—approximately the area occupied today by speakers of the Nobiin and Kenzi languages.

Southern Nubia refers to the Nile Valley between the Third and Fourth cataracts—approximately the area occupied by the Dongolawi (pl. Danagla) and their neighbors the Shaiqiya, who also spoke a Nubian dialect as late as the eighteenth century (Crawford 1951:44).

Central Sudan, a more inclusive term, refers to the Nile Valley and to the adjacent inhabited hinterlands, from the Third Cataract in the north

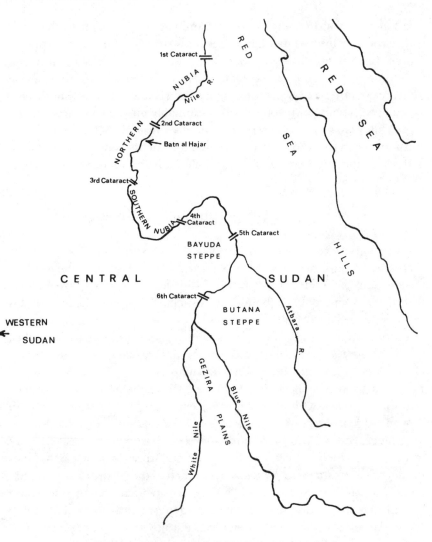

Map 1. Place-names and geographical subdivisions of the
middle Nile Valley.

to the southern limit of the Gezira in the south. This area encompasses
both southern Nubia and the area to the south of it which was occupied by
Nubian speakers until the end of the Middle Ages.

   Middle Nile Valley, a still more inclusive term, encompasses both
Northern Nubia and the central Sudan, that is, the whole area from
Aswan to the southern Gezira which was once occupied by Nubian
speakers.

Western Sudan refers specifically to Kordofan and Darfur.

Other, more geographically restricted toponyms that I employ include the Butana steppeland between the Nile and Atbara rivers; the Gezira plains between the Blue and White Niles; the Bayuda steppe west of the Nile and partly enclosed by the great reverse bend of the river; and the Batn el Hajar ("Belly of Stones"), the rugged stretch of mountains and rapids extending southward from the Second Cataract for about 70 miles. (For further clarification of these terms see map 1).

A word must also be said about ethnic and linguistic labels. For the sake of consistency I retain the names Nobiin and Dongolawi which Thelwall applies to the two Nile Nubian languages, although in other writing I usually use the terms Mahas-Fadija (for Nobiin) and Dongola-Kenuz. When it is necessary to differentiate I refer to the northern dialect of Dongolawi as Kenzi and to the southern as Southern Dongolawi.

The terms commonly applied to the speakers of these languages are not quite the same as the names for the languages themselves. The speakers of Southern Dongolawi are known collectively as the Danagla, and the speakers of Kenzi as the Kenuz. The speakers of Nobiin are most commonly known in the Sudan as Mahas (sing. Mahasi), and in Egypt as Fadija. In places where I am talking specifically about peoples and not about their languages I employ these familiar ethnic terms in my text.

The Evidence of Indigenous Texts

Evidence of linguistic discontinuity in Nubia is of three sorts: the direct evidence of written texts in the ancient and medieval languages, the inferential evidence of place-names, and the indirect evidence afforded by ethnic labels which were applied to different Nubian peoples by their neighbors.

The earliest Nubians were of course nonliterate. Although they lived for over 2,000 years in the shadow of Pharaonic Egypt, it was not until they passed under direct Egyptian colonial rule, between about 1500 and 1000 B.C., that the art of writing became known to the peoples of the middle Nile. The surviving records from the colonial period are, however, entirely in the ancient Egyptian language (hieroglyphic and hieratic scripts), and they furnish no clue to the indigenous speech of the region. This remained true even after the cessation of direct Egyptian control. Around 850 B.C. the Nubians established their own independent and long-enduring Empire of Kush, which extended from the First Cataract at Aswan far into the interior of the Sudan. Its government and institutions were closely modeled on those of Pharaonic Egypt, and for many centuries the rulers of Kush continued to employ exclusively the Egyptian language for their monumental proclamations and religious dedications.

Over the centuries familiarity with the Egyptian language gradually lessened, as is attested by a series of increasingly garbled and finally almost meaningless hieroglyphic texts. Then, apparently in the second century B.C., we begin to find for the first time royal annals of the Kushite rulers written in a native language. At first a hieroglyphic script was used, but it soon gave way to an alphabet comprising twenty-three characters, as well as the world's first written punctuation marks. Because the capital of the Kushite empire was by this time established at the fabled city of Meroe, the indigenous language of the late Kushite texts has been given the name Meroitic by modern scholars.

The Meroitic alphabetic characters are recognizably derived from the Demotic script of contemporary Egypt, and consequently their phonetic values are at least approximately known. A great many proper names—of Egyptian deities and of Kushite rulers, for example—can quite readily be identified. In spite of these advantages, however, the Meroitic texts have thus far resisted all efforts at decipherment. Part of the difficulty evidently lies in the very limited range of subject matter they cover. A few of the longest texts are, it appears, the royal proclamations of Kushite rulers, but by far the larger number are relatively short funerary biographies of nobles and officials, which evidently follow a set formula (Griffith 1911; Hintze 1959; Trigger 1970*b*). This difficulty may in time be overcome as a result of the ongoing excavations at Qasr Ibrim, which are producing the first substantial quantity of Meroitic textual material that may be of a purely secular nature (Adams, forthcoming). Study of this material is only just beginning, however, and its eventual decipherment, if it can be accomplished at all, undoubtedly lies far in the future.

For the time being the one point about the Meroitic language which seems to be clearly established is that it is not closely related to any other known language, ancient or modern. In particular there is no demonstrable relationship to any of the modern Nubian dialects, although Trigger (1964, 1977) has suggested a few points of affinity with the Eastern Sudanic family as a whole.

Meroitic became, and thereafter remained, the sole written language of Kush during the last centuries of the empire. Its use extended from the Kushite-Roman frontier in the north (which was established at Maharraqa, about 70 miles upstream from the First Cataract) at least as far southward as the junction of the Blue and White Niles. When the empire collapsed in the early fourth century A.D., however, the Meroitic system of writing seems to have disappeared almost at once. The entire Sudan was plunged into a dark age from which, over the next three centuries, there are almost no written records at all. In the far north of Nubia, on the frontiers of Egypt, there is also evidence of a drastic decline in literarcy, but here a few of the petty chieftains who seized power in the post-Kushite era have left us inscriptions in highly barbarized Greek (Kirwan 1937*a*; Skeat 1977). There is also some evidence of the use of Coptic, which along with Greek was the language currently employed in Egypt (Plumley et al. 1977).

The conversion of Nubia to Christianity in the sixth century was concurrent with the rise of extensive and powerful new kingdoms: Nobatia in northern Nubia, Makouria in southern Nubia, and Alwa in the region around the confluence of the Blue and White Niles. A little later we observe once again the emergence of an indigenous written language, which has come to be called Old Nubian. Written in a modified form of the Greek alphabet, it first appears in a religious graffito dated in the year 795 (Griffith 1913:5). Thereafter Old Nubian was employed to some extent in religious, legal, and administrative texts at least until the year 1484 (Adams 1977:533). It was not, however, the sole or even necessarily the official language of medieval Nubia, for both Greek and Coptic also appear frequently in religious texts, and Arabic was widely employed in commercial dealings with Egypt (Frend 1972; Shinnie 1974).

Old Nubian is recognizably ancestral to the Nobiin language spoken today by the Mahas and Fadija Nubians, and all the known manuscripts in Old Nubian seem to have originated in the area where Nobiin is now spoken. The medieval kingdom where it was developed had, however, a much wider territorial extent, including also the districts where both the Kenzi and the southern Dongolawi dialects (both variants of the same language) were spoken. The seat of government was in fact at Dongola, which is in the Dongolawi-speaking rather than in the Nobiin-speaking part of the kingdom. No Old Nubian texts have been found at Old Dongola, and for this reason scholars are hesitant to suggest that Old Nubian had any special or official status in the medieval kingdom. It should be noted, however, that a few Old Nubian graffiti have been found much farther to the south, in the Butana region (Griffith 1913:5), and one inscription is also known from Kordofan (Arkell 1951). It has been suggested that these may represent a different dialect from that found in the much more extensive manuscript material from the north (Griffith 1913:5).

To sum up the written textual evidence, we have Meroitic as the sole written language of Nubia and the central Sudan until sometime early in the fourth century, then a dark age in which no indigenous language was written, and finally the appearance of Old Nubian, alongside Greek and Coptic, through most of the Middle Ages. Before discussing this anomaly further we must turn briefly to two other lines of evidence—place-names and ethnic labels.

The Evidence of Place-Names

Place-names can furnish suggestive but seldom conclusive evidence in regard to population movements. In Nubia they seem to argue both for and against a change of population between ancient and medieval times. As evidence against a population change Ali Osman points out that place-names of apparent Nubian origin occur all up and down the Nile between the Second Cataract and Khartoum (Ali Osman 1973). Many of the named settlements are of no great antiquity; they could have been founded subsequent to the migration of Nubian speakers to the Nile Valley. Priese (1968, 1973b) believes, however, that he has identified names of Nubian origin, particularly in the region between the Third and Fourth Cataracts, in texts dating all the way back to the fifth century B.C. On the other hand, some of the oldest settlements in northern Nubia— Faras, Gebel Adda, and Qasr Ibrim—have names that are not of Nubian derivation but can be traced back to Meroitic antecedents (Griffith 1925; Adams 1977:349, 752–753).

The Evidence of Ethnic Labels

The rulers of ancient Nubia referred to their empire as the Land of Kush, preserving therein a toponym of much earlier Egyptian origin.[2] We do not know what label, if any, they applied to themselves as a people. Nowhere in their annals, however, can we recognize any word that appears to be cognate to "Nubia."

Classical writers, on the other hand, introduce us to a people called the Nubae as early as the second or third century B.C. We hear of them first in a passage from the geographer Eratosthenes which is preserved in Strabo: "The parts on the left side of the course of the Nile, in Libya, are inhabited by Nubae, a large tribe who, beginning at Meroe, extend as far

---

[2]The name Kush first appears in Egyptian texts of the XI Dynasty, around 2000 B.C., though at that time it referred only to a localized area in northern Nubia (see T. Säve-Söderbergh 1941:63).

as the bends of the river, and are not subject to the Ethiopians but are divided into several separate kingdoms" (trans. in Kirwan 1937*b*). "Ethiopians" in the foregoing passage, as in many classical texts, refers specifically to the inhabitants of the Empire of Kush—the people who presumably spoke Meroitic. It is clear from the words of Eratosthenes and Strabo that the Nubae were a separate people from the Kushites, living to the west of them across the Nile, and were not subject to their political hegemony. In the middle of the first century A.D., Pliny the Elder spoke of the "Ethiopian Nubae" as living along the Nile somewhere apparently to the north of Meroe; their principal "city" was called Tenupsis. Some scholars have identified this with ancient Egyptian Pnubs, situated on the island of Argo just above the Third Cataract (Kirwan 1937*b*). A century later Ptolemy's *Geography* placed the Nubae both east and west of the Nile, that is, partly within the Kushite dominions in the Butana steppe.

We next hear of the "Noba" about two hundred years later, not from a classical source but from an indigenous African one. In the middle of the fourth century A.D. the Abyssinian empire of Axum was at its height, and the Axumite ruler Aezanas launched a major campaign against the peoples of the middle Nile Valley, ostensibly because they had broken an agreement with him and had raided his territories. Aezanas erected in his capital city a series of monumental stelae proclaiming the details of his campaigns and triumphs. The longest of the inscriptions, and the source of most of our information, is in Greek, and it is conventionally dated in the year 350 A.D. (Kirwan 1937*b*; Hintze 1967). Although the text contains a number of ambiguities, it is evident that the primary enemies whom Aezanas encountered and put to flight were not the Kushites but the Noba. By inference it would appear that they had overrun large tracts of the Butana steppe, formerly the heartland of the Kushite empire, and had taken possession of some of its brick-built cities.[3] The text seems to suggest that the normal dwellings of the Noba were grass houses; they lived in cities of brick only when and where they had seized these from the earlier inhabitants. Aezanas concluded his campaign with a foray northward as far as the territory of the "Red Noba," a people who evidently lived along the Nile somewhere to the north of the ordinary Noba. The relationship between the two Noba groups is not made clear, but we are told that the ordinary Noba were in the habit of attacking the northern ("Red") group before the appearance of Aezanas.

The people of Kush (Kasu) are mentioned separately from the Noba

[3]Hintze (1967:83), however, disagrees with this interpretation, placing the Noba much farther to the south.

on the stelae of Aezanas. The Axumite ruler fought and defeated the Kushites in a battle near the junction of the Nile and the Atbara. They do not otherwise figure very prominently in the account of the campaign, and it seems evident that by this time the Noba and not the Kushites were the dominant force in the central Sudan. The lack of any specific mention of a Kushite ruler is taken as presumptive evidence that the Empire of Kush had already come to an end before 350 A.D., the presumed year of Aezanas's campaign (Monneret de Villard 1938; Kirwan 1960).

A short time later we begin hearing, in northern Nubia, of another ethnic group called variously the Annoubades, the Noubades, or the Nobatae. They appear first in a letter, datable to the second quarter of the fifth century, in which the Bishop of Aswan asks for troops to protect the Egyptian frontier against the combined attacks of the Blemmyes and the Annoubades (Kirwan 1937a). A few years later the historian Priscus recounts how the Roman General Maximinus negotiated a treaty with the two peoples on the island of Philae. Both the Blemmyes and the Annoubades (Noubades in the text of Priscus) are identified in the texts as residents of Nubia immediately to the south of the Egyptian frontier. The Blemmyes we know to be the Beja, a mostly nomadic people whose principal habitat since time immemorial has been the Red Sea Hills (Kirwan 1937a). The Noubades on the other hand are a new group, whose name surely identifies them as a member of the Nubian linguistic family.

By the sixth century the Noubades had clearly emerged as the dominant force in northern Nubia and as the successors to the power of Kush. A certain Silko, self-proclaimed "King of the Noubades and of all the Ethiopians," left an inscription in Greek in the Lower Nubian temple of Kalabsha, recounting how he had expelled the Blemmyes from the Nile Valley and established his dominion from the First to the Second Cataract. Silko's inscription is undated, but there is both external and internal evidence to suggest that it was written sometime around 500 (Kirwan 1937a,b). The historical reality of Silko's campaigns has recently been verified by a letter in Greek found at Qasr Ibrim, in which a certain King Phonen of the Blemmyes complains to a King Abournai of the Noubades about the depredations of Silko (Plumley et al. 1977; Skeat 1977).

Around 545 A.D. the Byzantine historian Procopius described the region immediately to the south of the First Cataract as being in the hands of the Nobatae. According to him they had been invited to settle in the Nile Valley by the Roman Emperor Diocletian, toward the end of the third century, as a buffer against attacks by the Blemmyes. Formerly they had dwelled "about the City of Oasis" (see Kirwan 1958), that is, presumably somewhere in the western Egyptian desert. Procopius, however, wrote two and half centuries after the event he purported to describe, and it has been pointed out that there is no mention of Noubades or Nobatae in any contemporary document from the time of Diocletain (Kirwan 1937*b*).

Christian missionaries, arriving to convert the Nubians in the middle of the sixth century, found the whole of the middle Nile Valley occupied by three major kingdoms. The most northerly of them, called Nobadia or Nobatia, extended from the First Cataract to a point somewhere between the Second and Third cataracts. This was, of course, the kingdom of which Silko was an earlier ruler, if not the founder. Most archaeologists also assume that it was the pre-Christian rulers of Nobatia who constructed the resplendent series of royal tombs at Ballana and Qustul, a short distance north of the present Egyptian-Sudanese frontier (Kirwan 1958).

To the south of Nobatia lay Makouria, whose inhabitants were called the Makoritae.[4] In them we can probably recognize the Makkourai who were named by Ptolemy as nomads dwelling west of the Nile in the second centry A.D.[5] The capital and geographical center of Makouria was in southern Nubia. Much farther upstream was the kingdom of Alwa, centered in the region around the confluence of the Blue and White Niles where its capital city of Soba was located. This territory was much the same as that invaded by Aezanas 200 years earlier, and we therefore have to assume that the subjects and presumably also the rulers of this kingdom were the Noba. Indeed, Alwa is specifically mentioned on the stela of Aezanas, not as a country but as one of the cities the Noba had occupied (Kirwan 1960).

All the Nubian kingdoms were successfully converted to Christianity before the end of the sixth century. About a hundred years later Nobatia and Makouria were merged into a single kingdom, the political center of power remaining in Makouria. The more northerly district, however, retained its separate name and identity throughout the Middle Ages; it was governed by a kind of viceroy whose title in Nubian was eparch of

---

[4]The first mention of this kingdom and its history is found in the sixth-century ecclesiastical histories of John of Ephesus and John of Biclarum, recounting the conversion of the Nubians to Christianity (see Trimingham 1949:48–59).

[5]*Geography* IV:2, 19. Monneret de Villard (1938:92), however, points out that the M-k-r root occurs in ethnic names recorded from North Africa in classical times, and it seems unlikely that they can all be the same people.

Nobatia or eparch of the Nobatae (Adams 1977:464–466). It was specifically within the territory of Nobatia that the Old Nubian language came principally into use, as we have seen.

The Evidence of Archaeology

The historical and philological evidence discussed thus far suggests an obvious and straightforward interpretation. During the time of the Kushite empire the lands east of the Nile were occupied by the Meriotic-speaking subjects of Kush, while the territory west of the river, presumably extending continuously westward into Darfur, was the home of various independent Nubian-speaking tribes. Then, with the decline of Kushite power, the Nubians seized the opportunity to overrun the former territories of the empire. The Noba pushed dirctly eastward into the Butana, the Red Noba took up a position somewhere to the north of them, and the Nobatae took possession of the lands in the far north. This interpretation of Nubian history has indeed been the prevailing view among scholars until the recent past. We must, however, turn—belatedly—to the testimony of archaeology, to see how fully it is congruent with the evidence of philology and history.

In the central Sudan, once the heartland of the Kushite empire and later of the Kingdom of Alwa, we encounter relatively few contradictions between archaeological and linguistic evidence. There does indeed seem to be a clear break in the continuity of development between Kushite and post-Kushite times. The temple-cities of the Butana—Musawwarat, Naqa, Meroe, and others—show few if any signs of continued occupation after the downfall of the Kushite empire; there are in fact no further signs of monumental building of any sort for several centuries. At the same time the Meroitic systems of writing and of decorative and canonical art disappeared, and even the manufacture of wheel-made pottery came to an end. There was, finally, an abrupt change in mortuary practice, from the use of extended burials with pyramidal superstructures to contracted burials with mound superstructures. All these changes are obviously coherent with the theory that the relatively "advanced" Kushite population and culture were overrun and subjugated by the more "barbarian" Noba in the fourth century.

Hintze (1967) suggests, nevertheless, that the picture may not be quite so simple. He points out that in the fourth century not all the Noba were rural or nomadic; on the evidence of the Aezanas inscriptions some of them were living in brick-built towns, cultivating grain and cotton, using vessels of bronze, and worshiping in temples. Presumably these were the Noba who had long been settled near, and perhaps even within, the territories of Kush, as is suggested by the earlier evidence of Ptolemy. Consequently any invasion that put an end to town dwelling and to temple building in the central Sudan should not, it would seem, be attributed to these relatively advanced and "Kushized" Noba. Instead we have to think of both the sedentary Noba and their Kushite neighbors as being overrun by a new wave of more rustic Noba from the west.

Archaeology has for the time being little to say about developments in southern Nubia, between the Fourth and Third cataracts. This region was apparently politically unimportant and economically backward during the last centuries of Kushite rule and for a considerable time afterward. There is nothing to foreshadow its emergence a little later as the center of the most powerful and extensive of the medieval kingdoms. Up to now, however, there has been so little excavation either in Kushite or in post-Kushite remains that we can say nothing of consequence about continuity or lack of continuity between the two.

It is chiefly in northern Nubia—the territory of Nobatia—that we encounter serious discrepancies between the archaeological and linguistic records. There were indeed important political changes following the collapse of the Kushite empire, most notably the replacement of centralized control from Meroe by locally based chiefdoms which dispensed with the more complex bureaucratic and symbolic trappings of Kush. Yet it is apparent that at least some of the post-Kushite rulers regarded themselves as the legitimate heirs to Kushite power, for they retained some of the Kushite royal insignia, particularly in their crowns (Trigger 1969). We may recall too that Silko styled himself "King of the Noubades and of all the Ethiopians."

In the discussion of northern Nubian archaeology I refer to the late Kushite period and culture as the Meroitic, and to the immediate post-Kushite period and culture as the Ballana, those being the terms most commonly employed by archaeologists and historians today. (The Ballana people and culture were for a long time known as the "X-Group," but this unsatisfactory term, with its implication of a separate population group, is finally being discarded.)

There are, it must be recognized, cultural discontinuities between the Meroitic and Ballana periods in northern Nubia; they are particularly conspicuous in the area of mortuary ritual. Thus it was that the early salvage archaeologists, who concentrated almost exclusively on mortuary sites, became convinced that they were dealing with the remains of two separate peoples. Later excavation in habitation sites has revealed, however, that there are far more continuities than discontinuities between the two periods. Many of the Meroitic towns and villages continued to be occupied in post-Meroitic times, with no immediate change in housing patterns. Domestic manufactures such as weaving, basketmaking, woodwork, and the production of handmade pottery were hardly affected by concurrent political changes, and there was no interruption in the importation of a wide variety of goods from Roman and Byzantine Egypt.[6] Wheel-made pottery does indeed exhibit a revolutionary change, but it is not one that we would expect to result from the intrusion of nomads from the south or the west. Ballana pottery represents an abrupt and complete triumph of purely Roman canons—long prevalent in neighboring Egypt—over an older Nubian tradition which derived from the art of Pharaonic Egypt (Adams 1964a).

Even the Meroitic cemeteries continued in use, with no interruption in their orderly pattern of growth. Ballana graves are unmistakably different from Meroitic graves both in type and in content—like the Noba graves farther south they frequently have contracted burials and mound tumuli—but the two occur side by side in the same cemeteries, and Ballana graves begin where Meroitic graves leave off. It may be pointed out, moreover, that an equally sudden and drastic change in burial ritual occurred two centuries later when the Nubians were converted to Christianity, but no one has suggested a change of population at that time. More than fifty years ago the great anthropologist A. L. Kroeber (1927) observed that burial customs in many cultures have been quite unstable, and that they are not always closely correlated with other domains of culture.

In earlier times racial evidence, specifically the evidence of comparative skeletal anatomy, was often cited in support of theories of population replacement in Nubia. This was true of the "X-Group," as the Ballana people were originally called, who were thought to exhibit more Negroid characteristics than did their Meroitic predecesors (Elliot Smith and Derry 1910). However, the more scientific and less subjective analytical methods of modern times have failed, in the view of most anthropologists, to substantiate any difference between the Kushite and post-Kushite populations (Adams 1977:391). This does not of course prove that there was no movement of peoples, for the genetic pool was probably pretty much the same throughout Nubia and the central Sudan. It does mean,

---

[6]Continuities between the Meroitic and Ballana periods have been particularly well established by the recent excavations at Qasr Ibrim, which are not yet published in detail. For preliminary reports see Plumley and Adams (1974:212–238), Plumley (1975), and Plumley, Adams, and Crowfoot (1977).

however, that skeletal remains cannot be cited as positive evidence in favor of a migration.

When we turn back to the linguistic evidence, however, we still find the same awkward discontinuity confronting us. There seems to be little room to doubt that Silko and his fellow rulers in the Ballana period were Nobatae, as were the majority of their subjects. Consequently there can also be little doubt that they spoke the language that later became Old Nubian and later still became the Nobiin of today. Yet just a little earlier the only written language of Nubia had been Meroitic, which cannot be identified as a member of the Nubian family. Its use dates back at least to the second century B.C., clearly antedating the appearance in the Nile Valley of any of the ethnic groups whom we have identified as Nubians. How and when, then, did the Nubian speakers enter the northern territories of Kush, if it was not at the time of the empire's collapse? Interestingly enough, I think that archaeology suggests an answer to this question, though it is not an immediately obvious one.

The extensive surveys necessitated by the Aswan dams have revealed, at least to the satisfaction of archaeologists, that northern Nubia was largely uninhabited throughout the last millennium B.C. The reasons for this are, in my view, attributable to a lowered average level of the Nile,[7] but in any event the archaeological evidence, or rather the lack of it, is quite convincing. In archaeology the "argument from silence" is not often a safe one, but when a region more than 300 miles in length has been examined inch by inch, and when the surveys have recorded hundreds of sites from the second millennium B.C. and from the first millennium A.D., but fewer than a dozen from the intervening millennium, then I think we can speak with confidence about a general depopulation. Contrary to the suggestion of some philologists (Priese 1973*b*), this idea is not refuted by the fact that the early Kushite ruler Taharqa built temples at Qasr Ibrim, Buhen, and Semna, that later Kushite as well as Ptolemaic rulers built temples at Dakka and Debod, or that small garrisons were maintained at Qasr Ibrim and perhaps other strategic points. Temple building was the accepted way of "showing the flag" (that is, proclaiming sovereignty) in ancient Egyptian and Kushite times; and control of the Nile Valley in Nubia, the lifeline of communication and trade between Egypt and Kush, was vital to the interest of both countries, even at a time when hardly anyone lived there (Adams 1976*b*).

Qasr Ibrim is in the most literal sense the "exception that proves the

---

[7] I developed this thesis originally in Adams (1964*b*); see also Adams (1977:242). Trigger (1970*a*) presents counterarguments.

rule" in regard to a general depopulation of Nubia in the last millennium B.C. Both historical and archaeological evidences suggest that this great hilltop fortress was in fact occupied during much if not all of the depopulation period. However, the excavations at Qasr Ibrim, which are just now beginning to penetrate into deposits from the last millennium B.C., are yielding pottery and other remains quite unlike anything known from other sites in Nubia (Plumley et al. 1977). I take this as evidence that no other Nubian sites were being occupied at the time when these pottery types were in use.

The general depopulation of northern Nubia came to an end soon after the beginning of our Christian era. There was a virtual land rush of reoccupation, resulting in a string of flourishing villages throughout the region by the third century A.D. I have elsewhere given my reasons for believing that the reoccupation was associated with the introduction of the *saqia*, or ox-driven waterwheel, making irrigation possible in portions of the Nile Valley which had not been accessible to cultivation since the higher Nile levels of the Egyptian New Kingdom (Adams 1964*b*, 1976*b*:15).

The newcomers who settled in northern Nubia became, de facto, the subjects of Kush, since the empire was already maintaining strategic control over the region through garrisons at Qasr Ibrim and perhaps elsewhere. They also came to share a good many cultural traits with the more southerly inhabitants of the empire, including the use of the Meroitic language at least for written communication. There are, however, conspicuous and important differences in culture between Meroitic Nubia and the remainder of the empire, which I have discussed at considerable length in another essay (Adams 1976*b*). In particular, the basis of government and administation appears to have been much more secular and less theocratic in Nubia than in the heartland of the empire. The fortress rather than the temple and the royal tomb was always the primary symbol of authority in the north, and we hear almost nothing of the lion-god Apedemark who was the chief tutelary of the ruling family at Meroe. These conditions suggest to me that the northern and southern Kushites did not share, or at least fully share, in a common ideological tradition.

At the same time the Meroitic Nubians seem to have outstripped their southern neighbors in a number of material respects, most notably in the production as well as in the importation of luxury goods. They were, of course much closer to the Roman-Egyptian frontier and could benefit both from technical innovations in the northern country and from the closer proximity of a trading partner. Thus many of the luxury goods found even in the royal tombs at Meroe seem to be of northern manufacture, whereas the graves of ordinary folk in the north exhibit a much higher level of material prosperity than is reflected in the southern provinces of Kush (Adams 1976:40–42).

My belief, in short, is that the "Nobatian invasion" of northern Nubia was in fact the general repopulation of the first and second centuries A.D. Arrived in their new habitat the immigrants became—if indeed they were not already—subjects of the Empire of Kush which had long been in strategic control of the region. Government remained in the hands of a small, elite cadre of Meroitic nobles and officials, and Meroitic remained the language of written communication. On the other hand, the mass of the immigrant population, according to my interpretation, spoke the Nobatian language which they had brought with them from their previous home. With the subsequent collapse of the Kushite empire the essentially foreign Meroitic language, which was perhaps understood by only a small minority of the population, ceased to have any legitimizing function, and its use soon disappeared. It is noteworthy, on the other hand, that the local rulers in the subsequent period did not begin immediately to write their own language. To the extent that they required a medium of written communication they borrowed the Greek of neighboring Egypt, though with less than perfect comprehension (Kirwan 1937a; Skeat 1977).

I have to acknowledge that a version of the foregoing theory was put forward by Millet (1964) eighteen years ago. He suggested, however, that there were two Nubian migrations to the northern region, one of pre-Dongolawi speakers in the third century B.C. and one of pre-Nobiin speakers in the third century A.D. Archaeology does not really support the idea of two separate migrations in the north, nor is there anything to suggest a general reoccupation as early as the third century B.C. It is also unlikely in my view that the Dongolawi speakers came to the Nile earlier than did the Nobiin speakers, a point to which I will return a little later.

It would be foolish to suggest that the interpretation I have put forward here resolves all difficulties. For one thing we cannot speak of the immigrant Nubians (Nobatians) as being "Meroized" or "Kushized" after their arrival in northern Nubia. To the extent that the culture of Meroitic Nubia shows affinities with the remainder of the Kushite empire, those affinities are present at the outset; they do not gradually increase over time. For that reason I think we have to rule out any idea that the immigrants came directly from the wilds of Kordofan or Darfur, that is, from the ancestral Nubian homeland. I think they must have been previously settled on or close to the Nile, where they had already absorbed a good deal of Kushite culture, prior to their movement into northern Nubia. Bearing in mind Priese's (1968) identification of Nubian names in southern Nubia as early as the fifth century B.C., and Ptolemy's mention of Nubae along the Nile to the north of Meroe, I think we have a basis for assuming that the northernmost *inhabited* district of the Kushite empire, between the Third and Fourth cataracts, already had a Nubian-speaking population in the last centuries B.C. (maps 2 and 3). In my view it was these people who moved northward into the formerly depopulated region of northern Nubia after irrigation was made possible by the *saqia*.

The most serious objection that can be raised against my interpretation is that it does nothing to account for the present, anomalous distribution of the Nile Nubian languages. Between Maharraqa (about 70 miles above the First Cataract) and the Third Cataract we have the Noblin language, while both to the north and to the south of it are the closely related Kenzi and Southern Dongolawi dialects of the Dongolawi language. It is to this anomaly that I address myself in the concluding section of this paper.

The Problem of Modern Distributions

The correspondence between particular language families and particular cultural traits or culture types is not always a close one. Consequently archaeology, in and of itself, can shed only an uncertain light on linguistic distributions, and vice versa. In Nubia, however, the conjunction of historical and archaeological evidence allows us some suggestive inferences about the distribution of the present-day Nubian dialects.

The point that seems to me most clearly established by all available evidence is that the Nobiin of today are the Old Nubian speakers of the Middle Ages and the Nobatae of the late Kushite and post-Kushite periods. The geographical distribution is very much the same in all three cases; that is, the area occupied by the modern Nobiin corresponds closely to the area in which Old Nubian texts are chiefly found, and to the earlier territory of Nobatia. This is also the area of the post-Kushite Ballana culture, which I think we can confidently associate with the Nobatae people (Kirwan 1937*b*; Millet 1964). These identifications are important, for, if my interpretation is correct, they establish the Nobiin not merely in the Nile Valley but in their present specific habitat as early as the first century A.D.

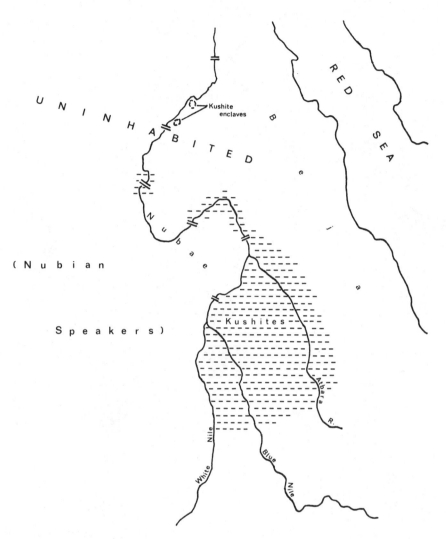

Map 2. Hypothesized distribution of language groups in the
second century B.C. in northern Sudan.

What then of the other Nile Nubians, the Danagla to the south of the
Nobiin and the Kenuz to the north of them? These peoples speak dialects
that are generally regarded as constituting a single language; they are
much more similar to each other than they are to the intervening Nobiin.
Consequently their anomalous distribution north and south of the Nobiin
has been the subject of a great deal of speculation and of differing

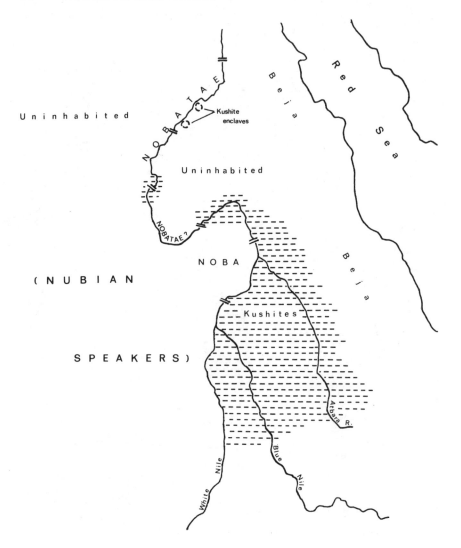

Map 3. Hypothesized distribution of language groups in the
second century A.D. in northern Sudan.

historical interpretations. It has been variously suggested that the Kenuz
represent a northward migration of Danagla (Fernea 1979) that the
Danagla are a southward migration of Kenuz (Adams 1966), or that the
later intrusion of the Nobiin opened a gap between two formerly contiguous peoples (Millet 1964).

    If we accept the identification of the Nobiin with medieval Nobatia and its people, I think we can similarly accept an identification of the Danagla with medieval Makouria and its people. Their name is, after all, derived from that of the historic capital of Makouria (Old Dongola), and their geographical range (excluding the Kenzi dialect) corresponds fairly closely with the territory of Makouria. Moreover, we have the direct testimony of the medieval traveler Ibn Selim el Aswani that in his time, toward the end of the tenth century, the peoples of Nobatia and Makouria were already separate "races" speaking separate languages. His account, preserved in an excerpt in Maqrizi's fourteenth-century geography, refers to "the city of Yosto . . . the last of Merys[8] [Nobatia] and the beginning of the country of Mokra [Makouria]. From this place to the frontiers of the Moslim country [i.e., Egypt], the inhabitants speak the Merysy language." Ibn Selim further states categorically that "the Noubas [Nobatians] and the Mokras [Makourians] are two different races, with two different languages" (Burckhardt 1819:495). From a close reading of Ibn Selim's account, Kirwan (1935) has placed Yosto (i.e., the frontier between the Nobatians and Makourians) at a point slightly to the north of the Third Cataract, which corresponds almost exactly to the present language boundary between Southern Dongolawi and Nobiin.

The identification of the Danagla with the Makourians has further important implications, for it seems evident that the Makoritae were already a separate people with a separate kingdom, and in their present locality, when they were first contacted by Christian missionaries in the sixth century. Their antipathy to the Nobatians was in fact so strong that they opted deliberately for the orthodox Melkite sect of Christianity after their neighbors had been converted to the rival Monophysite sect (Trimingham 1949:56–57). We may note additionally that the post-Kushite Ballana culture, which is found throughout the territory of Nobatia, has no apparent counterpart in the territory of Makouria. Thus if we can argue for the moment from archaeology to language, we have a basis for inferring that the distinction between the Nobatae and the Makoritae goes back at least to the fourth century A.D. Indeed, the mention of Makkourai by Ptolemy raises the possibility that they were already a distinct people in the second century (map 3). Although these identifications become increasingly speculative as we go back in time, we have at least a good reason to believe that the linguistic split between Nobiin and Dongolawi goes back substantially earlier than the 1,100 years estimated

[8]Ibn Selim employs the term (usually transcribed Maris) by which medieval Egyptians usually referred to Nobatia. It is derived from the Coptic word for "south."

by Greenberg (Trigger 1966) or the 1,300–1,400 years implied by Thel-wall's percentages. Thelwall in his companion paper (chap. 3, below) provides a satisfactory explanation of why Dongolawi vocabulary evidence might give the appearance of a more recent split from Nobiin than is the case, namely, that the dominant political and literary standing of Old Nubian deeply influenced vocabulary retention and change in the contemporary "Old Dongolawi," greatly damping down the apparent rate of divergence.

The origin of the Nobiin-Dongolawi split still remains to be considered. The linguistic frontier just below the Third Cataract, though it has evidently remained stable for the best part of a thousand years (i.e., since at least the time of Ibn Selim), does not coincide with any significant cultural or political boundary since the merger of Nobatia and Makouria at the beginning of the eighth century. Nor is there any physical barrier or topographical change in the Nile Valley at this point. On the contrary, the Dongolawi-Nobiin frontier cuts quite arbitrarily across a string of nearly continuous farming villages which are in other respects indistinguishable from one another. If the language difference between the Mahas and the Danagla developed within the Nile Valley, subsequent to the in-migration of the Nubian group as a whole, it is impossible to explain why it developed at this particular point and not in some more inhospitable and unpopulated district. Some connection with the nearby Third Cataract of the Nile might be postulated, but in fact the Third Cataract is much less an impediment to navigation than are several of the rapids farther north, within the territory of the Nobiin speakers.

If the Nobiin-Dongolawi split did not originate in its present site, the alternative is surely to imagine that there was once a geographic gap between the two peoples larger than that of the recent past. We would then have to picture two different Nubian migrations at different times: one of Nobatae/Nobiin and one of Makoritae/Danagla. In that event I think the evidence points clearly to the prior arrival of the Nobiin and the subsequent arrival of the Danagla, within the area that is now their common homeland (map 4 and 5).

I suspect therefore that the present Nobiin-Dongolawi frontier is the result of a secondary intrusion of Danagla not from the west but from somewhere farther up the Nile. We have the early historical records of the Nubae/Noba as well as the accounts of medieval travelers to indicate that, until the end of the Middle Ages, Nubian languages were spoken along the whole length of the Nile, at least from Aswan to the site of modern Khartoum (Adams 1977:558–563; Trimingham 1949:17). There were

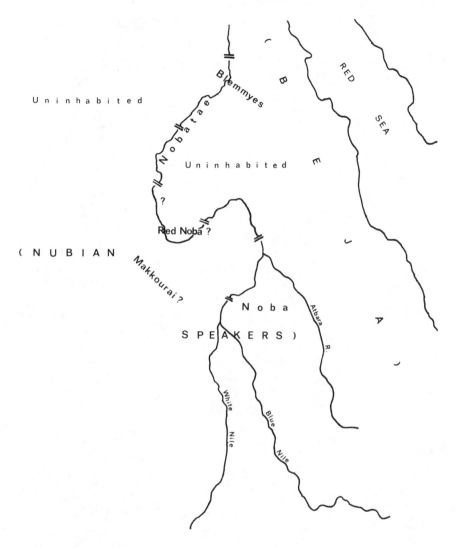

Map 4. Hypothesized distribution of language groups in the fourth century A.D. after the breakup of the Meroitic empire.

also apparently Nubian-speaking nomad groups in the immediate hinterland of the Nile, especially in the Bayuda steppe. I suspect that all their languages were once closely related, but that dialect differences may have arisen between peoples in widely separated areas, and especially perhaps between the nomads and the riverain farmers. The Danagla in their

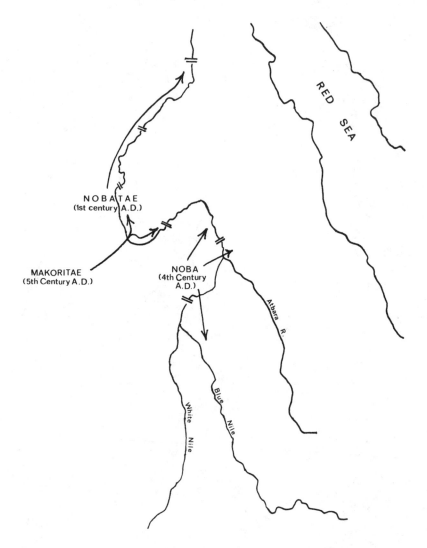

Map 5. Hypothesized sequence of Nubian migrations
in the Nile Valley.

present habitat would, in my view, represent most probably the northward migration of what was originally a more southerly riverain group, or
the settlement in the river valley of a formerly nomadic group from the
immediate hinterland. I lean slightly toward the nomadic hypothesis,
partly because there is so little evidence of pre-Christian settlement in the
Dongolawi area and partly because the Makkourai/Makoritae are identi-

fied as nomads both in Ptolemy's geography and in the account of their conversion to Christianity written in the sixth century by John of Biclarum (Trimingham 1949:56–57).

We should not forget that even in the Nile Valley we are dealing only with fragmentary and vestigial linguistic evidence. The Kenuz, the Nobiin, and the Danagla represent collectively a rapidly shrinking island surrounded by Arabic. Their neighbors, the Shaiqiya, the Rubatab, the Manassir, the Ja'aliyin, and all the other peoples between Debba and Khartoum, also spoke Nubian languages until two or three hundred years ago; unfortunately, their ancestral dialects have been lost as completely as have many of those in the western Sudan. All these peoples were, we assume, the descendants of the original Nubae/Noba, but whether at the end of the Middle Ages they spoke one language or a series of languages, and how closely those languages were related to Dongolawi and Nobiin, is anybody's guess. Thus we lack the evidence that might help us to identify an earlier homeland for the Danagla, prior to their entry into their present territory (maps 6 and 7).

What, finally, of the Kenuz, isolated and seemingly forgotten in the north? If the situation of the Danagla is somewhat enigmatic, theirs is infinitely more so. Lower Nubia (between the First and Second cataracts) has been a continuous highway of travel and trade throughout its history, and it has nearly always been under one political rule and has manifested, archaeologically, a homogeneous culture. There is no logical reason whatever why it should today be cut across the middle by a linguistic boundary.

The one point that I think we have already established about the Kenuz, by inference, is that they cannot have been for very long in their present habitat. The dialect split between Kenzi and Southern Dongolawi surely dates back no more than four or five hundred years, and we have seen that the Dongolawi speakers were already established to the south of the Nobiin in the tenth century, and very probably in the sixth. We have also ruled out the possibility that the Nobiin represent a later intrusion driving a wedge between the formerly contiguous Dongolawi groups. The only remaining hypothesis is, then, that the Kenuz represent a northward movement of Dongolawi speakers in the relatively recent past.

Insofar as we have any key to the history of the Kenuz it is to be found in the folk traditions that link them to the late medieval Beni Kanz (Banu'l-Kanz). This was originally an Arabized Beja tribe, which in the tenth century gained effective control over Aswan and the neighboring district of upper Egypt. They subsequently established their dominion

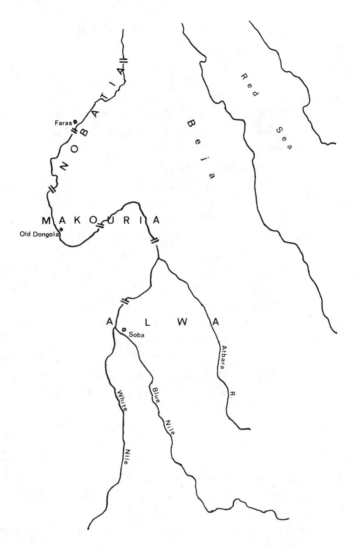

Map 6. The medieval Nubian kingdoms.

over the northernmost portion of Nubia as well. When in later centuries they were expelled from Aswan by the Ayyubids and Mamelukes, they fell back upon Nubia which became their principal base for warlike operations both in Egypt and in the Sudan (MacMichael 1922:I,149—151; Hasan 1967a:58—60, 1967b).

The Beni Kanz are said to have become Nubianized through inter-marriage with the native population in northern Nubia (Trimingham 1949:68, 84). This does not, however, explain why their descendants

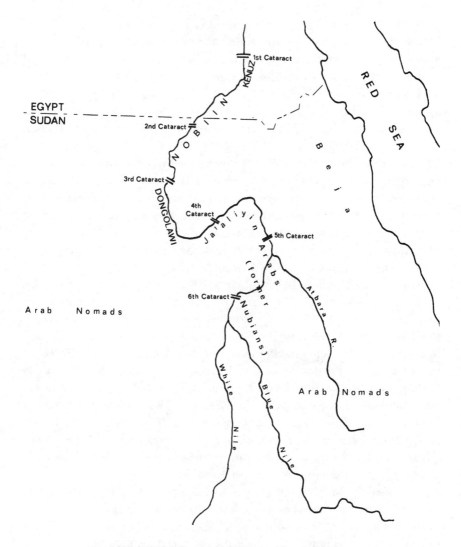

Map 7. Distribution of Nile Nubian languages
in the twentieth century.

spoke Dongolawi and not the Nobiin language which was indigenous in
the far north. I think the most plausible explanation for this anomaly
offered thus far is that of Fernea (1979). He points out that the Beni Kanz
initially established their hegemony in northern Nubia through an agreement with the rulers of Makouria. This alliance was eventually cemented
by a network of intermarriages with the Makourian ruling family, even
though the Beni Kanz were Moslems and the Makourians at that time

were still Christians. So strong did the linkage become that eventually one of the Beni Kanz leaders succeeded to the throne of Makouria itself, apparently as a result of the rule of matrilineal succession which prevailed at medieval Nubia.[9] According to tradition this accession to the throne took place in 1323 (Adams 1977:529). Fifty years later, however, it appears that the Beni Kanz had lost their control at Dongola and had returned to their more usual base of operations in the far north (Hasan 1967a:118–120).

Fernea evidently believes that during the brief period of their sovereignty large numbers of Beni Kanz came to Dongola to share in the spoils, that they contracted marriages with local women there, and that after their expulsion these women were carried by their husbands back to northern Nubia, where they taught their own Dongolawi dialect to their offspring. He correctly points out that throughout the Islamic world children are taught to speak exclusively by their mothers, so that a migration of females alone could be sufficient to account for the transplantation of the Dongolawi dialect. If we are to imagine a complete linguistic change in northern Nubia originating from such small beginnings, however, I think it can only be because the returned Beni Kanz became a ruling elite in their home district. The dominance of their language over time would therefore be a reflection of their social and political dominance over their Nobiin subjects. Fernea makes the telling point that for a considerable time the relationship between the Beni Kanz/Kenuz and their Nobiin neighbors was that of slavers and enslaved, a relationship that was justified initially because the Kenuz were Moslems whereas the Nobiin were Christians. Under those circumstances there would surely have been an advantage in exhanging Nobiin for Kenzi identity.

Fernea's hypothesis was greeted with a certain skepticism when it was first presented, perhaps because it is so far removed from the tradition of mechanistic and deterministic explanation which is now firmly established in anthropology. It is nevertheless the only suggestion thus far offered which places the arrival of Dongolawi speakers in northern Nubia within a linguistically acceptable time frame—that is, not much more than 500 years ago—and which is consistent with the complete lack of evidence for ethnic or cultural diversity in the north at an earlier date. The author goes on to cite additional cultural evidence which he sees as supporting his position. I have no further space to discuss his arguments here, but I hope to see them more fully explored in subsequent research.

[9]This event is historically attested by several contemporary authors (see Hasan 1967a:121).

3 | Linguistic Aspects of Greater Nubian History

ROBIN THELWALL

MY AIM IN THIS PAPER is to present a classification of the Nubian language group based primarily on the comparison of basic lexicon. This comparison is used as a starting point for proposing hypotheses on the earlier geographical location of Nubian-speaking peoples and their possible movements. It also serves as a check on other hypotheses on the origin and movements of the Nubian languages.

The initial brief background to comparative linguistic study in Africa is intended for nonlinguists who need to bear in mind the extent and limitations of the generalizations being made. The detailed presentation of internal Nubian language relations then given is followed by a consideration of possible external links. The final summary of historical arguments is based on the above.

The fact that the classification rests almost entirely on the lexicostatistics of basic vocabulary should not mislead readers into assuming that I accept this as a method for subclassification. The justification for its presentation and its use in hypothesis forming is that we do not yet have sufficient comparative data for other reliable subclassifications. The method used is systematic and methodologically more or less transparent. The strengths and weaknesses of the method are discussed at relevant points in the article. Those who would dismiss this method out of hand would make a better contribution by collecting sufficient new data to refute the conclusions and/or the method in this African context.

Background to the Classification of Sudan Languages

The systematic description of Sudan (and African) languages began in the nineteenth century as a natural extension of the Indo-European comparative movement. Two major factors conditioned the course of comparative African language studies: (1) the absence of ancient textual material in Africa (except for Egyptian, Ethiopian Semitic, and Nubian);

(2) the inaccessibility of the languages, which meant that the selection of languages to be described resulted from the random presence of particular African language speakers in Europe or of particular European scholars in Africa (for an insight into these matters, see Andrzejewski 1968).

The selectivity and the paucity of the data did not, however, deter linguists from proposing general classification schemes. Their schemes were conditioned by their views on the interrelationship between racial theory and genetic and typological linguistic features, and not until quite recently have scholars been able to disentangle these factors, in terms of both nomenclature and methodology. (McGaffey 1966 and Trigger 1978 present recent discussions of these matters.) Meinhof's (1912) and Westermann's (1911, 1927) classifications are prime examples of the early comparative work.

For eastern, southern, and western Africa the data base for comparative work and classification has expanded hugely, particularly since 1945. For the Eastern Bilad al-Sudan (from Chad to Ethiopia), however, both research and publication have been more sharply limited, except for Ethiopia, which since 1967 has been the subject of extensive and intensive investigation as shown by Bender et al. (1976), Bender (1976), and numerous articles. For the Sudan in particular, there is the large manuscript collection of R. C. Stevenson, many of whose grammatical data are included in Tucker and Bryan's (1966) comprehensive volume. Of approximately 100 languages spoken primarily in the Sudan, however, not more than twenty have published grammars and dictionaries. For the other eighty or more languages varying and lesser amounts of vocabulary and grammatical information have been published. In addition, the number of active linguists is still small when compared with the number of workers elsewhere in Africa, though it is a good sign that a number of Sudanese now have completed or are completing linguistics training.

The Current Situation in Sudan Language Classification

The three proposed classifications of Sudan languages in existence are based on significantly more data than are Meinhof's and Westermann's: Greenberg (1963); Tucker and Bryan (1966), the latter of which forms the basis of this geographical area for Dalby's (1977) "referential" classification; and Bender (1976). Greenberg provides a comprehensive hypothesis of the hierarchical relationships from individual language groups up to the major family (or phylum) level. Dalby presents "a revised classification of African languages, based on *known* levels of historical relationship" (my emphasis). The latter half of this statement refers to the reevaluation of Greenberg's hypotheses, possible because of the expansion of data available, and a comparative analysis, as well as an extensive argument about the methodology of language classification in Africa and elsewhere.

The question of whether Greenberg's classification is supportable on the evidence and methods he used has become less important than the stimulus it has provided for the collection of new data and the general reevaluation and refinement of genetic and typological classification methods. But it is certainly true that the uncritical acceptance by many nonlinguists of Greenberg's (or any other) classification, along with their use of it as supposedly solid collateral for the reconstruction of culture history, has been a dangerous spin-off. It is in this context that Dalby has argued cogently over several years for a "neutral" geographically based classification. Unfortunately, in the preliminary publication of his *Language Map of Africa* (1977), he has not really done this kind of classification; numerous traces of older racial-genetic-based classifications remain for which there is now no valid evidence, such as the tendentious retention of the term Para-Nilotic.

What is important is that nonlinguists should be aware of the controversies still surrounding much of African language classification. This is not to take an archconservative linguistic view toward Greenberg (as is not unknown among European Africanists), but rather to emphasize that controversy on the classification of African languages, fruitful and essential as it is for the advancement of the field, is primarily to be evaluated by linguists. Those from other disciplines who wish to join in the arguments must be prepared to evaluate critically the linguistic data and methodology instead of simply accepting the conclusions of any proposed classification. The same principle applies equally to linguists who actively participate in culture reconstruction and attempt to relate linguistic data to history.

Lexical Comparison

The major (and controversial) methodological addition in the field of comparative vocabulary analysis, which from the first has been the basis for Indo-European reconstruction both of protovocabulary and of the sound-change rules, has been lexicostatistics. Hymes (1960) gives the most balanced discussion of the method(s), and work by Gleason (1959),

Dyen (1965), Bender (1969, 1976), Henrici (1973), and Thelwall (1978) indicates both the growing usefulness of these methods and the critical reexamination of their validity and their limitations.

Lexicostatistics of "basic" vocabulary is also the basis of the much more controversial glottochronology. I will merely say here that where a relative chronology of linguistic relations can be established and can be correlated with an absolute or relative chronology derived by any other method and linked with the glottochronological scale (by the standard formula), then I see no reason for not using the glottochronological scale for dating the rest of that relative chronology, subject of course to counterevidence at any particular point without vitiating the whole scale. Discussion on this matter with specific reference to Nubian follows in the last section of this paper.

The issue of the incidence of chance similarity within basic vocabulary I take to have been examined by Bender (1969) and the probabilities to have been established. The issue of whether a specific pair of related lexical items are present in a pair of languages as the result of resistance to loss since the time of the protolanguage, or alternatively are present as a result of borrowing from one language to another, is ever present, and it can be even partly resolved only by checking sufficient comparative data. We are not yet in a position to attempt a thorough investigation of this problem for the Nilo-Saharan languages.

Current Models of Nilo-Saharan Relationships

As stated above, there are only three proposed groupings of Nilo-Saharan languages, those by Tucker and Bryan (1966), Greenberg (1963), and Bender (1976). In a sense, as Greenberg (1973) himself has pointed out, his classification and Tucker and Bryan's groupings are not in direct conflict since they start from different methodological bases, the one genetic and the other typological, and they coincide at the lowest level of relationships. Since it is genetic classifications which are *historical* classifications, the two explicitly genetic schemes of Greenberg and Bender are the ones that must be presented here, as background to understanding Nubian relationships.

Greenberg (1963): Nilo-Saharan

A. Songhai
B. Saharan

C. Maban
D. Fur
E. Chari-Nile
    1.   Eastern Sudanic
    1.1 Nubian: (*a*) Nile Nubian, (*b*) Kordofanian Nubian, (*c*) Meidob, (*d*) Birked
    1.2 Murle (Beir), Larim, Didinga, Suri, Mekan, Murzu, Surma, Masongo
    1.3 Barea
    1.4 Ingessana (= Tabi)
    1.5 Nyima, Afitti
    1.6 Temein, Teis-um-Danab
    1.7 Merarit, Tama, Sungor
    1.8 Dagu of Darfur, Baygo, Sila, Dagu of Dar Dagu, West Kordofan, Njalgulgule, Shatt, Liguri
    1.9 Nilotic: Western (1) Burun, (2) Shilluk, Anuak, Acholi, Lango, Abur, Luo, Jur, Bor, (3) Dinka, Nuer; Eastern (1) Bari, Fajulu, Kakwa, Mondari, (2*a*) Jie, Dodeth, Karamojong, Teso, Topotha, Turkana, (2*b*) Maasai; Southern: Nandi, Suk, Tatoga
    1.10 Nyangiya, Teuso [IK]
    2.   Central Sudanic
    2.1 Bongo-Baka, Morokodo, Beli, Gberi, Sara, Vale, Nduka, Tana, Horo, Bagirmi, Kuka, Kenga, Disa, Bubalia
    2.2 Kreish
    2.3 Binga, Yulu, Kara
    2.4 Moru, Avukaya, Logo, Keliko, Lugbara, Madi
    2.5 Mangbetu, Lombi, Popoi, Makere, Meje, Asua
    2.6 Mangbutu, Mamvu, Lese, Mvuba, Bfe
    2.7 Lendu
    3.   Berta, Malkan, Sillok, Tornasi
    4.   Kunama
F. Coman: Koma, Ganza, Uduk, Gule, Gumuz, Mao

Bender (1976 with his own modifications): Nilo-Sahelian

A. Songhai
B. Saharan
C. Maban
D. Fur
E. Eastern Sudanic (Greenberg's E 1.1–1.8)

F.   Nilotic
G.   Nyangiya, Teuso, Tepeth
H.   Central Sudanic
I.   Berta
J.   Kunama
K.   Koman
L.   Gumuz

Bender, who has carried out the most extensive assembly and colla-tion of existing and new data, emphasizes that his scheme is provisional, because of both the continuing expansion of the data base and the devel-opment of the comparative methodology. His scheme, nevertheless, represents a more critical reappraisal of Greenberg than Dalby's (1977). The weakness of the Chari-Nile hypothesis had been previously pro-posed by Goodman (1971) on the basis of Greenberg's own evidence, but this hypothesis now rests on Bender's new data and analysis. Also to be noted are the revisions in Eastern Sudanic. The internal situation in Nilotic can now be reevaluated as a result of extensive recent work, particularly by scholars from Cologne University, though Bender concurs with Greenberg in accepting a three-way split at the next level down.

The Nubian Group

The major impact of the introduction of the Arabic language and Islam to the eastern Sudan began with the fall of Christian Nubia in the period after A.D. 1000, and the expansion of the use of Arabic ever since has created a situation today in which not only are speakers of many Nilo-Saharan languages interpenetrated and even isolated by Arabic mono-linguals, but they are also by and large bilingual with Arabic as at least a second, and increasingly a first, language. Thus it is often impossible, or at least very difficult, to estimate the previous distribution of Nilo-Saharan languages, particularly for the areas that at the present time are solely Arabic-speaking, or where the presence of non-Arabic speakers may be owing to recent migration. It is nevertheless surprising to observe how few of the Nilo-Saharan languages have either become extinct, or are on the verge of extinction, since 1920, the point from which the recorded information on the peoples and languages of the Sudan starts to achieve some sort of overall coverage (maps 8 and 9).

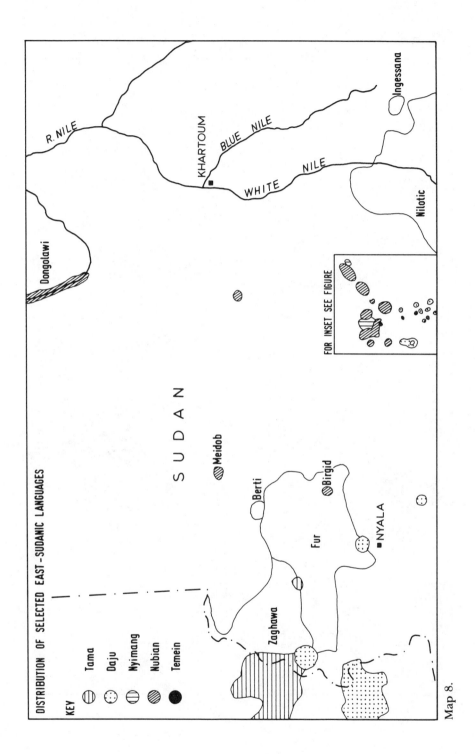

Map 8.

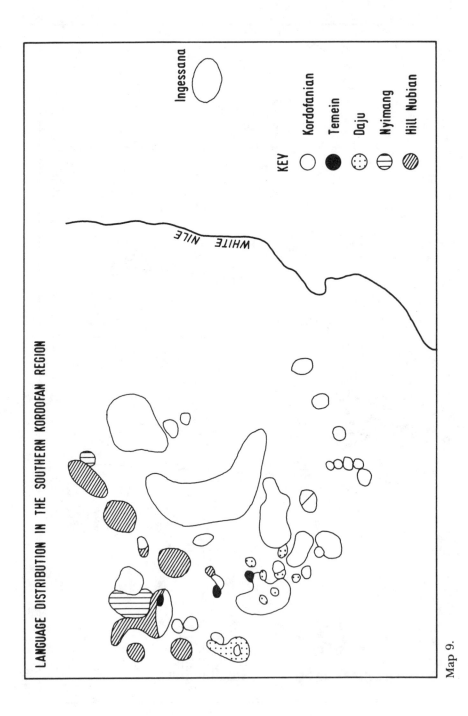

LANGUAGE DISTRIBUTION IN THE SOUTHERN KORDOFAN REGION

Ingessana

WHITE NILE

KEY

Kordofanian
Temein
Daju
Nyimang
Hill Nubian

Map 9.

Internal Relations in the Nubian Language Group

The Nubian languages are, of course, important carry-overs from the pre-Arabic eras, and tracing their earlier history is an important part of our understanding of Sudanese history in the last millennium B.C. and the first millennium A.D. The most succinct summary of ideas about the history of the Nubian languages and possible migrations of Nubian-speaking peoples is given by Trigger (1966:19): "The principal debate concerning the history of the Nubian languages has been whether they spread to the Nile Valley from Kordofan and Darfur or moved in the opposite direction." Basically MacMichael (1922) and Arkell (1961) argue that the presence of Nubian-speaking groups in Kordofan and Darfur resulted from the incursions of Ethiopians or the Arabs and Islam on the Nile Nubians. Zyhlarz (1928), relying on an evaluation of the linguistic evidence available to him, argues for a Kordofan origin. Of the various modified forms of these hypothesis which have been proposed, the only pertinent one is Greenberg (1963). He supports Zyhlarz, arguing tentatively, on the basis of a glottochronological study, that any split between "Hill and Nile Nubian more recent than 2,500 years B.P. [before present] is incorrect."

Ultimately the choice among hypotheses depends on the establishment of a reliable subclassification of the Nubian languages. Although it has been known, at least since MacMichael (1922), that the Nubian language group comprised Nobiin (Mahas), Dongolawi-Kenuzi, Hill Nubian (South Kordofan), Birgid, and Meidob, and that the two Nile Nubian dialects were closer to each other than to any other member, it was only with the collection of new data on Birgid and Meidob and the systematic comparison of basic vocabulary across the whole group (Thelwall 1978) that a serious reappraisal of internal subgrouping could take place. The cognate counts of the 100-item list were submitted to cluster analyses, and tree diagrams based on five different methods were derived (Thelwall 1981). The trees yield the same derivation for the following relations: (1) Meidob is the most distant member of the group; (2) Kadaru and Debri are the closest-knit pair and, at 87 percent cognate, may be treated as dialects of one Hill (Kordofan) Nubian unit; and (3) Dongolawi-Kenuzi and Nobiin are closer to each other than either is to any other language. Crucial qualifications to this last statement are taken up below.

What is not consistent from the tree diagrams is the hierarchical relationship among Birgid, Kadaru, Debri, and Nile Nubian. The basic anomaly is the difference in the percentages between Dongolawi as against Nobiin and Birgid, Kadaru and Debri. If we take only the highest figures for either Kadaru or Debri, excluding the other on the basis that two cognate counts for such closely related languages will distort the figures, we still get a mean or average of 53 between Dongolawi and Birgid-Debri as against 40.2 between Nobiin and Birgid-Kadaru. It is less for Nobiin:Birgid-Debri. This 13 percent difference is not plausibly explained as random differential retention of common core Nubian Lexicon.

One plausible hypothesis is that the percentages for Dongolawi with Birgid, Kadaru, and Debri more accurately represent retained common vocabulary and that the Dongolawi:Nobiin percentage is discordantly high because of borrowing by Dongolawi from Nobiin so early in the history of Nubian differentiation that loan status is not easily discernible. In support of this interpretation we may argue first that place-names of probably Nobiin origin exist in an area that is now either Arabicized or inhabited by Dongolawi speakers. Second, the political dominance of Nobiin as the administrative and religious language (the extant texts in "Old Nubian" are closer to Nobiin than to any other present-day Nubian language) shows that Nobiin had a prestige advantage which would explain continuing vocabulary interference from Nobiin through the medieval period, with a resulting higher proportion of Nobiin loans in present-day Dongolawi. A third argument is that in the first millennium A.D. Nobiin and Dongolawi would still have been sufficiently mutually intelligible for the selection of alternative lexicon on the basis of prestige to have been sociolinguistically easy and not to require special pleading. If we discount the Dongolawi high score with Nobiin, the pattern of percentages may be reasonably interpreted as a dialect chain with the low range in the 40 percents, representing more distant members, and the 50 percents, the nearer members in a chain or network.

Figure 1 presents a schematic version of present geographical distribution of the Nubian languages with the glottochronological dates inserted. The dates are not proposed deterministically but merely for hypothesis building and testing.

In summary, the lexicostatistical relations, with the overhigh Dongolawi:Nobiin figure attributed to contact influences, suggest that in the last millennium B.C. Nubian communities, presumably pastoralists in subsistence, spread out widely across the steppes between northern Darfur and the Nile. The possible position of Meidob in its own group

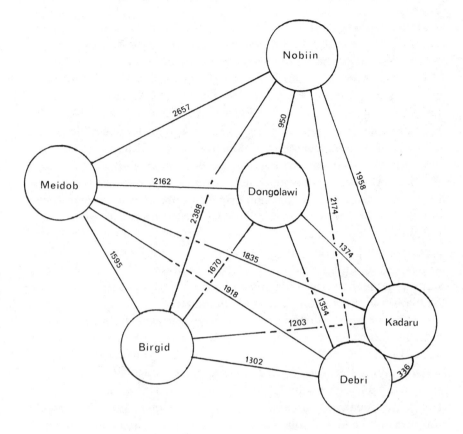

Fig. 1. Schematic representation of Nubian geographical positioning and glotto-chronological distance (in years B.P.).

coordinate with the group made up of the other four Nubian languages suggests that the movement was principally from Darfur eastward. The pre-Nobiin were the first Nubians to settle in the upper and lower Nubian Nile stretches, perhaps even in the latter part of the last millennium B.C. The pre-Dongolawi were a slightly later intrusion of nearby Nubians displacing the pre-Nobiin in Upper Nubia. If pre-Dongolawi were replacing the still very similar (at that time) pre-Nobiin, that would further enhance the movement of Nobiin vocabulary into Dongolawi and thus add to the appearance of special resemblance between the two which, it has been argued, was caused by the medieval prominence of Old Nubian. A recent examination of vocabulary evidence for Nubian contact with the Nile is given in Behrens (1981). W. Y. Adams (chap. 2, above) adduces evidence from texts which indicates the history of Nubian settlement is strikingly parallel to that reached from the linguistic sources.

Some corroborating nonlinguistic information supporting this conclusion is a migration tradition of the Shaiqiya tribe, who are part of the greater Jaali group, presently Arabic-speaking, along the Nile upstream from Dongola and who are considered arabized Nubians. This tradition recounts that the Shaiqi came from western Sudan and first settled on the White Nile near Ed-Dueim, 120 kilometers south of Khartoum, and then at a later date moved north across the Bayuda steppe to their present position (Ali Osman, personal communication). It would be a very aberrant and thus believable tradition even for a present-day Nubian-speaking community, let alone an Arabic one, since the historical importance of the Nubian kingdoms and the desire to manufacture a respectable Islamic and Arabian pedigree combine to give many peoples in the central and western Sudan migration-from-the-east traditions. The Meidob, for instance, hedge their bets by having both a tradition linking them to the Nile Nubians and a tradition of Hilāli Arab origin.

We are left with one remaining major puzzle. The Kenuz speak a Nubian tongue barely distinguishable from Dongolawi, and yet they are located primarily in Upper Egypt north of Wadi Halfa, with the Nobiin situated along the Nile between them and the Dongolawi. According to some scholars, the presence of Nobiin sandwiched between two groups of Dongolawi speakers supposed the incursion of Nobiin, probably from the southwest. The lexical subclassification and the argumentation based on it above go strongly against this hypothesis and instead indicate that the presence of Dongolawi speech among the Kenuz is due to a northward movement of Dongolawi speakers, and a relatively recent movement at that, unless the lines of communication between the two remained exceptionally strong and constant. Fernea (1979) has argued cogently that "the language, belief system, tribal organisation and distinctive architecture among the Kenuz . . . [were] a legacy from the Dongola region." Supporting evidence from medieval sources such as Ibn Khaldun (Hasan 1967a: 127) tells us that as the Christian kingdoms of Nubia were collapsing, many Nubian women were given in marriage to Arabs. Kanz al-Dawla, who was of both Dongolawi and Arab descent and from whom the Kenuz take their name, after being made king of Dongola in the late fourteenth century, subsequently retired with his followers to estates near Aswan (Hasan 1967a:119). The collusion of historical and contemporary evidence would seem to resolve the puzzle (see also Adams on this point in chap. 2, above).

External Links with the Nubian Language Group

What was the earlier background of the proto-Nubians of the first millennium B.C.? Since Greenberg (1963) offers no details of subgrouping within Eastern Sudanic, except for Nilotic, comparisons were made with seventeen other languages belonging to six other Eastern Sudanic groups and Berta (Thelwall 1981:169–171). Two sets of comparisons are significant:

	Range	Median	Average
Nubian:Tama	19.6–24.7	22.1	22.2
:Nyimang	9.8–19.8	14.8	13.4
:Afitti	10.7–16.7	13.7	12.5

For Tama, the lowest figures are with the geographical outliers of the group, Meidob and Nobiin, and the highest figure is with Dongolawi. If the relationship with Tama was primarily the result of proto-Eastern Sudanic retentions combined possibly with variations owing to subsequent contact with Western Nubian groups, we would expect a cline falling from Darfur Nubian through Kordofan to Nile Nubian. The pattern given indicates instead that, at one stage of the development of Eastern Sudanic, Tama and Nubian formed a distinct subgroup. The present geographical position of Tama, centered on the Chad-Sudan border zone north of Geneina (see map 1), and its linguistic position separated from other Eastern Sudanic languages by at least Zaghawa and Fur indicate two things. First, they support the Darfur origin hypothesis for Nubian. The glottochronological figures range from 3,668 to 3,315 years ago, placing the Tama-Nubian breakup in the earlier second millennium B.C. Second, they raise the probability that Tama diverged from Nubian by a movement to the west, even if we allow for possible movement of Fur as well as of Zaghawa speakers into intervening areas. The figures and the derived tree diagrams strongly support Nubian-Tama as a distinct subgroup within Eastern Sudanic.

The relationship of the Nubian group with Nyimang-Afitti is more tenuous, and at these percentages the confidence level decreases. Given the geographical location near to Hill Nubian of the two languages, again we would expect the highest figures with these; however, the highs are rather with Dongolawi and Nobiin, farther away, a fact that strenthens our confidence in the indications of the percentages. The location of Nyimang and Afitti puts their earlier homeland in or near Kordofan and suggests that the Tama-Nubian homeland should be somewhere nearby, perhaps between Darfur and Kordofan.

The remaining figures for Nubian relationships, which are all lower, merely support Bender's revised model for Nilo-Saharan with a number of coordinate branches going back a long way in time. Clearly lexicostatistics has little to offer in the way of deep-time subgrouping here. The next advances will come from detailed comparisons and reconstructions; the examination of borrowing, particularly in culture vocabulary; and the development of hypotheses about environmental and culture-contact relations.

Acknowledgments

This paper could not have been completed without generous access to Roland Stevenson's word lists and Lionel Bender's word lists and ongoing grammatical analyses. It was written during a sabbatical visit to the Sudan from the New University of Ulster, with the generous support of a British Academy research fellowship. Local facilities in Khartoum were kindly provided by Dr. Mustafa Abdel Majid of the Linguistics Department, University of Khartoum. W. Y. Adams was instrumental in encouraging me to turn my main attention to the Nubian group. I am also grateful to Ali Osman for stimulating discussions and unpublished information.

Part II

Equatorial Africa

OVERVIEW

For much of equatorial Africa—defined broadly here to include Cameroon, Gabon, Congo, Central African Republic (CAR), southern Sudan, Zaire, and parts of Zambia and Angola—the possibility of effective correlation of language and archaeology exists only for the eras of the spread of food production. Throughout the forest and the formerly forested savanna zones of the Congo Basin, the Lupemban tool industry and its derivatives persisted down to the agricultural threshold and, in some instances, for a while after that, alongside the industries of agriculturists. The obvious candidates for the aboriginals who produced those tool kits are the ancestors of the Pygmy hunter-gatherers of the rain forest and its margins. But the language correlation will have to remain unknown because the Pygmies of today all speak versions of the languages spoken by communities of farmers presently or formerly living near them. Only around to the northeast, in the southern Sudan, and to the south, in the southern savanna belt, can preagricultural language affiliations possibly be probed. In the southern Sudan the Late Stone Age hunters and fishers may often have been Nilo-Saharan in language; in the southern savannas, at least since the drying of the climate in the third millennium B.C., many of the hunters would have spoken Khoisan languages, in particular the makers of "Wilton"-type tool industries in Zambia.

Into such contexts in northern equatorial Africa, food-producing peoples of Niger-Congo languages—the Bantu and the Ubangians—and of Nilo-Saharan affiliations—the Central Sudanians and the Nilotes—were variously beginning to expand by probably the third millennium. It is with these and subsequent eras that the three articles of this section deal.

The opening two articles are by linguistic historians. The first, by Christopher Ehret (chap. 4), looks at the dominant early historical theme of the southern two-thirds of equatorial Africa, the expansion of the Bantu and the apparently concomitant introduction of food production to the region during broadly the last three millennia B.C. It is a theme that has generated more recent historical and linguistic publication than any other such African topic. But the solid historical conclusions that have repeatedly emerged from the debate often remain obscured because of the interjection early on of unfounded speculations, offered by scholars with the ostensible credentials but without the theoretical or methodological grounding necessary for the particular kind of work involved (most notably Malcolm Guthrie; see Flight 1980). What Ehret's chapter does, therefore, is to set out point by point what the evidence of Bantu relationships and vocabulary reconstruction, as it now stands, requires, what it allows, and what it does not allow.

The second article of the section, by Douglas Saxon (chap. 5), presents linguistic evidence for the remaining, northern third of equatorial Africa, in which the dominant populations today speak languages of the Ubangian portion of the Adamawa-Ubangian (Greenberg's Adamawa-Eastern) branch of the same Niger-Congo language family to which the Bantu belong. The Ubangian peoples, generally neglected by historians, were expanding through the woodland savanna just north of the equatorial rain forest during approximately the same eras as early Bantu settlement in the forest. Their spread was, in other words, a roughly contemporaneous northern counterpart of the first stages of Bantu expansion.

The third and final paper on equatorial Africa, by Nicholas David (chap. 6), is a sweeping and engrossing overview of archaeological knowledge of the whole region. David's interpretation of the scattered pre–Iron Age and Early Iron Age agricultural finds from the Congo Basin is remarkably close to the historical picture that emerges from linguistic analysis. His own fieldwork in the Central African Republic and the southern Sudan allows him to bring the Ubangian, Central Sudanic, and Nilotic peoples of those regions into his synthesis as well. David suggests that the one extensive later Ubangian spread, that of the Mundu-Ndogo which Saxon puts in the later last millennium B.C., may correspond to the spread of metallurgy evident by no later than mid-first millennium A.D. in the Central African Republic.

As for the Central Sudanic and Nilotic peoples of the far northeastern fringes of equatorial Africa, David's proposals again break entirely new ground and form a welcome turning of attention toward another neglected area of historical study. His discussion of possible Nilotic correlations with archaeology ties into (and at one point disagrees with) Ambrose's discussion in this volume (chap. 7) of areas farther south, in East Africa. David also suggests ways the archaeology of Western Nilotes may link up with the oral tradition of recent centuries, in particular for the Dinka and for the Luo expansion.

Linguistic Inferences About
Early Bantu History

CHRISTOPHER EHRET

THE HISTORICAL-LINGUISTIC STUDY of the Bantu lan-
guages has progressed to a point where several major generalizations
about the course of Bantu history can be made with considerable confidence and alternative postulations can be rejected. There continues to be
a lag in the communication of such advances to other historians of Africa,
not only because of the presumed abstruseness of the source material but
also because some historians, incorrectly assuming that their several
linguist-mentors have had equally adequate theoretical grounding in
their craft, have attempted to reconcile conclusions fundamentally at
variance (e.g., Oliver 1966). The variety of alternative possible arrangements of the main outlines of Bantu history have been progressively
reduced over the past decade and a half, and it is time to lay out as
succinctly and clearly as possible what can now be asserted about that
history, both to open the way to further advance and to provide historians
with a guide through the maze of literature on the topic. It should be
noted that what can be asserted are conclusions only about rough outlines
of change and about certain broad issues of Bantu history. The details
everywhere remain to be worked out.

The Proto-Bantu Homeland

The Bantu languages originated in the far northwest corner of their
modern distribution through the vast southern third of Africa. This first
conclusion is now so generally accepted that it may seem redundant to
bring it up again. But it lies at the core of the story, and it derives from
application of a fundamental linguistic-historical principle, the principle
of least moves.

Greenberg (1955) showed the relevance of this method of inference
by applying it to the external relationships of Bantu. Bantu, he demonstrated, belonged to the Niger-Congo language family, nearly all of whose
members other than Bantu were spoken in West Africa; and within that

family Bantu belonged in the Benue-Congo branch, all other members of which were found in a relatively compact region of Nigeria, some in the plateau areas of north-central Nigeria and the rest in the far east of the country adjoining the most northwesterly Bantu languages. The least-moves principle required the placing of the proto-Bantu homeland next to the nearest of the other Benue-Congo peoples, namely, in far eastern Nigeria or adjoining parts of Cameroon.

The conclusion is just as strongly supported by the evidence of internal relationship. Within the Bantu language group the primary divisions, as a variety of studies have put beyond doubt (Ehret 1964; Heine 1973; Henrici 1973; and others), are between languages spoken in the northwest portion of the Bantu zone and all the rest of the group. Even from the evidence of Bantu subclassification alone, then, the proto-Bantu homeland would have to be placed in or about the general region of southern Cameroon.

The Antiquity of Bantu Expansion

The spread of Bantu speakers out of that homeland began at least 4,000 years ago and possibly as long as 5,000 years ago. Though this conclusion was presaged in work done more than two decades ago (Meeussen 1956), scholars still sometimes try to compress the immense complexity of history encompassed by the generalization "Bantu expansion" into a shorter period. The lexical variance between the most distantly related Bantu languages, with cognation in basic vocabulary dropping into the low 20 percents and occasionally even lower, cannot be accounted for by any shorter period unless one supposes Bantu Africans to be somehow different in their linguistic behavior from other human beings.

By the same criteria the beginnings of the eastern and southern African stage of Bantu expansion belong to a later era, approximately the last millennium B.C. Among the eastern and southern African languages the minimum percentages of cognation in modified versions of the standard 100-word list of core vocabulary range in the high 30 and the 40 percents, markedly higher than their cognation with the northwestern languages or the cognation of different northwestern subgroups with each other. Experience elsewhere with human languages suggests that a maximum time depth on the order of about 3,000 years is adequate to account for this degree of diversity.

In both instances we are talking about the lower dating limits for the bare beginnings of diversification. The full working out of the process would last into subsequent centuries.

The Nature of Bantu Expansion

Bantu expansion, at least up to the threshold of the Iron Age and even often thereafter, consisted of the whole of successive advances from previously established frontiers of settlement. Time and again the effects of dialect chaining can be discerned in the areal distribution of features across the lines of genetic division within Bantu, in more than one instance confusing or obscuring the details of relationship, occasionally though not usually beyond recovery. Dialect chaining reflects a history of expansion of a people into a string or network of adjoining territories, with social unity breaking down gradually on a territorial basis but with intercommunity contacts continuing and particular cultural and linguistic changes spreading in differing degrees (according to practical advantages or social constraints) along those lines of contact. Thus repeatedly through Bantu expansion history the evidence implies contiguity and maintenance of contact for a period across expanding settlement areas.

Directions and Stages of Bantu Expansion

There are no linguistic grounds for supposing that early Bantu expansion went around the fringes of the forest (as Phillipson 1977*b* and elsewhere, among others, suggests) or that it included a dash through the forest to the other side (as Guthrie 1962 proposes). The only reason for continuing recurrence to such hypotheses seems to be an a priori reluctance on the part of scholars to accept the forest as a suitable ecological zone for early Bantu settlement. The most probable outline schemes of Bantu subclassification (Henrici 1973; Ehret 1964; Heine 1973), analyzed by the least-moves principle, all make parts of the equatorial rain forest the most likely region of initial expansion; and the evidence for gradual and progressive Bantu spread would militate against any long dash through, or a long encircling movement around, areas left unsettled.

The most inclusive effort so far at Bantu subclassification (Heine 1973) needs especially to be looked at because it has been used by one scholar (Phillipson 1977*b, d*) to argue forest-encircling and transit movements. By Heine's reckoning, proto-Bantu diverged at first into eleven branches. (More recently, Heine et al. 1975 reduces the number to eight, but the overall implications remain the same.) The modern distributions of the ten branches of limited spread depict a long irregular stream of early Bantu settlement extending from southern Cameroon and Gabon eastward across the northern equatorial forest about as far—neglecting a historically more recent eastern extension of Benge-Bira peoples

(McMaster 1977, 1978)—as Kisangani. The eleventh branch, Heine's "Kongo-Zweig," includes all the rest of Bantu. The homeland of the ancestral language of that branch must thus be placed somewhere adjoining the much more limited skein of territory marked by the other ten, in particular along the south side of the skein to account for the subsequent directions of dispersal. Since the Kongo-Zweig itself divides into nine subbranches, eight of which are limited to the areas between the Lualaba and the Atlantic while just one—Heine's Osthochland (the Eastern Bantu of Ehret 1973)—covers nearly the whole of the Bantu field east and southeast of there, the principle of least moves also places the proto-Kongo homeland in the western part of the continent. The point of origin was most probably in the areas near or south of the Congo-Ubangi confluence, because in and around those regions are concentrated five of the nine subbranches of the Kongo branch. This stretch of land includes rain forest and woodland savanna areas. The subsequent emergence of the Eastern (Osthochland) Bantu can best be placed off to the east of this zone, probably along the Lualaba near the forest/savanna interface, as it is there that the westernmost subgroups of the Eastern subbranch adjoin other members of the Kongo-Zweig. (See Nurse, chap. 10, below, for a summary of Heine's Eastern group.)

Heine's classification therefore does not at all suggest Bantu circumvention of the forest zone. It suggests rather an initial expansion across the northwestern and north-central rain forest, with one of the groups that emerged from the first stage of expansion subsequently embarking on its own complex and ultimately much vaster expansions, at first (in the proto-Kongo period) occupying parts of the forest and its southern savanna fringes, perhaps in an arc roughly describing the lower and middle reaches of the Congo River, and only later extending far into the regions east and south of the rain forest. Nothing in the evidence argues against the possibility of riverine routes of access to the forest zone. Heine's scheme, with its skein of eleven branches, several of them scattered along or near the Congo River stretches in northern Zaire, conforms quite well to a pattern of initial Bantu expansion and establishment along rivers, and the second stage of expansion required by this subgrouping, that of the Kongo-Zweig, also seems river-oriented. Other schemes of overall Bantu subclassification (Henrici 1973; Ehret 1964) support the implication of initial forest settlement; being less inclusive, they do not make a case for or against riverine access.

Bantu expansion, apparently gradual in the forest, did not immediately take off upon encounter with a woodland savanna environment around the southern and eastern edges of the rain forest. The evidence of dialect chaining in the early period of differentiation of Eastern Bantu is particularly strong (Ehret 1973), and it can be argued that for some centuries the early Eastern Bantu, while breaking up into a large number of small communities, expanded only slowly over a still relatively compact territory before spilling out into the great expansions that would eventually spread their descendants, the speakers of the modern Eastern Bantu languages, over nearly the whole of eastern and southeastern Africa.

Subsistence Practices in Bantu History

The oldest Bantu subsistence vocabulary so far reconstructible accords with postulation of a high-rainfall, tropical environment for the proto-Bantu homeland. No grain terms can be reconstructed, but there is instead a word for yam. Two or three possible root words dealing with the oil palm may also date to proto-Bantu, and the reconstructible proto-Bantu name for alcoholic drink apparently referred specifically to palm wine. At least one cucurbit, probably the bottle gourd, a pulse (the cowpea?), and probably the *Voandzeia* groundnut were also known to the proto-Bantu (Ehret 1974*a*). These three crops would all have been domesticated elsewhere than in the proto-Bantu homeland, but apparently they could be effectively grown in high-rainfall savanna and/or rain forest. (For modern occurrence of these crops in the forest, see Miracle 1967.)

A second indication of a high-rainfall environment is provided by the reconstructibility of fishing and boating vocabulary (Guthrie 1962, 1967–1972; Ehret 1972). Apparently the proto-Bantu made considerable use of riverine resources and lived where large perennial streams were commonplace.

Knowledge of two domestic animals, cattle and goats, can be reconstructed. The presence of a word for cow might mean the proto-Bantu lived in a tsetse-free area, such as the grasslands area of Cameroon, or near enough to such an area to be acquainted with the animal. Alternatively the trypanosomiasis-resistant West African strain of cattle might already have been developed. Whatever the cause of proto-Bantu knowledge of cattle, it was lost by those who expanded into the equatorial rain forest, for the proto-Bantu root *nyaka is found no farther south than some of the forest languages in which it was reapplied, in the absence of cattle, to the buffalo.

What particular kind of a high-rainfall environment did the proto-

Bantu live in? It is widely assumed that it was a woodland savanna environment; the reconstructible subsistence terminology would fit well with that postulation, but it does not rule out an actual rain-forest climate. The most probable areas of Bantu origin, in and about southern Cameroon, today include both forest and high-rainfall savanna; thus the proto-Bantu homeland may have straddled two climatic regimes. There is also the problem of the timing of the proto-Bantu era. If it lies as far back as 3000 B.C., much more of the probable homeland region would have been rain forest, and the proto-Bantu mainly forest people. If it lies in the later third millennium B.C., then Bantu expansion could have begun as the movement of Benue-Congo dwellers of the forest/savanna fringe southward with the retreat of the forest at the end of the wet phase, with some of them adapting more fully to the forest and so setting off the long chain of developments eventuating in the Bantu distributions of today.

The emergence much later of Bantu communities out of the southern and eastern fringes of the forest set off a new period of adaptation, pervasively reflected in the evolution of subsistence vocabulary in the Bantu languages of the southern savanna and eastern and southern Africa (Ehret 1974*a*). What appears from vocabulary change to have taken place at that time was the gradual adding of grains and other crops suited to the savanna to the Bantu agricultural repertoire. It is subsequent to this period that the Bantu expansion across eastern and southeastern Africa occurred because the words that mark this period of adaptation recur throughout the Eastern Bantu area.

Early Bantu Technology

Contrary to a widely held view, knowledge of ironworking cannot be linguistically reconstructed for proto-Bantu (de Maret and Nsuka 1977). The earliest stages of Bantu expansion appear therefore to belong to the Stone Age, as is to be expected from the probable dating of the proto-Bantu era to sometime in the third millennium B.C. By the beginnings, however, of Bantu expansion into eastern Africa, on linguistic grounds most probably during the last millennium B.C., metallurgical terms had come into use among at least the ancestral Eastern Bantu communities (Ehret, unpublished *b*). Hence the later stages of Bantu history most clearly do belong to the Iron Age, but the earlier stages seem as surely to have preceded it.

Causes of Bantu Expansion

What should now be clear is that "Bantu expansion" was no single on-going development. It began too early for the possession of iron to be the distinguishing advantage of Bantu speakers (as Wrigley 1960 and others suggest); it began too early and in the end encompassed too many quite different environments for the single adoption of the Indonesian or any other crop complex to have created the opportunity of expansion (as Murdock 1959 says). The dominant causative factors may have been and probably were quite different in different eras and areas of the spread of Bantu speech.

Several possibilities as to causation, speculative at this point, suggest themselves. The Bantu establishment in the forest could have amounted simply to the advance of the food-producing frontier at the expense of more scattered and less productive hunter-gatherers. In the southern savanna belt and in southern Africa, Bantu populations were generally again intruding into the lands of hunter-gatherers; the intervening complication would have been the necessity of the Bantu-speaking societies to have made subsistence adaptations, namely, the adoption of additional crops better fitting their food-production activities to the drier climates of those regions. In eastern Africa the Bantu settlers must, on the other hand, have frequently been moving in among preexisting agricultural populations. What can be suggested is that the settlers there may have been able to persist at first by taking up wetter, wooded ecological niches previously underutilized by the herders and grain cultivators who preceded them—areas such as Bukoba, parts of the Kenya and northeast Tanzanian highlands, and the East African coastal belt (Ehret, forthcoming *b*).

Archaeological Expectations

What should be expected as the archaeological correlate of the Bantu linguistic indications would be the spread of a particular culture or set of related cultures from Cameroon through parts especially of the equatorial rain forest (if Heine's classification bears some resemblance to the true picture of Bantu relationships), at least as early as the second millennium B.C. and probably beginning in the third millennium. The bearers of this tradition would be pottery makers but not ironworkers and would probably mix food-collecting pursuits, especially fishing, with cultivation and the keeping of some goats. Their distribution might bear some relation to the locations of the rivers of the Congo Basin, with early concentrations along and north of the east-to-west stretches of the middle Congo River and later extensions of population to the south down, and to the east up, the river. Expansion would probably have been quite selective, leaving many parts of the forest zone to be settled by food producers only in still later times (map 10).

By the first millennium B.C., descendant forms of this set of related cultures would be beginning to extend into parts of the woodland savanna adjoining the forest proper, such as to the south where Kongo and early Western Savanna Bantu (partly equivalent to Heine's Westhochland) settlement must be accounted for (Papstein 1979). Of special importance at this stage would be the areas on the east side of the forest, between the Lualaba, Lake Victoria, and Lake Tanganyika. It is somewhere in this region and period that the ancestral language of most of the modern languages of the eastern half of the Bantu area should best be located on linguistic grounds. Two major additions to the cultural complex should start to turn up at that point in the archaeology—ironworking and new crops, especially sorghum and finger millet—after which time derivative cultures would begin to spread, all about the same time, widely and relatively rapidly through regions to the east and south, and the new crops (and probably ironworking) would diffuse rapidly westward to the other, more distantly related cultures already beginning to penetrate the southern savanna zone.

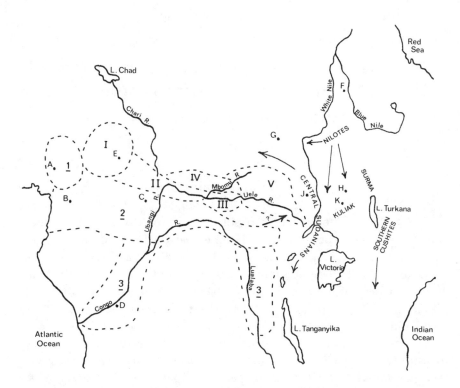

Map 10. Equatorial Africa, 3000–500 B.C.: Proposed linguistic expansions and key archaeological sites. I—Probable approximate Adamawa-Ubangian region, ca. 3000 B.C.; II—First stages of Ubangian expansion, ca. third millennium B.C.; III—Eastern Ubangian expansion, ca. early second millennium B.C.; IV—Mbomu-Uele expansion, ca. late second millennium B.C.; V—Mundu-Ndogo expansion, ca. second half of first millennium B.C.; 1—Proposed pre- and proto-Bantu region; 2—First Bantu expansions, ca. third millennium B.C.; 3—Second Bantu expansion, ca. second millennium B.C.; ✓ —Other expansions, in second or early first millennium B.C.

NOTE: In some southern parts of areas shown on the map to be within the Ubangian sphere, especially along the Ubangi River as far as the Mbomu-Uele confluence, Bantu-speaking communities may formerly have constituted a significant population element. (See McMaster 1977.)

Archaeological sites (from David, chap. 6, below); A—Sum Laka; B—Ebobogo; C—Batalimo; D—Pointe de la Gombe; E—Nana-Modé; F—Jebel Moya; G—Dhang Rial; H—Jebel Kathango; J—Jebel Tukyi; K—Lokabulo.

5 | Linguistic Evidence for the Eastward Spread of Ubangian Peoples

DOUGLAS E. SAXON

Ubangian Expansions

THE DISTRIBUTION OF SPEAKERS of Ubangian languages has long been recognized as indicating that they spread eastward to dominate the drainage basin of the Ubangi River and its tributaries (Tucker 1940:29). Disputes have remained, however, regarding the time and sequences of the expansion of Ubangian speakers. G. P. Murdock (1959:222–236, map on p. 15) asserts that their spread, spearheaded by the Zande, took place since 1500 A.D. C. C. Wrigley (1962:271), on the other hand, recognized that the Zande expansion was recent and did not constitute the first eastward spread of Ubangian languages. But even Wrigley felt that the Ubangian speakers expanded at the expense of Central Sudanic speakers, breaking up their contiguous settlement from the Shari Basin south to the edge of the Congo forest. More recent work on Ubangian and Central Sudanic history has shown that Central Sudanic peoples did not in general precede Ubangians in the Ubangi Basin and that Ubangians were probably the first food producers in most of their early areas of settlement (Ehret et al. 1974). Drawing on a more extensive collection of evidence than was available to earlier authors, I propose a revision of the classification of Ubangian languages and a revised history of Ubangian expansion.

The initial step was to establish the percentages of cognation in a standard basic vocabulary of each pairing of languages within the group (see tables 1 and 2). From this information a tree of historical relationships and diversification of the Ubangian group can be drawn. The tree model (fig. 2) shows the linguistic history of the Ubangians as a series of steps. To the left of the diagram the approximate period of each step is noted. The dating is based on an average rate of change within core vocabularies of various languages in the world, where the history is known. A slightly modified form of the 200-word list (dropping "snow" and "ice") was used. In some cases less than the full word list was available, but for only a few

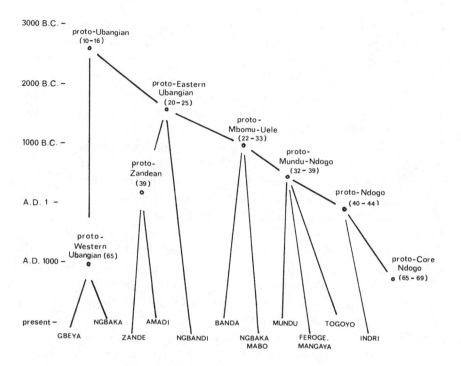

Fig. 2. Ubangian language relationships.

languages, most notably Mundu-Ndogo, do the samples contain markedly less than 200 words. (The languages in the Ubangian chart in table 2 are ones for which full or relatively full lists exist.) Since percentages of cognation theoretically follow a normal distribution curve, extremes of ranges are disregarded in estimating dates, though off-range scores may also reflect historical contacts. It should be reiterated that the datings shown are only rough approximations based on the state of the art today; these dates could therefore be subject to alteration when adequate archaeological work has been completed.

If the model is examined more closely it will be noted that the nodal percentage ranges (table 1) overlap by a few points. This apparent discrepancy underlines the correct way to view the charts. The nodes, while they represent stages in the historical development of the modern Ubangian languages, also reflect the cultural existence of peoples who for a period of time shared a common set of culture features and spoke a common language. Gradually, over time, those peoples grew apart, losing their ability to understand one another's speech. This development would not have been uniform for all the component parts of the community. Populations that lived closer together would have retained the ability to communicate with one another longer than those on the far fringes, for example. Therefore if the chart shows the lack of a sharp break between emerging language divisions, notably for the nodes from proto-Eastern to proto-Mbomu-Uele, that lack would reflect social realities rather than a defect in the chart.

Examination of the chart for the Ubangian languages as a whole (table 2) would leave the position of Mundu doubtful since it has similar scores with Banda, Ndogo, and Ngbaka Mabo. The Banda and Ngbaka Mabo figures, higher with Mundu than with other Mundu-Ndogo languages, must be understood to reflect continuing proximity of the pre-Banda and pre-Ngbaka Mabo with the early pre-Mundu-speaking fringe of the proto-Mundu-Ndogo territory. The pre-Mundu language must have diverged on the western edges of that region, with the pre-Ngbaka Mabo to one side and the pre-Banda to the other. Although Mundu itself is found today far to the east near the Uele headwaters, the presence of Gbanziri and Monjombo, which belong to the Mundu subgroup (Greenberg 1963:9), respectively on the lower Uele and west of the lower Ubangi supports Mundu derivation from near the great bend of the Ubangi, near to the Ngbaka Mabo on the west or southwest and to the southern edge of Banda territory on the north or northeast.

The slightly higher-than-range scores between Gbeya-Ngbaka and Ngbaka Mabo (table 2) may be laid to borrowings that occurred when Ngbaka speakers moved through in relatively recent centuries and settled on lands that were previously Ngbaka Mabo in speech. The above-range Gbeya and Ngbandi count probably reflects some similar history, since the Ngbandi have been important in recent centuries.

To summarize, the stages of Ubangian history presented by the linguistic classification are four in number. The proto-Ubangian society began to break into two sets of communities, proto-Western and proto-Eastern Ubangian, during the third millennium B.C. Proto-Eastern Ubangian then split into three daughters, proto-Mbomu-Uele, pre-Ngbandi, and proto-Zandean, sometime roughly in the earlier second millennium. Over the later second millennium B.C., proto-Mbomu-Uele unity in turn broke down, as the pre-Banda, pre-Ngbaka Mabo, and proto-Mundu-Ndogo societies emerged. Finally, over the course of the last millennium B.C., proto-Mundu-Ndogo broke into Mundu, Tagoyo, Mangaya-Feroge, and Ndogo subgroups. The last stage of Mundu-Ndogo expansion was marked by the separation of pre-Indri from Core Ndogo about 2,000 years ago. The Core Ndogo breakup into a number of descendant communities is a much more recent event, dating not more than about 1,000 years ago (map 10).

The first two stages of Ubangian expansion, occupying roughly the third millennium B.C., seem to amount to a progressive eastward movement from west of the great bend of the Ubangi. The split of proto-Eastern from proto-Western Ubangian can be seen as the result of a move of some of the proto-Ubangians east toward the confluence of the Mbomu and Uele rivers; the next split, of proto-Eastern into proto-Mundu-Ndogo, pre-Ngbandi, and proto-Zandeans, can be understood as a further move of Ubangians, with the proto-Zandeans moving eastward beyond the Mbomu-Uele confluence. The early Ubangian expansions appear contemporary with and parallel to the Bantu expansions to the south of them and similarly show a tendency to follow rivers (see Ehret, chap. 4, above).

The first divergences among the Mbomu-Uele peoples concentrated probably on the areas between the Ubangi bend and the Mbomu and Uele confluence. They involved differentiation among Ubangians already in place and in contact with one another. The Mundu-Ndogo expansions of roughly the second half of the last millennium B.C. were, however, an immense reexpansion of Ubangians, carrying from the bend of the Ubangi through most of the Mbomu and Uele basins to the edges of the Nile watershed—across the Central African Republic and far northern Zaire as far as the southwest part of the Sudan, where Tagoyo, Indri, and Core Ndogo communities were taking shape 2,000 years ago. The Mundu-Ndogo spread may or may not have correlated with river routes of movement. At about the same time the proto-Zandeans were dividing into proto-Zande-Nzakara and pre-Amadi groups. Why the Zandeans persisted in the midst of the vast Mundu-Ndogo expansion is not evident. It may be that the Mundu-Ndogo settlements intruded between different Zandeans and so was responsible for breaking up proto-Zande into two descendant communities.

By 2,000 years ago the Ubangian territory had reached almost its full present extent. The expansion of the Zande proper during the past few hundred years was not generally a further extension of Ubangian speech but a replacement of the earlier Ubangian languages of the region by another Ubangian language whose ancestral form, proto-Zandean, had survived as perhaps an enclave in the midst of Mundu-Ndogo expansion. Who preceded the Ubangians in most of their areas cannot presently be determined. Central Sudanic people were clearly encountered by the

Core Ndogo who crossed well into the Nile drainage system but do appear to be an early factor elsewhere. Bantu influences in areas near and west of the Mbomu and Uele confluence, through settlement and diffusion since the Ubangian establishment, are prominent; a few Bantu may have preceded the Mundu-Ndogo spread in a few areas at the far east of the Ubangian expanse (Mary McMaster, personal communication).

It is appropriate at this point to examine each of these stages in greater detail to see what language can say about the way of life of the speakers of Ubangian languages.

The Proto-Ubangians

For the proto-Ubangian period, as for the others to follow, there are two main concerns: the location of the community in time and space and the examination of reconstructible vocabulary for a glimpse of the life-style of the community.

As previously noted, from the linguistic evidence available this period corresponds roughly to the early third millennium B.C. In order to solve the problem of positioning the community we must look at the major division of the Ubangian family into the Western and Eastern branches. The Western languages are located north and west of the great bend of the Ubangi River. Among the Ngbaka, the sole exception, oral tradition still recalls their relatively recent crossing of the river. The other primary division, the Eastern Ubangian, focuses on the areas between the bend of the Ubangi and the juncture of the Mbomu and Uele rivers. The next closest related languages of Ubangian, the Adamawa group, are spoken to the west and northwest even of the Western Ubangian languages, thus pulling the origins of the Ubangians as a whole back to the west and northwest of the bend of the Ubangi. Thus the proto-Ubangians probably inhabited some part of the modern Western Ubangian region.

The evidence for proto-Ubangian subsistence is as yet weak, but the people appear to have been cultivators and fishers. Cowpeas and sesame were probable seed crops, and a word for yam is reconstructible and also a word for calabash. The pan-Niger-Congo word for cow did not apparently last into proto-Ubangian, but the word for goat did (Greenberg 1963:16, 19). A proto-Ubangian root *lu "to plant" could be cognate with Bantu *-lim- "to cultivate," if *i went to *u because of the following labial *m and final *m* was then lost; if so, a proto-Ubangian verb for a food-producing activity would have to be reconstructed. The proto-Ubangians lived in villages, which indicates possession of a fairly productive set of subsistence techniques, and made earthen pots. They also probably fished and used canoes if the proto-Eastern Ubangian root for paddle (*kapi) preserves an older Niger-Congo root and is not a borrowing from Bantu. The proto-Ubangians seem thus to have resembled their contemporaries, the proto-Bantu, in many ways (see table 3).

Early Eastern Ubangians

By sometime in the third millennium B.C. at least two groups had formed from the previous proto-Ubangian people. West of the bend of the Ubangi River was the group that much later became the modern Gbeya, Ngbaka, and Mandja peoples, namely, the proto-Western Ubangians. Perhaps settled to the east toward the Mbomu and Uele confluence were the rest, whom we have called the Eastern Ubangians. This latter group is the more important for they represent the spearhead of the eastward expansion of the Ubangian peoples.

The proto-Eastern Ubangians seem to have had millet, yams, calabashes, and perhaps the oil palm. Their word for oil palm seems to be a loanword from Bantu and to reflect diffusion of the crop from the south or southwest (see table 4). They also drank beer, strongly indicative of significant grain cultivation. Evidence of some kind of hereditary chiefship is adducible.

By or before the mid-second millennium the Eastern Ubangians had expanded further, diverging into proto-Mbomu-Uele, probably near the bend of the Ubangi, pre-Ngbandi near the Uele-Mbomu confluence, and proto-Zandeans up the Uele east of the confluence. Later in the second millennium the proto-Mbomu-Uele society began to divide into pre-Banda, pre-Ngbaka-Mabo, and proto-Mundu-Ndogo sets of communities. This development had emerged fully by the end of the millennium, at which time the center of Mbomu-Uele settlement may have been near and to the east of the Ubangi bend. The whole period from the breakup of proto-Eastern Ubangian to the beginning of Mundu-Ndogo spread as yet offers no significant evidence of major subsistence change or of additions, unless of a hard groundnut, probably *Voandzeia* (table 5).

When the Mbomu-Uele communities broke up into the three groups mentioned above, it was owing to the beginnings of an extensive geographic displacement of the daughter societies. The Ngbaka Mabo group moved perhaps down the Ubangi, becoming the ancestors of the present-day riverine peoples in the region of the Ubangi bend. The pre-Banda settled probably north of the Mbomu and Uele confluence. The Mundu-

Ndogo communities thrust themselves eastward, generally along the Mbomu drainage system toward the region of the Nile-Congo watershed and far east toward the uppermost Uele drainage. By the time of Christ their eastern outliers extended even into the southwestern Nile watershed. At these fringes of Mundu-Ndogo advance Ubangians seem to have been reintroduced to cattle, and some groups even to milking, or at least to knowledge of the practice by others. New words for cow and for "to milk" appear among the Ndogo languages and in Mundu proper, reflecting changes in knowledge dating probably to the late last millennium B.C. (see table 6).

Implications

From these data several important implications arise. First, the history of the Mbomu-Uele expansions indicates that the Ubangian peoples were occupying much of the territory they occupy now as early as the late first millennium B.C. Their expansion was not a development of the past few centuries.

Second, although Central Sudanic peoples by then definitely occupied a portion of this territory, they did not occupy nearly as much as Murdock and others have previously thought. They were limited rather to the northern and eastern fringes of drier climate. They cannot have occupied the southeastern fringe areas of rain forest, where Mangbetu and Lese-Mamvu Central Sudanics live today, because they lacked the means to penetrate the forest; that is to say, they could not have had the Malaysian agricultural complex at this early date, and they can only just have been introduced by the intrusive Ubangians to aspects of the West African agricultural complex that would enable them in the future to penetrate the forest. The advantage of this explanation is that instead of having the people with the superior agriculture and presumably the larger numbers retreating before the people to whom they were imparting this knowledge, we have the reverse. According to Murdock (1959:225), the Central Sudanic peoples

played the role of mediators in a long series of important diffusion processes. . . . In passing on the Malaysian food plants, therefore, they were playing no unaccustomed role. . . . The . . . members of this linguistic subfamily form a fringe . . . around the northern, eastern, and southeastern borders of the Eastern Nigritic [Ubangian] province. This suggests that they have been pressed back by the inhabitants of this province and extruded from a portion of their former territory.

What our evidence indicates, on the contrary, is the arrival of the Ubangian peoples with the guinea yam and other crops superior to the grain crops of the Central Sudanic speakers in this particular area. Emphasis on cattle raising would also have restricted Central Sudanic occupation. The Ubangian groups, spearheaded by the Mundu-Ndogo communities, successfully advanced as far as the Nile watershed, in some places at the expense of Central Sudanic speakers. Only with the full absorption of root crops by sections of the Central Sudanic peoples would the Mangbetu cluster of Central Sudanic speakers and the Lese-Mamvu have been able to reverse the trend and penetrate the forest fringe area.

Another implication of the data is that the spread of the Ubangian peoples was not one simple and continuous eastward push that ended with the Zande in the precolonial period; rather, there were three major episodes of expansion. The first eastward wave was that of the early Eastern Ubangians, of whom one descendant people, the proto-Zandeans, pressed as far east as the middle Uele Valley before 1000 B.C. The key advantage the first Ubangian settlers probably possessed was that of being the first food producers of the region. The second even wider spread was that of the pre-Ngbaka Mabo, pre-Banda, and proto-Mundu-Ndogo, beginning perhaps before 1000 B.C., but only taking off later on. What accounts for the ability of these Ubangians to expand against their neighbors must remain a mystery until either further linguistic inquiry or further archaeology provides us with more clues (but see David, chap. 6, below, who proposes knowledge of ironworking as the cause). The last expansion was that of the Zande which is recorded in the oral traditions and in the journals of European explorers. Much of the Zande expansion seems to have been at the expense of other Ubangian peoples rather than of Central Sudanic groups. The key to this expansion seems to have been a military advantage on the part of the Zande.

Thus, as we have seen, the expansion of the Ubangian people, Murdock's "Eastern Nigritic" people, took place earlier than most scholars have supposed. In addition, it took place in at least three major phases rather than in one continuous movement. Finally, we have examined some of the effects these new data have had on previous notions of the interaction between the Ubangian peoples and their Central Sudanic neighbors.

TABLE 1
Mbomu-Uele Cognation Percentages
(200-word list)

Ngbaka Mabo											
26	Banda										
37	40	Mundu									
24	31	33	Togoyo								
30	33	35	36	Sere							
28	38	36	41	73	Tagbu						
28	33	40	39	69	74	Ndogo					
30	33	39	36	67	69	86	Bai				
25	28	34	35	69	66	69	80	Bviri			
22	23	23	39	46	44	40	37	41	Indri		
20	21	33	31	37	34	34	31	32	43	Mangaya	
22	21	32	34	35	40	34	39	38	38	83	Feroge

TABLE 2
Ubangian Cognation
(200-word list)

Gbeya								
65	Ngbaka							
13	11	Zande						
10	15	39	Amadi					
20	14	17	21	Ngbandi				
17	20	16	20	21	Ngbaka Mabo			
11	13	22	23	22	26	Banda		
15	16	24	25	25	37	40	Mundu	
12	10	16	21	26	28	33	40	Ndogo

TABLE 3
Proto-Ubangian Cultural Vocabulary

Item or practice	Provisional reconstruction	Gbeya	Ngbaka	Zande	Ngbandi	Ngbaka Mabo	Banda	Mundu-Ndogo group
fishhook	*yango	yaŋgo			yòŋgō		yàngō	
eel	*(N)gbi	ŋmgbíím				gbigbì		
mortar	*kpo		kpŕ		kpwókpwó			
yam	*gue (cf. Bantu *-kua)			à-ŵra	guí			
"beans"	*war(a)	war		à-ŵra				
sesame	*sun(d)i	sunu			sìndì			
calabash	*gbeo	gbo						Feroge *gbèè*
field	*po	fɔ	fɔ̀		pútù (reused field)			
house	*toe (?)	tuwa	tɔa			tē		Tagoyo *tí*
village	*Re	ré	lē					Bai, Bviri *rā*
pot	*kɔrV	kɛrɛ		akɔrɔ				Ndogo *kaRa*
dance	*bia	bia (drum)	bia (song)			bè		
to dance	*do	do		dó	dɔ́dɔ́		dɔ	
spirit or shadow	*giRo	gíro	gɛ́là	gíriso (spirit)				
amulet	*basi		bésɔ̄		bisì			Ndogo *baàci*

TABLE 4
PROTO-EASTERN UBANGIAN VOCABULARY

Item or practice	Provisional reconstruction	Zande	Ngbandi	Ngbaka Mabo	Banda	Mundu-Ndogo group
to plant	*lu	r̄ú̧	lū		lū	
granary	*gɔlɔ		gɔ̀			Ndogo, Bai, Bviri *gálá
grindstone	*wili	wí̧rí̧				Feroge, Mangaya wulu
millet	*ngiRa	ngiria			ngaa	Indri ngireka
beer	*pi	(Pambia) fi			ípí	Mundu fí (i); Core Ndogo *pe
calabash	*kasi	kasi				Ndogo keci
yam	*gbaRa	gbara			gbaa	
oil palm	*mbira	mbi̧rä	mburu	mbia		
house	*da		dà			Indri da(a); Mangaya, Feroge dää
paddle	*kapi	kə́pí̧	kāpī			
chief	*gbia	gbɨa	gbīā			
drum	*kVnV		kānā			Togoyo kuni
soul or spirit	*tɔrɔ	tɔ̀rɔ	tɔ̄rɔ̄			

TABLE 5
PROTO-MBOMU-UELE VOCABULARY

Item or practice	Provisional reconstruction	Ngbaka Mabo	Banda	Mundu-Ndogo group
"hard" groundnut	*v̂i		àvì	Mangaya v̂ikpí; Ndogo vo-kpolo "peanut"
wild yam	*ngasa		ngāšá	Core Ndogo *ngaca
knife	*mba	mbà		Core Ndogo *mba
rope	*ku	ku		Mundu ku
fence	*ngaRa	ngala	ānga	
canoe	*gbaa		agbwa	Ndogo gbáá; Indri gbaká
drum	*kporo		ə́kp(ɔ)rɔ́	Core Ndogo *kpóró
medicine	*ye	yē	āyɔ̄	Core Ndogo *(i)yè

TABLE 6
Proto-Mundu-Ndogo Vocabulary

Item or practice	Provisional reconstruction	Feroge	Mangaya	Indri	Togoya	Mundu	Core Ndogo
to milk	*pī			fī(yā)	fiŋ	fĩ	Ndogo pḕē
cattle	*mbúu	mbú(u)			mbú(u)		
to cultivate	*jú			jí		*ju; *njú "field"	
mortar	*to(n)guli	tŵn(g)ūli	togŏle		tingil(i)		
grindstone	*ué			'uá	ue	uó	Ndogo v̂u
flour	*zúu			zúa	zú(u)	zú(u)	*njú-ko
fish spear	*dɔɛ	dŵ	dé(ɛ)	dɔka	diŋ	dó	
mat	*duá			duáka			Ndogo duú
song	*cī	ci	ci			ci	Ndogo cè
chief	*ŋwana	wāna	(ŋ)wāna	(w)uŋ(w)a			
war	*go				gŵ	gŵ	Ndogo go

6 | Prehistory and Historical Linguistics in Central Africa: Points of Contact

NICHOLAS DAVID

IN THE CURRENT STATE of archaeological knowledge of central Africa, any attempt to account historically for the distribution of its major cultural-linguistic groupings must necessarily be speculative. Archaeologists cannot afford to ignore the results of historical linguistics, which can help to orient their fieldwork and serve as an alternative structuring of past events against which to test their own conclusions. I do not repeat here the corresponding contributions that archaeology makes to linguistics; nor do I review the theoretical and practical difficulties inherent in any attempt to relate archaeological and linguistic entities either to each other or to other aspects of culture (see David, forthcoming). I have limited my aims in this paper to summarizing the results of recent archaeological work, suggesting points of contact with linguistic reconstructions, and, since some gross aspects of economic prehistory can be inferred even at a preliminary stage of archaeological investigation, raising important questions about the dynamics of the diversification and spread of languages.

The cultural map of Africa as we know it has its origins in new systems of interaction between man and his environment which developed during the Holocene. For most of the period under consideration there were no chiefdoms or more complex forms of political organization; neither was there trade on any significant scale. Since we have no access as yet to the social or ideological realms, we are constrained to adopt a heuristic model in which subsistence economy and demography are the prime determinants of the fate of peoples and languages. My working premise is, therefore, that more productive economic systems tend to expand at the expense of the less efficient, and that in small "face-to-face" societies transformation of the economy stimulated by new technology is normally accompanied by the spread of language, whether by an increase in the birthrate and emigration of participants in the more productive system or by incorporation of neighboring groups, or both. The rate of expansion in the main depends upon the viability of the expanding system in the surrounding territories, or its adaptability, and upon the relative efficiencies of competing systems. The greater the disparity, the more likely it is that the more productive will spread as a coherent though not unchanging system, embracing—besides the economic—social, cultural, and other aspects of behavior. In complex environments where two or more complementary economic adaptations can persist side by side, numerous examples from Africa and elsewhere suggest that the kinds and intensity of interaction within and between the different systems and relative population densities become the crucial factors in determining the future of the languages represented.

Nilo-Saharans: The Central and Eastern Sudanic[1] Subfamilies

Sutton (1974) has argued that the achievement, in some areas as early as the eighth millennium b.c., of an economic adaptation that combined hunting with, for the first time, intensive exploitation of wild grains and aquatic resources, is correlated with the initial spread and diversification of Nilo-Saharan. I deplore Sutton's use of the term "civilization" to describe what is in fact a highly variable technocomplex, and there is a strong case arguable on distributional and other grounds that Niger-Congo and Afroasiatic speakers also participated in what was, during the early part of the main Holocene wet phase, a vast diffusion sphere. But the time depth of the archaeological entity seems not inconsistent with the degree of diversification within Nilo-Saharan and, at least in the central and eastern Sahara, the correlation holds good. The breakup of Nilo-Saharan may have been accelerated, in its early stages, by the very success of an adaptation that in spite of the absence of food production allowed the development in favored areas of a semisedentary village way of life. Temporary deterioration of the Saharan environment in the sixth millennium b.c. would have accelerated the process, predisposing certain groups to take up a pastoralist way of life as cattle, sheep, and goats diffused southward, and some to experiment with the domestication of plants. The most important of these was *Sorghum bicolor*, believed on botanical evidence to have come under cultivation perhaps in several places within a "noncenter" extending at about 15°N latitude from Lake Chad across to the Nile (Harlan 1971). *Pennisetum americanum*, bulrush

---

[1] I follow Thelwall's modification (see chap. 2, above) of Bender's (1976) classification of Nilo-Saharan subfamilies and branches, which excludes Nilotic from the Eastern Sudanic subfamily.

millet, is also likely to have been domesticated slightly farther north and within the supposed area of Nilo-Saharan distribution.

The Kadero-Zakyab group of sites (Krzyaniak 1976, 1977, 1978, 1979; Haaland 1978, 1979; Tigani el Mahi 1979), whether or not occupied by Nilo-Saharans, provides the best evidence to date of agricultural development about 4000 b.c. Kadero, a village site 18 kilometers north-northeast of Khartoum, was occupied perhaps throughout the year and certainly in the rainy season, during which sorghum and perhaps a wide range of other crops, including eleusine, *Pennisetum*, teff, and even possibly barley were cultivated (Klichowska 1978). Herds of cattle and sheep and goats were pastured round about. In the dry season, smaller camps, of which Zakyab is one, were established a few kilometers away on the Nile in order to provide the herds with pasture and water and to exploit aquatic resources. The provisional identification of eleusine and teff carries the suggestion of contact with Ethiopia, where there is direct evidence from the Axum region that at least the former crop was already being cultivated (Phillipson 1977a).

Just as the spread of Afroasiatic Chadic languages in the Chad Basin can best be explained as accompanying the diffusion of mixed farming (Olderogge 1956; David 1976:257–258), so it can be argued that development of the economy exemplified by Kadero and variants of it accounts for the original expansion of certain subfamilies of Nilo-Saharan. The suggested time depth and the distribution of prehistoric rock art and of Eastern Sudanic languages today (Ehret 1974a: preface; Butzer 1971: 326–329; also see Thelwall, chap. 2, above)—although the latter distribution is affected by later movements of the Nubian branch (Adams, chap. 3, above) and by the Semitic incursions of this millennium—suggest that during the Neolithic period Eastern Sudanic languages spread over large areas of the Sudan Republic, extending from Darfur in the west across to the Nile. The eastern limit of their distribution in prehistoric times is uncertain, but they probably extended into the Blue Nile drainage. The Eastern Sudanic Nara (Barea) live today in Eritrea, and the various Surma people live along the southwest of Ethiopia, so their spread may have penetrated partway into the Ethiopian highland fringes. Far to the west, competition from Chadic and other Nilo-Saharan speakers may explain the restricted distributions of the Maban and Fur subfamilies.

Use of the least-moves principle places the Central Sudanic homeland "broadly in the Upper Bahr-el-Ghazal watershed, to the west of the Nile and possibly as far south as northwestern Uganda" at a date "broadly in the third millennium b.c." (Ehret et al. 1974:87–88). I challenge this and, by extension, other applications of the least-moves principle on the ground that the progressive desiccation and southward retreat of the vegetation belts began to affect the northern tropical and equatorial zones at about this time (van Zinderen Bakker 1976; Street and Grove 1976). Reconstruction of proto-Central Sudanic subsistence terms suggest that the people cultivated sorghum and possibly bulrush millet and herded cattle, which were milked, and also goats (Ehret et al. 1974:86). An economy based on these staples could almost certainly not have been practiced in the moist forest environment inferable for third-millennium upper Bahr el Ghazal. An area perhaps as far as 10°N, just south of the territory of Eastern Sudanic speakers from whom the Central Sudanic group would have obtained their main domesticates, is more suitable. During the period of climatic deterioration Africans were forced to choose, over a period of centuries, between their homes and their environments. If they clung to the former, as did the inhabitants of Dhar Tichitt in Mauretania (Munson 1976), adaptation, albeit painful, was essential; if the latter, then they might, by moving house, retain their life-style.

For the proto-Central Sudanians, the second alternative had much to recommend it, above all the opportunity to expand their territorial range into areas previously lacking food production. Thus expansion would have taken place to the southwest (the West Central Sudanic branch) and to the south and southeast (the East Central Sudanic and hypothesized South Central Sudanic branches), while their former territory came to be occupied by representatives of the more northerly subfamilies. Although some adaptation to moister environments would have taken place, Central Sudanic speakers seem either not to have reached or, lacking the yam, to have failed to penetrate the moist forests of the Congo Basin, where they may also have found themselves confronting early Bantu (see below). The Adamawa-Ubangian and Chadic blocks meanwhile inhibited further expansion to the west.

Although there are as yet no archaeological phases that can unequivocally be attributed to the period of Central Sudanic expansion, the assemblages from the lower levels of the Jebel Tukyi rock shelter (5°19′N; 30°27′E), located in Moru territory in western Equatoria Province, show some of the predicted characteristics (David, Harvey, and Goudie, in press). Large domestic cattle together with wild animals are here associated with an undiagnostic flaked quartz component and pottery that is a variant of the comb-impressed tradition that goes back to the "Aquatic Technocomplex." A single date of 180±220 b.c. (GU-1306) argues for an early spread of cattle to a locality that is even today only 100 kilometers north of moist lowland forest (Wickens 1975:52). Given that the region would have been more heavily wooded in Ceramic Later Stone Age times, it would be surprising if some form of cultivation had not also been practiced. The absence of direct or indirect evidence from the site is scarcely significant, as only 7 square meters were excavated.

It is conceivable that the little-known Kansyore Ware of the Lake Victoria Basin could represent the arrival of Central Sudanic speakers in that area, but the associated culture is as yet undefined, the dates are problematic (Soper and Golden 1969:40–41; also see Ambrose, chap. 7, below), and its pottery has been insufficiently described and illustrated to determine its relationships within the comb-punctate tradition.

For reasons discussed below, Central Sudanic speakers have, after their initial success as food producers and with exceptions that include the Baghirmi, played a passive role in central African history. The Nilotic subfamily has on the other hand undergone several episodes of expansion.

The Nilotes

In the southern Sudan and northern Uganda and Kenya, the narrowing of the ecological zones, the more irregular relief of the landscape, the unique characteristics of the Sudd and surrounding wetland savanna, and the proximity of Ethiopia and its peoples have led to complex interactions between cultures. These are amply documented by ethnography and history and, in Kenya, by archaeology. Ambrose's contribution to this volume (chap. 7, below) includes well-argued correlations of, among others, the Elmenteitan Culture with early Southern Nilotic penetration of the western Kenya highlands, and of the Pastoral Iron Age facies characterized by fiber-rouletted wares of Lanet type with the later arrival of Eastern Nilotes. These equivalences are by no means proven and the second is probably wrong; nevertheless, Ambrose's paper testifies to a state of archaeological research that will not be attained in neighboring countries in the foreseeable future. I therefore restrict myself to two questions: Is there evidence from the southern Sudan that relates to his thesis? Does such evidence as is now available help to explain the dynamics of Nilotic migrations into East Africa?

Current views of Nilotic history within the Sudan Republic are based for the later periods mainly upon the synthesis of oral traditions (Cohen 1974), and for earlier phases upon linguistic inference. Ehret (1974*b*: 50–51) and Ehret et al. (1974:90) suggest a third-millennium date for proto-Nilotic and a homeland located in the southeast portions of Sudan.

Believed to be associated with the proto-Nilotes in a somewhat earlier move from the north are representatives of another Nilo-Saharan branch, Kuliak, and of the Surma subdivision of Eastern Sudanic. The arguments for the siting of the homeland are based upon "the dating of both proto-Eastern Cushitic contacts with an Eastern Sudanic [*sensu lato*, including Nilotic] people and of Nilotic contacts with early Southern Cushites" (Ehret 1974*b*:50). The inference must be considered exceptionally fragile since even the status of the Cushitic branches or subfamilies and their relationships to Omotic and other subfamilies of Afro-Asiatic are still in dispute (see, for example, Bernal 1980), and their locations during the third millennium are open to question. Reconstruction of proto-Nilotic subsistence terms reveals an emphasis on cattle keeping which, although presumably combined with hunting and fishing and perhaps also with a limited form of cultivation, clearly contrasts with the more balanced form of mixed farming ascribed to speakers of proto-Central Sudanic. As the proto-Nilotes or their immediate ancestors are most likely to have obtained their domesticates from the north, a case can be made for a homeland immediately south of the Eastern Sudanic block, perhaps on the White Nile lake that extended north of the Bahr el Ghazal confluence during the period in question (Wickens 1975:62 and fig. 5). Of possible relevance here is the characteristically Nilotic trait of evulsion of lower incisors practiced by some of the population of Jebel Moya (Addison 1949:53–55). This site is only 270 kilometers south of Khartoum and within the orbit of Meroe, though occupation is known to go back at least into the late third millennium b.c. (Clark and Stemler 1975). Adaptation of economic strategies to allow exploitation of the wetland savanna, especially east of the White Nile, is surely a critical but as yet archaeologically undocumented factor in the first phase of Nilotic expansion into an area previously inhabited, if at all, only by hunter-gatherers. The linguistic evidence does not appear inconsistent with the concept of a dialect chain within which, from north to south, the Western, Eastern, and Southern branches were beginning to diversify. Such a reconstruction differs only in emphasis from that of Ehret and his colleagues. It offsets the proto-Nilotic area somewhat farther north than they seem to place it; the point is worth noting because the archaeological evidence seems to favor a late survival of hunter-gatherers in the drier savanna of the extreme southeastern Sudan.

Lokabulo rock shelter (4°33′N; 33°21′E), near Kapoeta, has given a Later Stone Age sequence estimated by four radiocarbon dates to extend from the fourth to the end of the first millennium b.c. It thus covers much of the second part and of the closing stages of the Holocene wet phase. Pottery of the comb-impressed tradition, stylistically different from the Jebel Tukyi materials, appears during a period of soil formation dated to 1830±120 b.c. (GU-1304), and thus several thousand years later than in some neighboring areas (David, Harvey, and Goudie, in press). The associated faunal remains are indicative of a hunter-gatherer economy and an environment more humid than that of today. We found no evidence of plant or animal domesticates. The culture represented may be considered a late variant of the Aquatic technocomplex adapted to savanna rather than lacustrine or riverine conditions. Preliminary results of the 1980 B.I.E.A. expedition suggest that it may be widespread in the drier parts of eastern Equatoria Province (Robertshaw and Mack 1980: 38–39).

The end of the Later Stone Age may be connected with the arrival of cattle-herding Nilotes; as yet, however, there is still a gap in the regional sequence covering the period during which Southern Nilotes may be supposed to have passed through on their way south. The succeeding phase is not represented at Lokabulo but at an ash mound on the slopes of Jebel Kathangor (5°45'N; 33°59'E) some 150 kilometers to the north-northeast. This site produced Turkwel pottery, characterized by grooved decoration, and its discovery considerably extends the geographic range of this tradition, previously known from sites clustered west and south of Lake Turkana with outliers in eastern Uganda and one immediately north of the lake in Ethiopia. Dates from the Kenyan sites excavated by Lynch and Robbins (1979) indicate that this pastoral tradition, Iron Age in at least its later phases, persisted in that area from a.d. 450 or earlier to about a.d. 1100. The same authors attribute the complex to early Eastern Nilotes, citing both historical and linguistic evidence in support of a correlation that must be strengthened by the new evidence from Sudan. As mentioned above, the correlation suggested by Ambrose is between Eastern Nilotes and pastoral Iron Age occurrences with Lanet Ware, decorated by twisted-cord roulettes. While I would agree with Ambrose and other authors (e.g., Posnansky 1967a:637) that the use of twisted-cord roulettes diffused to East Africa from the north and that they were adopted by Eastern Nilotic and other peoples, the available radiocarbon dates (see Bower et al. 1977:131–145) leave considerable room for doubt as to whether they had arrived in East Africa before a.d. 1000. Although much more work is required on the Eastern Nilotic question, the Lynch and Robbins interpretation is to be preferred. In the southeastern Sudan the appearance of fiber roulettes, though as yet undated, certainly precedes the adoption of carved wooden roulettes, presently the favorite tool for pottery decoration among the Larim (Boya) and some other Surma-speaking peoples who, together with the Eastern Nilotic Toposa, occupy the area today.

Cohen (1974) provides a convenient summary of the fifteenth-century and later Western Nilotic Luo migrations into Uganda and neighboring parts of Kenya, Zaire, and Tanzania. Archaeological data of relevance to these movements come from the numerous village mounds in Dinka territory around Wun Rok, 160 kilometers north of Wau, the capital of the Bahr el Ghazal Province. These mounds were first noted by Titherington (1923), and several new sites were located in 1979. Test excavations at Dhang Rial mound (9°N; 28°21'E) produced a two-phase Iron Age sequence overlying traces of an earlier Ceramic Later Stone Age occupation characterized by rocker-stamped comb-decorated pottery (David, Harvey, and Goudie, in press). The Early Iron Age phase, dated to a.d. 765±85 (GU-1240) and a.d. 1220±74 (GU-1308), is estimated to have begun about a.d. 500. It was during this phase that most of the mound accumulation occurred through the collapse of buildings, the renewal of floors, and the deposition of domestic rubbish. The early Iron Age inhabitants herded domestic cattle, fished, and hunted and may be presumed, though we lack evidence, to have cultivated sorghum and other crops. They made bone tools but wore iron jewelry and also necklaces made of mollusk-shell beads ground, as stone is lacking, into disc shape on potsherds. Besides pottery sparingly decorated with twisted-cord roulettes, they manufactured stylized terra-cotta figurines of their humpless cattle. The dead were buried in shallow graves, lying in an extended position on the left or right side with heads to the west. The summary disposal of at least fifteen adults at one moment in the phase suggests intervillage raiding or feuding. Our amateur observations on the poorly preserved skeletal materials lead us to believe that the people were tall and probably of "Nilotic" physical type. Dental evulsion, however, was not practiced, and we cannot affirm that they spoke a Nilotic language.

Changes from early to later Iron Age at Dhang Rial include the replacement of humpless by humped cattle, indicated by the figurine evidence, and the restriction of settlement to the perimeter of the mound. Although homesteads are sometimes built on mounds today, use as rainy-season cattle camps or sorghum fields is far more common. This change in the pattern of utilization is likely to go back to the start of the later Iron Age. Shell beads were no longer made, but the pottery differs only minimally from that of the preceding phase. Unfortunately no late

Iron Age burials were found within the excavated area. According to Dinka Tuich traditions, the mound builders were the "Luel," a cattle-herding and iron-using people, some of whom were driven out while others were assimilated when, long ago, the Dinka arrived in the region from the east. There seems no reason to deny a substantial measure of truth to these traditions. There is no detectable break between the later Iron Age and the Dinka occupation; neither need the difference between the early and late Iron Age phases imply any major population replacement. Instead, a change in economic adaptation and an accompanying process of "Niloticization" are indicated by the new breed of cattle and change in use of the mounds. Thus we suggest that the "Luel" of the early Iron Age developed into the Dinka Tuich of today.

The role of cattle and of different breeds of cattle in Nilotic and other pastoralist expansions has not as yet received the attention it deserves from culture historians. Because *Bos* has a much shorter generation length than man, cattle populations have the potential of increasing much more rapidly. As they are more specialized in several respects, including diet, they are at the same time more susceptible to catastrophic population decline. Any economic system that places a large measure of reliance upon cattle (and indeed other forms of) pastoralism is therefore inherently unstable. Times will occur when the herds come greatly to exceed the carrying capacity of the lands exploited by their owners; migration then becomes one among several options. Stress of this kind internal to the system could have provided a dynamic for early Nilotic expansions (though knowledge of ironworking may be a factor in that of the Eastern Nilotes), but if so it will take a long time before data sufficient in quantity and quality are accumulated for this to be demonstrated in the archaeological record.

Let us then return to the humped cattle of Dhang Rial and their significance. Here we get into difficult waters because remarkably little is known of the history of cattle in Africa except from iconography, always a suspect source, and the "physical bovinology" of recent breeds, a study with a distinctly old-fashioned air about it. There are very few archaeological assemblages that allow distinctions to be made among the wild ancestor, *Bos primigenius*, its domesticated descendant, *Bos taurus*, and the humped zebu, *Bos indicus*, if indeed these are the valid and only taxa anciently present in Africa. With this disclaimer, we may proceed to state that the cattle first herded in North Africa were of *Bos primigenius/taurus* types. At a much later but still uncertain date came the first of several introductions of zebu to the continent from Asia (Epstein 1971:I, 505 ff.).

Generalizations are dangerous, as the local races of hybrids between *B. taurus* and *B. indicus* are highly variable; but, following Epstein, we may say both of zebu and, to a lesser extent perhaps, of the humped cross-breeds known as sanga, that they are better adapted to arid and semiarid zones in some or all of the following characteristics (Epstein 1971:I, chap. 4): better regulation of body heat; lower water requirements; greater resistance to ectoparasites (ticks, etc.) and to some other diseases, including rinderpest; harder hooves and lighter bones, making them better fitted for travel over long distances; ability to store fat to some extent in their humps for use in the dry season; and ability to browse and survive on nutritionally inferior plant foods.

Zebu and sanga cattle are thus better suited than *B. taurus* to such systems involving long-distance transhumance as those practiced by Dinka and other peoples in many of the harsher African environments. Thus the replacement of humpless by humped cattle may well be a significant causative factor in the abandonment of the nucleated mound villages of the Wun Rok region and the spread into this and other areas of essentially modern patterns of Nilotic pastoralism.

When did these patterns emerge? Zebu are first documented in Egypt, where they never became common, as early as the twentieth century B.C., having been brought from Mesopotamia (Epstein 1971:I, 505). It has been suggested but not demonstrated that their main influx into Eritrea and northern Ethiopia occurred at the time of the first Semitic migrations across the Red Sea, perhaps as early as the seventh century B.C. In the Horn of Africa, camels and humped cattle are represented only in the latest rock art. Clark (1954:315; 1977:76) is inclined to the view that these animals began to enter Ethiopia in any numbers only after A.D. 330 with the expansion of the Christian kingdom of Axum. He also notes a bronze figurine of a humped bovid found at Zaban Kutur, near Cohaito, and believed to date to the period immediately before the Axumite adoption of Christianity. The many representations of Meroitic cattle all show humpless animals (Shinnie 1967 and personal communication). Humped cattle are, however, depicted in the art of Christian Nubia and it would be extraordinary if the northeasternmost Nilotes had not been exposed to zebu cattle by the tenth or eleventh century, whether from Arab sources via the Nile or through Ethiopia (see Hrbek 1977:69–75). Epstein (1971:I, 417) is of the opinion that "of the two principal cattle types in the Sudan, i.e. zebu and sanga, the sanga is undoubtedly the older," implying an earlier source of zebu genes in Nilotic cattle. However, this cannot be demonstrated in the absence of detailed genetic studies.

According to Cohen (1974:141), the first Lwo migrations were stimulated "probably as a result of pressure from peoples to the east." On a broader frame, the immigration of Arabs into the northern cattle-keeping zone during the thirteenth and fouteenth centuries (Hrbek 1977:78–80) is likely to have affected the Western Nilotes as a whole. It is tempting to conclude that the latter's possession of a superior breed of cattle strongly influenced their later successes. A fourteenth- or fifteenth-century date for the early to later Iron Age transition at Dhang Rial accords with the radiocarbon evidence and, together with the fact that the mounds are the only permanent man-made landmarks in that flat and featureless country, may account for the vividness of Dinka Tuich memories of the Luel. In East Africa, to which zebu cattle might have been introduced from the coast, humped cattle are now ubiquitous, with only a few doubtful records of humpless cattle persisting into recent times (Epstein 1971:I, 265). Nevertheless, the earliest date for zebu in the interior is surprisingly late. At the Lanet site near Lake Nakuru they are dated to a.d. 1574±100 (Y-570) (Posnansky 1967b; Sutton 1973:118), while at the Hyrax Hill Northeast village overlooking Lake Nakuru they are associated with a trade bead (Leakey 1945:305–365, 370) and are certainly no earlier. Again we may wonder whether the fifteenth-century and later Maasai spread from the Kerio River Basin south of Lake Turkana (Jacobs 1975:411) was not assisted by zebu cow power.

Ubangians

A glance at the distributions of the two branches of Adamawa-Ubangian reveals a striking contrast. Whereas a dense cluster of Adamawa languages in north Cameroon extends from the Adamawa Plateau to the Benue and across the borders into Nigeria, Chad, and the northwestern Central African Republic (C.A.R.), Ubangian languages occupy vast tracts of the central African savannas and the northern forest-savanna mosaic. These patterns are indicative of a long, more or less in situ differentiation of Adamawan languages and of relatively recent and rapid Ubangian expansion. In an earlier paper, David and Vidal (1977) argue that it was iron that gave the Ubangians a technological edge over their competitors and momentum to their expansion. Saxon's (chap. 5, above) revision and amplification of Ehret et al. (1974:96–100) demonstrate that the early stages of the process go back into Later Stone Age times. Food production may therefore have been the critical factor; as in the proto-Central Sudanic and proto-Nilotic spreads, the proto-Ubangians may be seen as pushing before them the frontier, which lay to the east, between food-producing and food-extracting economies. Early Ubangian terms have been reconstructed for sesame (which may have replaced or substituted for the oil palm in upland environments), "hard groundnut" (?*Voandzeia* or *Kerstingiella*), calabash, "millet," and yam—all likely elements of early agriculture north of the equatorial forest. On ecological and distributional grounds it is probable that the Guinea yam and, in most areas, the oil palm were staple crops.

It is more questionable whether the hierarchical evolutionary model that Saxon uses to generate his tree of relationships, and from which by application of the least-moves principle he derives a succession of proto-homelands, is at all precise or even appropriate in the Ubangian case. If, as is generally acknowledged, the main thrust was toward the east, differentiation may be supposed to have occurred among languages relatively stationary in the west, among others still shifting gradually eastward, and among still others that were spoken by those farthest east who were actively extending the limits of Ubangian colonization. The data on vocabulary are less than perfect, and Saxon suggests, as I would also, that besides genetic relationships the factor of geographic proximity is structuring the data, in particular the centrality of the Ngbandi, Ngbaka Mabo, and Banda groups as opposed to the marginality of the Western Ubangian, Zandean, and Mundu-Ndogo.

The archaeological evidence from the C.A.R. and northern Zaire is, as elsewhere in central Africa, wholly insufficient to support a detailed critique of Saxon's tentative reconstruction. Work carried out over the past five years has, however, produced evidence of Later Stone Age and Iron Age phases of expansion and resulted in the correction of earlier misinterpretations. The "civilisation mégalithique de Bouar" (Vidal 1969) in the westernmost C.A.R. postdates the proto-Ubangian phase and, being distributed near the boundary between the Adamawa and the Ubangian branches, cannot be ascribed to one rather than the other. Excavations in 1975 (David, n.d.) produced new radiocarbon dates (Calvocoressi and David 1979:9) and allowed reassessment of the sites previously excavated by Vidal. The culture, now placed firmly in the first millennium b.c., is as yet represented only by its monuments, the megalithic *tazunu*. It occupies part of the Yadé massif, the delimitation of the megalithic zone apparently reflecting more definite ethnic boundaries than obtain in the area today. The size of many *tazunu*, which are so numerous as to suggest that they express individual or family status and are funerary in function, is such as to require that they were built by a population of food producers. Small finds are excessively rare in *tazunu*, but include a ground-stone ax and grindstones which provide indirect evidence of the use of grain. Occasional objects of iron or of indubitably Iron Age date are in all instances likely to be intrusive. The small sample of potsherds clearly represents a different tradition from the comb-punctate wares of the Ceramic Later Stone Age of the Nilo-Saharan zone. The pottery is thicker and less carefully made; decoration is less common and sparingly applied, and, while comb decoration is present, grooving/incision is the more common technique.

Saxon suggests that by 2000 B.C. Ubangian advance had reached the Mbomu-Uele confluence and that by that time the Ubangians were already in contact with Bantu, from whom they borrowed a word for oil palm. Although iron metallurgy is now firmly dated in the Nigerian Nok Complex to the sixth century b.c. (Calvocoressi and David 1979:10–11), the *tazunu* dates preclude the diffusion of iron to the C.A.R. before 400 b.c. at the very earliest. Independent development of ironworking or diffusion from some other source is in the highest degree unlikely. The Nana-Modé village site (6°19′N; 15°6′E), dated to the seventh or eighth century a.d., exemplifies a culture with an already well-established metallurgical tradition, and which in its unknown ancestral form replaced that of the *tazunu* builders in the Bouar region.

The Nana-Modé pottery is decorated almost exclusively by impressions of carved wooden roulettes, and the excavators (David and Vidal) have shown that the technique appears very commonly on pottery made by Adamawa-Ubangian speakers. The use of carved wooden roulettes seems to have originated in the Nok Complex, perhaps because the carving of the roulettes, made in special woods, requires sharp iron tools for ease of execution. Although the technique spread in other directions, its main extension was to the east. It appeared early in Cameroon and, on published evidence, arrived in East Africa around a.d. 1500, although according to P. Schmidt (personal communication) a date some centuries earlier is suggested by his Buhayan materials. Study of its present distribution shows that around a core area occupied by Adamawa-Ubangian speakers, all or almost all of whom practice roulette decoration, it extends into southern Chad, the southern Sudan, Uganda, western Kenya, and Zaire. In these peripheral areas the technique is practiced by speakers of various Central and Eastern Sudanic, Nilotic, and Bantu languages who have little in common with one another beyond their proximity to the Ubangian block.

I would therefore contend that there are two main phases of spread of the technique to and among the Ubangians, during and succeeding both of which there was limited diffusion to their neighbors. In the first, knowledge of carved wooden roulettes accompanied by iron metallurgy diffused rapidly within the Adamawan branch, and from Adamawans to Ubangians already settled in the C.A.R. perhaps as far east as the Mbomu-Uele confluence. In the second phase, which may be correlated with the differentiation and spread of Mundu-Ndogo languages, knowledge of iron became the prime determinant of the expansion of Ubangians into savanna and forest-savanna mosaic previously occupied by other Ubangians and perhaps, even at this time, by Bantu-speaking peoples (Oliver 1978:405−406). We do not yet know when this phase began or ended, but it must have been proceeding by the middle of the first millennium A.D.

On present evidence it would seem that the expansion of Ubangian is similar to that of Bantu (next discussed) in that following a long-drawn-out period of expansion consequent upon the development of food production, rapid diffusion of metallurgical techniques between peoples speaking related languages and sharing many other aspects of culture led to a second and, in the case of the Bantu, explosive wave of colonization. The difference between the destinies of the Bantu and the Ubangians is largely explicable by the fact that the Bantu were less in competition with other food producers and, at the time they received iron, still had available to their south and east immense territories occupied only by hunter-gatherers.

Bantu

The linguistic evidence reviewed by Ehret (chap. 4, above) favors a Benue-Congo homeland dating to before 3000 B.C. in central Nigeria, where African yams and the oil palm were available for domestication and came to form the basis of a highly productive forest economy that required very different exploitative techniques from those of the cereal farming and cattle herding practiced farther north (Harris 1973, 1976). After the Saharan climatic optimum and the southward shift in the vegetation belts, it is likely that food production spread rapidly in southern Nigeria, bringing Benue-Congo peoples to the southeastern Nigerian−southwestern Cameroon border area.

Archaeological evidence in support of these assertions is as yet very limited. In southeastern Nigeria the Ezi Ukwu Ukpa I rock shelter at Afikpo may span the changeover to an agricultural way of life, but the results of the Hartle (1966:15–16; 1967:139–141; 1972:3–6) and later excavations by Andah and Anozie (1976) are strikingly different and cannot be reconciled without more information. It may, however, be noted that the pottery of Andah and Anozie's middle cultural level, in which possible agricultural stone tools first appear, is characterized by various grooved designs. Widespread and locally abundant traces of "Neolithic" stoneworking in western Cameroon and in the formerly forested zone that extends across southern Cameroon at about 5°N (Marliac 1973:13–17) can be read to indicate the expansion of early Bantu into these regions at a period unlikely to be later than the second millennium b.c. Indeed, latest indications suggest a Ceramic Later Stone Age presence in the Cameroonian grassfields at a much earlier date.

At Sum Laka rock shelter (5°52′N; 10°5′E), test excavations by de Maret (1980) have produced an assemblage that includes an abundant flaked-stone industry with a single implement of "ax hoe" type, pottery, and faunal remains that include gorilla. Three radiocarbon samples from a previous sounding at the site give dates ranging from the early sixth to the late fourth millennium b.c. A comparable assemblage was found at Abeke rock shelter 10 kilometers to the northeast. It is hoped that analyses now in progress will determine the type of economy practiced. The grassfields were endowed with exceptional advantages for early food producers: light, easily cleared forest, fertile soils, lower incidence of several serious diseases, including sleeping sickness and malaria, and in general an excellent potential even for a mixed farming economy, though there is as yet no direct evidence of cattle. Then, as today, the population densities generated in this region were predictably high enough to stimulate emigration into the less favorable but sparsely inhabited forests to the east. The presence of Kwa speakers at a similar technological level would have militated against migration to the west, while either Adamawan peoples had already colonized the plateau or its poorer soils discouraged Bantu expansion in this direction.

Ehret (chap. 4, above) believes that Bantu colonization of the Congo Basin may have begun as early as 3000 b.c. The archaeological evidence, while remaining inconclusive, has substantially increased in recent years. Polished- and ground-stone tools are known from forest and coastal Cameroon (Marliac 1973) and, if the paucity of research is taken into consideration, are quite common in Gabon (Blankoff 1969). In Bas-Zaïre, over 200 polished-stone axes, collected in some instances with perforated schist discs and poorly flaked tools of quartz, were attributed by Mortel-mans (1962a) to a "Léopoldian Neolithic." The vast majority are surface finds and therefore suspect both in their associations and as evidence of a Neolithic presence, since in some parts of Africa stone continued to be used for heavy-duty tools into the ethnographic present (e.g., Jeffreys 1948). Cahen's (1976) excavations at the Pointe de la Gombe, Kinshasa, where a polished ax had previously been found, produced an assemblage from near the top of the sequence which comprised pottery, flaked-stone, and grindstone fragments, besides bits of iron slag that may be intrusive from an occupation of the eighteenth century A.D. A single date of 1575±35 b.c. (GrN-7279) for this level may testify to an early Bantu movement deep into the Congo Basin. That such a penetration had occurred before the end of the first millennium b.c. is now almost certain, with six dates from five sites in Bas-Zaïre in the fourth-to-first-century b.c. range, but it is not clear whether the associated assemblages are late Neolithic or Early Iron Age (de Maret 1976). Their pottery is further discussed below.

As to the "how" of this population movement, like other forest-adapted food producers the Bantu had African yams and the oil palm as staples, other crops that probably included *Voandzeia*, possibly even sorghum, and goats and fish to supply animal protein, together, we may suppose, with game and forest products in part obtained by barter from Pygmies. Movements of people were almost certainly canoe-borne by coastal and riverine routes. Archaeological distribution patterns are not yet adequate to demonstrate this point, but there is limited support in proto-Bantu vocabulary (see Ehret, chap. 4, above), from the association of several groups, especially within the Kongo branch of Bantu (Heine 1973; Heine, Hoff, and Vossen 1975), with major rivers and their basins; and, last but not least, from comparison with the Macro-Arawakan expansion in the similar environment of the Amazon Basin (Lathrap 1970:70–78).

A seventh-century b.c. date for iron smelting in Niger and the sixth-century dates from Nigeria mentioned above push the introduction of metallurgy to sub-Saharan Africa back in time and support the view that it diffused via a central Saharan route (Calvocoressi and David 1979:10). I argue elsewhere (David, forthcoming), on technological, typological, and cultural-ecological grounds, that the second-millennium and ninth-to-fifth-century b.c. dates for early ironworking at the Rugamore Mahe site in Tanzania (Schmidt 1975) should all be rejected. Fourth-century dates for iron at the Ise Dura rock shelter near Ussongo in the Katsina Ala region of southeast Nigeria show that metallurgy was being practiced at or before that time within the territory of Bantoid speakers (Calvocoressi and David 1979:11). Once within the Congo Basin knowledge of iron-working could have been transmitted extremely rapidly along the rivers from one group of Bantu farmer-fishers to another. Iron tools and weapons would in their turn have facilitated further advances, including that of about the first century b.c. which brought Bantu into East Africa for the first time. These migrants are represented archaeologically by the Urewe phase assemblages clustered around the western and northern Lake Victoria Basin. That is where we should expect to find them since much of the basin at this time was still under deciduous and evergreen forest (Kendall 1969:127, 162–164). It was in effect an eastern extension of the Congo Basin which required little in the way of new adaptation on the part of the Bantu immigrants.

The archaeological evidence in support of this scheme of events, discussed at length by David (forthcoming), includes an analysis of ceramic traits from assemblages in and around the edges of the Congo Basin. These include Group VI wares from the Bas-Zaïre sites noted above (de Maret 1976; Mortelmans 1962b); materials from the Ebobogo (or Obobogo) site at Yaoundé first excavated by Jauze (1944) and redis-covered by de Maret (1980); materials from Batalimo on the Lobaye River in the C.A.R. (de Bayle 1975:206–220), which site has given a thermo-luminescence date of a.d. 380±220 (OxTL 154a4) and must have been located near the Bantu-Ubangian frontier; and finally the pottery of the earliest phases, Urewe and Chondwe, of Phillipson's (1975) eastern and western streams. In spite of variable data quality, the analysis—a presence or absence study based upon that applied to the Early Iron Age by Soper (1971b)—showed that there were substantial similarities in the decorative techniques employed, especially in formal and technical characteristics of horizontal band impressions, and that some highly specific motifs were shared between the northwestern and eastern series. Although there was no basis for grouping the pottery according to vessel morphology, the similarities in decoration were found to be strongly suggestive of cultural relationship. It is of interest in this connection that Soper (chap. 11, below) has also noted similarities between the Ise Dura pottery and that of the Urewe phase.

The analysis showed no indication of serial developments from one assemblage to another, nor did the degree of similarity between assem-blages appear to be influenced by distance. The loose network of relation-ships implied by this admittedly gross and insensitive form of analysis is congruent with a spread of Bantu along the river systems of the Congo Basin. In short, the appearance of Bantu equipped with iron in East

Africa can most economically be explained by a "model" that (1) derives people, language, pottery, and iron from a single source area in the northwest; (2) requires only one adaptive shift on the part of the peoples involved, that is, from a dry forest-savanna woodland to a moist forest environment; (3) does not require the migrants to compete with other food producers but only with Pygmy hunter-gatherers practicing a subsistence economy that is to some extent complementary; (4) allows sufficient time for Bantu expansion into the forest and for the diffusion of iron through it; (5) respects natural diffusion routes; (6) requires the diffusion of a new technology to take place only among speakers of closely related languages living in similar environments; and (7) accords with the pattern of genetic relationships revealed by historical linguistics, with comparative ethnology, and with the archaeological data available. Alternative explanations (e.g., Phillipson 1977b:216–225) fall down on several of these criteria—in particular a route from West to East Africa lying north of the equatorial forest now seems definitively blocked by Ubangians— whereas the interpretation offered above shows a satisfactory degree of correspondence with Ehret's (chap. 4, above) linguistically derived views. The later phases of Bantu expansion in East Africa are discussed by Collett and Soper in their companion papers (chaps. 9, 11, below).

I am as aware as anyone else of the tenuous nature of the above review. There is no reason to lend it greater concreteness by summarizing what is in essence a summary. My intentions will be amply satisfied if the paper stimulates enlightened anxiety among the culture historians, of whatever discipline, whose task it is to design and undertake future research.

Acknowledgments

I am grateful to Christopher Ehret and Merrick Posnansky for making it possible for me to attend the conference at which I presented a draft paper hastily prepared on my return from the southern Sudan. This expanded version owes a considerable debt to the papers of Stanley Ambrose and Douglas Saxon. My fieldwork in the southern Sudan was undertaken as part of the British Institute in Eastern Africa expedition of 1979, and that in the Central African Republic was supported by the National Geographic Society of Washington.

Part III

Eastern and Southern Africa

OVERVIEW

Eastern and southern Africa seem to have been fairly anciently the home of peoples speaking Khoisan language. The Khoisan family, it seems increasingly probable from recent work, will eventually be accepted as comprising the languages Greenberg (1955) attributed to it, with the possible exception of Hadza of Tanzania, which is still poorly known because of the lack of publication by those who have studied it. The assumption of the correlation of Khoisan speakers with the makers of the various microlithic tool industries loosely grouped under the label "Wilton" has long been made. Munson (1978) also accepts that correlation. Radiocarbon dating now shows up to 20,000 years of antecedent development in Later Stone Age tool making, leading down to the more recent industries which were fashioned by undoubted Khoisan communities. Such a dating for the initial expansion of Khoisan hunter-gatherers is not at all out of the question, for the depth of divergence in the family could well be as great as for Afroasiatic or Nilo-Saharan.

The agricultural transformation in East Africa, which started in the third millennium B.C., has two early sources, one among Nilo-Saharans in the Sudan belt and the other among the Cushites of the Horn. The Nilo-Saharan contribution, via Central Sudanic and Nilotic peoples, is touched on by Saxon and David (chaps. 5 and 6, above). Its earlier roots lie in the Sudanic development of food production of the fifth or sixth millennium B.C. (discussed in overview to Part I, above), to which the early expansion of the Eastern Sudanic peoples is probably also connected. The Southern and Eastern Cushites, and also the Nilotes who settled in East Africa, are the central concern of Stanley Ambrose's analysis (chap. 7, below) of the linguistic and archaeological correlations in the Later Stone Age.

Ambrose's contribution offers a synthesis of the east African "Neolithic." He distinguishes three major archaeological groupings of cultures in Kenya over the last three millennia B.C., tying them by correlations of location, dating, and material features to the three major pre-Bantu populations of the country identifiable from the linguistic evidence: Eburran Culture with possibly the Khoisan, Savanna Pastoral Neolithic with the Southern Cushites, and Elmenteitan with the Southern Nilotes. He deals also with the extension of some of these correlations into northern Tanzania, and he goes on to propose archaeological identification of the settlement of the Maa-Ongamo, an eastern Nilotic people, in central Kenya, an event that linguistic evidence suggests belongs to the first millennium A.D.

In southern Africa a limited form of food production, the herding at first of sheep and then of cattle as well in some areas, also antedates the close of the Stone Age. Ehret's article (chap. 8, below) shows that the expansion of known Khoisan-speaking peoples can adequately account for the archaeology. The material remains of the communities, possibly Central Sudanic in language, who carried livestock raising south from East Africa as far as the Zambezi, where the Khoisan adopted the trait, are, however, yet to be located.

But what effectively ties eastern and southern Africa together and requires their consideration in a single section of the book is the vast spread, beginning in the north apparently in the latter first millennium B.C., of one set of extremely closely related cultures. Known as the Early Iron Age Industrial Complex, it came in the space of a very few centuries to extend from southern Uganda and parts of Kenya as far south as the Ciskei in modern South Africa. South of northern Tanzania the Early Iron Age Complex spread mostly over areas that would seem previously to have been the domain of Khoisan-speaking hunter-gatherers with "Wilton"-related tool kits. It can confidently be accepted that the complex was the work of a set of still very closely related Bantu-speaking communities, specifically speaking dialects attributable to the Eastern Bantu subgroup, as Ehret's article (chap. 4, above) shows. Phillipson (1977*b* and elsewhere) has proposed that there was a second equally wide Later Iron Age expansion which actually brought in the Eastern Bantu tongues. It now seems clear that, while there were a number of regional Later Iron Age Bantu expansions on the eastern side of Africa which rearranged Eastern Bantu language distributions (e.g., Huffman 1978), there was no single vast Later Iron Age movement (cf. the continuities from Early to Later Iron Age periods described by Soper in chap. 11, below, for the Mt. Kenya and Kilimanjaro regions).

Collett's article on Bantu expansion in eastern and southeastern Africa (chap. 9, below) explores the possible ways in which the Early Iron Age settlement could have advanced through that portion of Africa; he finds that a discontinuous-spread model best fits the archaeology. According to this model people at first spread out rapidly to the natural limits of a less densely populated area, then stay relatively unmoving while population gradually builds up to the carrying capacity allowed by technology and the environment. What is especially exciting about Collett's conclusion is that the discontinuous-spread model fits the pattern of rapid initial scattering out projected by the linguistic evidence. Collett's paper was one of the two papers not presented at the conference, and so the congruence of his findings with the linguistic implications are all the more arresting.

Two other articles carry the story on into the eras of Bantu establishment in East Africa. Derek Nurse (chap. 10, below), from his classification of the East African Bantu languages, based in large part on his own extensive field research during the 1970s, argues convincingly for the sort of wide initial scatter, just mentioned, of Bantu settlement across the eastern portions of the continent during one relatively short period of time. Many later, lesser expansions took place among descendants of the peoples established by that first scattering out, but no other similarly vast and rapid expansion. In this respect Nurse's article stands as an important corrective to Phillipson's notion that there might have been two vast Iron Age expansions, one by Bantu as late as 900 years ago. Nurse enhances the usefulness of his work for nonspecialists by opening with a nontechnical introduction to his assumptions and procedures.

Robert Soper (chap. 11, below) provides the archaeological overview on the Early Iron Age, showing the overall fit of that expansion with the Bantu spread documented by Nurse. What is important for East African historical studies is the presentation side by side of Soper's succinct layout of archaeological evidence and Nurse's new and up-to-date linguistic overview of Bantu spread into East Africa proper. Together the two papers lay the basis for attempts at drawing more specific correlations between particular versions of the Early Iron Age Complex and particular Eastern Bantu subgroups and extending such correlations into more recent periods, thus leading historical invesigation into new and important domains.

For the areas south of the Zambezi, the most up-to-date thinking on the correlation of particular versions of the Iron Age Complex with particular divisions of Eastern Bantu has already been published elsewhere. The reader is directed especially to recent articles by Huffman (1978) and Ehret and Kinsman (1981). Huffman has shown convincingly the correlation of the Zimbabwean Later Iron Age with Shona-Speaking Bantu; Ehret and Kinsman find additional support for that link and go on to suggest where the archaeological parallels for other linguistically attested Bantu settlements in southeastern Africa might be sought. Huffman traces the Kutama cultures of the early Shona back to the Lydenburg tradition of the South African Early Iron Age; Ehret and Kinsman, for their part, hypothesize that the makers of the at least equally early Silver

Leaves and Matola wares (see chaps. 9 and 11, below) of eastern Transvaal and southern Mozambique were the proto-Southeast Bantu, from whose dialect of early Eastern Bantu derive the later Nguni, Sotho, Tsonga, Venda, and Nyambane languages.

An untenable variant view of the Early Iron Age has been offered by Gramly (1978), who opines that what took place was the diffusion of iron and food production to Bantu populations that had already been in southern Africa for some thousands of years. In the mid-1960s his article would have had considerable heuristic value; today it is simply a red herring. It shows a superficial and outdated acquaintance with the archaeology, a lack of knowledge of the human genetic indications, and a disturbing willingness to overlook the linguistic evidence, in which Gramly admits a lack of grounding. But because the article was written by an otherwise reputable archaeologist and published in a reputable journal, it may be given unwarranted credence by nonspecialists in the Early Iron Age. Its antimigrationist stance also appeals to a strong current of thought in North American anthropology. For these reasons the doubts it raises need to be laid immediately to rest.

Gramly's suggestions in fact fly in the face of the evidence. What takes place with the inception of the Early Iron Age in southern Africa is not just the spread of ironworking and some associated features of material culture, as Gramly's hypothesis would require, but the rapid and abrupt establishment, across more than 2,000 miles, of an entire cultural complex that is new to those regions and whose essential unity, despite its immense spread and consequent development of local variations, is clear beyond cavil. The physical anthropology of modern southern Africa peoples, in keeping with the archaeology, shows in varying degrees the superimposition of a new gene configuration (of more northerly connections) onto patterns resembling those of the remaining Khoisan speakers. The first skeletal indications of the new configuration appear in sites of the Early Iron Age Complex, whereas Khoisan-like indications are general in the pre—Iron Age skeletal materials. Finally, to place Bantu languages in southern Africa further back than 2,000 to 3,000 years ago, at the most, is linguistically insupportable. Moreover, that dating leaves the Khoisan languages, a demonstrable substratum to Bantu in many if not all parts of southern Africa, as an unaccounted-for anomaly.

Migration is of course not the sum of history; it is is just one of the vehicles of culture change and is itself generated and sustained by more fundamental motive factors. No important scholar of the Early Iron Age in southern Africa would argue otherwise. But the diffusion of items, even with the added movement of a few blacksmith clans, as per Gramly, is a wholly inadequate explanation of the completeness and abruptness of the break between the Early Iron Age cultural package and what came before it. The cultural complex was spread by the movement of people, a not inconsiderable movement of people at that.

7 | Archaeology and Linguistic Reconstructions of History in East Africa

STANLEY H. AMBROSE

Introduction

EVEN THE MOST CURSORY survey of ethnic and linguistic groups in East Africa reveals an astonishing degree of heterogeneity. This mosaic of ethnic groups is situated with an equally diverse array of physiographic, ecological, and climatic settings (table 7). The four major language phyla of Africa, Khoisan, Afroasiatic, Nilo-Saharan, and Niger-Congo, are all represented in this corner of the continent (table 8; Map 11). These cultures have economies based on pastoralism, agriculture, fishing, and hunting and gathering, occasionally in pure form, but mainly to varying degrees and in all possible combinations. When first encountered by European explorers, most of these groups seemed well adapted to their environments, implying very long histories. Many language families, however, showed disjointed distributions, suggesting that former tribal boundaries and culture areas may have been remarkably different and indicating a long history of migrations and population expansions by some groups at the expense of others. Some languages, such as Oromo and Maasai, were found to be relatively uniform over vast regions, implying recent common origins, where others, such as Kalenjin and Somali, were fragmented into dialects that were not always mutually intelligible, implying longer histories of local differentiation. The complexities of human geography in East Africa thus present an intriguing challenge to oral historians, historical linguists, and archaeologists alike, all of whom have attempted to document the places of origin and the times and directions of movements and contacts.

In the past two decades the pace of work in all these fields has accelerated. The historical reconstructions proposed within the past twenty years can be reexamined in the light of the large body of recently compiled empirical evidence. It is my purpose in this paper to outline the present understanding of regional archaeological successions and the

TABLE 7

CLIMATIC, REGIONAL ARCHAEOLOGICAL, AND LINGUISTIC SEQUENCES IN EAST AFRICA

AGE B.P.	CLIMATE IN HIGHLANDS	NORTHERN KENYA LOWLANDS	HIGHLANDS & RIFT VALLEY IN KENYA & TANZANIA	VICTORIA BASIN & LOWLAND TANZANIA	HISTORICAL LINGUISTIC EVIDENCE OF LANGUAGE FAMILY LOCATION	AGE B.P.
0				Carved & plaited roulette wares (7 5)	Western Nilotes at L. Victoria ~400 (7)	0
	similar to modern ~3,000 - 0	Pastoral Iron Age (6 4 3)	Pastoral Iron Age (6 3) 1,300 - 0, Lanet Ware			
1,000			Deloraine Farm Pottery 1,300 - 1,000 (3)		Eastern Nilotes in Highlands by ~1,250 (6)	1,000
1,500			Iron Age, Kwale Ware 1,800 - 900 (5)			1,500
2,000		Turkwell Ware Neolithic & Namoratunga ~2,300 (4)	Akira Ware ~2,000 (2)	Lelesu Ware 1,800 (5) Urewe Ware ~2,200 (5) Iron Age (5)	Bantu in Victoria Basin by ~2,000 (5)	2,000
			Maringishu Ware ~2,000 (2)		Eastern Cushites in Northern Kenya Lowlands ~2,300 (4)	
2,500		?	Narosura Ware ~2,800 (2)		Southern Nilotes in Western Kenya Highlands by ~2,300 (3)	2,500
			Elmenteitan Industry 2,500 - 1,300 (3)			
			Eburran Phase 5 (?1 2 3)			
3,000			Savanna PN Industry 3,300 - 1,300 (2)		Southern Cushites in Highlands by 3,000 - 4,000 (2)	3,000
4,000	Drier than modern 5,600-3,000	Savanna PN, Nderit & Narosura Wares by ~4,500 (2)	?	Kansyore Ware by ? ~4,700 (1)		4,000
5,000	Gradually drying by ~5,600		Hiatus ~5,600 - 3,300		Southern Cushites in Northern Kenya by ~5,000 (2)	5,000
8,000	Wet ~10,000	Early Ceramics & Bone Harpoons by ~9,000 (?1)	Eburran Phases 1-4 ~12,000-5,600 (?1)	Quartz based Industry ~8,100 - ~1,000 (1)	Click speakers indigenous to Subsaharan Africa and (?) East African Highlands (1)	8,000
	Dry ~11,000 Wet ~12,000	Later Stone Age		?		
12,000		?		Hiatus to ~8,100 Later Stone Age ~18,000		12,000
20,000	Hyper-arid 12 - 17,000		Later Stone Age by ~21,000			20,000

correlations implied with the historical linguistic sequence outlined by Christopher Ehret (1971, 1974*b*) and others (Fleming 1964, 1969; Heine et al. 1979; Vossen 1977).

The Nature of the Evidence and Methodological Considerations

Although what follows may appear to be a comprehensive, all-inclusive correlation of the succession of archaeological and linguistic groups in East Africa, it should be considered only an approximation allowed by present knowledge of the archaeological succession. Many crucial regions are still archaeologically unknown, and other areas have prolonged and sometimes stubborn gaps in their records, posing intriguing questions which require investigation. Archaeological cultures, as yet unknown, may fill these gaps. Moreover, many of the presently known archaeological cultures are poorly defined. When more precise definitions become available, and the occurrences attributed to them are reexamined, meaningful divisions may be revealed which may have correlates with linguistic groups and cultures. The "Stone Bowl Neolithic" has proved to be a significant example. Thus, although the proposed reconstruction that follows may assign a single archaeological culture or sequence of genetically related cultures to a single language family, without excluding any language groups or archaeological cultures, the recognition of new language families or archaeological entities could easily invalidate many of the proposed correlations.

Advances in the understanding of the history of language groups and their interactions are moving far ahead of archaeological reconstructions of regional industrial sequence. Historical linguists have already begun to reconstruct dialect geographies within language groups such as Southern Cushitic, which may be equated with cultural entities at the "tribal" level. On the other hand, archaeologists cannot at present make meaningful, valid distinctions beyond the level of industries and industrial complexes. These archaeological taxa may encompass many prehistoric groups that, although sharing material cultural traits and a common origin, may have seen themselves as composed of many discrete cultural entities at the "tribal" level.

One should notice that the dates given by linguists for the appearance of language families are very generalized. Dates obtained by lexicostatistical and glottochronological methods yield only an approximate estimate of age with a wide margin of error, a margin of error so large that the estimate appears useless in comparison with that obtained from radiometric dating techniques. The evidence derived from loanword strata, however, give an unambiguous view of the relative age of these contacts and movements. The stratigraphic dating method based on the principle of superposition as used in archaeological interpretation is equally applicable to loanword evidence. When complete linguistic and regional archaeological successions are obtained and compared, attempts can then be made to correlate archaeological cultures to linguistic groups. If the fit of the archaeological and linguistic sequence as a whole excludes no industries or cultures and generates the modern distribution of language families, then one can propose correlations with confidence.

In theory, correlations must conform to this rigorous procedure: if successive archaeological cultures 1, 2, 3, and 4, with geographic distributions A, B, C, and D, with economies a, b, c, and d, are paralleled by an equal number of successive major linguistic groups $1'$, $2'$, $3'$, and $4'$, with geographic distributions A', B', C', and D', and a', b', c', and d', then one can say that archaeological culture 1, of area A, with economy a represents linguistic group $1'$ of area A' with economy a', and so on. Correlations are valid only if one is dealing with complete archaeological and linguistic sequences. If these requirements are fulfilled, then correlation of the entire succession, from earliest to latest, should generate the modern distribution of language families and their associated material cultures. I am fairly confident that this reconstruction of the archaeological record is complete in outline and that further work will simply reinforce and elaborate upon the reconstruction proposed below. I place the same confidence in the work of historical linguists.

The basic assumptions upon which this whole pursuit ultimately rests must be stated explicitly: that there is in most instances a correlation among language, culture, and material culture, and that in most instances the boundary of a suite of material culture items correlates with a cultural boundary. The pessimist would say, "But pots and stones cannot speak!" and would thus conclude that such correlations are futile. Although there are significant exceptions to the generalizations outlined above, and there is never a simple one-to-one correlation among an ethnic group, a language, and an artifact assemblage, the exceptions cannot invalidate the intuitively obvious principles on which this exercise rests. The identification of cultures on the basis of *fossils directeurs*, as in the case of the "Stone Bowl Culture," may result in the construction of a false archaeological entity. By the same token, the use of functional criteria—that is, inferring ethnic affiliation from similarities in the proportions of shaped stone tools, a measure of activity differentiation—may lead one to infer cultural differences (Haaland 1977). Polythetic definitions (Clark 1968:358–398), based on the co-occurrence of stylistically distinct lithic and ceramic assemblages, settlement patterns, economies, mortuary traditions, and so on, must be employed when proposing such correlations.

These generalizations about the covariance of language and material culture seem particularly appropriate for East Africa. Where there is competition for land and resources owing to population presure and/or environmental deterioration, ethnic boundaries become canalized (Hodder 1979). Although individual members of ethnic groups may cross these boundaries in intertribal marriage and there may be a free exchange of goods, ethnic differences across these boundaries are not diluted (Barth 1969:11; Hodder 1977, 1978, 1979; Spencer 1973). Empirical evidence that supports these axioms is illustrated by the recent work of Ian Hodder (1977, 1978) among the Tugen, Pokot, and Camus (Njemps) in the Baringo district of Kenya. He has demonstrated that material culture items, and stylistic differences among shared items, may serve as a means for signaling tribal identity. This effectively prevents the diffusion of artifact styles from group to group, keeping intertribal boundaries sharp and clear. In this case, intertribal stylistic heterogeneity is maintained even in the face of intensive intertribal exchange and intermarriage. The work of Paul Spencer (1973) among the Rendille and Samburu of central and northern Kenya also demonstrates stability of ethnic group boundaries despite the free movement of individuals between tribes and the simultaneous membership of individuals in both tribes.

Close inspection of table 7 reveals that some pottery traditions are presently associated with more than one language family; such associations would seem to invalidate the aforementioned assumptions. These cases may be explained by the diffusion of selected traits across ethnic boundaries after long periods of contact. This must have happened in the past as well. Adoption of a new language also occurs under such conditions. For my purposes here, however, the final critical assumption is that the initial appearance of a discrete archaeological culture represents a single linguistic group. Historical processes of assimilation, acculturation, and diffusion of technology, particularly in areas where competition is not maintaining ethnic differences, tend to blur some distinctions, given long, enduring, intensive intertribal contacts.

The efficacy of historical reconstructions in East Africa is owing in large part to an accident of geography. The diverse range of environments has made it possible for discrete groups practicing different economies to live side by side without intensive, overt competition. Thus it is possible for pastoralists to live on the tsetse-free open savanna while agriculturalists are farming the adjacent woodlands and bush. Hunters and gatherers can avoid competition with herders and farmers by exploiting ecological zones, such as montane forests and arid bush, and by developing exchange relationships with their neighbors.

Hunter-gatherer languages are particularly useful for historical reconstructions. As hunter-gatherer/food-producer relationships develop and intensify, the indigenous hunters usually adopt the language of their food-producing superiors. After a review of the Dorobo and Elmolo of central Kenya, Paul Spencer found a pattern of hunter/food-producer relationships which suggested that for an indefinite period, many of these Dorobo groups "(a) have formed reciprocal relations with certain neighboring tribes; (b) have spoken the same language as these tribes and observed some of their customs (e.g., loosely acknowledging their age-set systems); (c) have to a certain extent intermarried and intermigrated with these tribes, albeit on a small scale" (Spencer 1973:204–205). In regard to Dorobo land tenure, Spencer (1973:205) writes:

A recurrent feature is that with the territorial advances and tactical withdrawals of the pastoral tribes, the Dorobo groups tend to remain closely tied with their traditional hunting grounds and to adapt themselves socially to their surroundings. In this way they may be absorbed . . . ; they may retain a certain degree of separateness . . . ; or they may retain their Dorobo characteristics while entering into a new reciprocal relationship with their new neighbors.

This pattern is clearly evident among the Okiek and Yaaku of western and central Kenya, the Dahalo and Ariangulo of eastern Kenya (both called confusingly Sanye), and the Asa and Aramanik of northern Tanzania (Ehret 1974b; Fleming 1969).

When the local food-producing group competes for resources with another group with a similar economy and is displaced or absorbed, the hunting and gathering groups usually remain and develop similar relationships with the new groups. If the language of the new group is adopted it often retains features of the language previously spoken. When neighboring groups maintain different languages, regardless of their respective economies, the nature, duration, and intensity of their interactions may be reflected by the size and number of loanword sets in both languages. Thus, through the study of vocabularies, the imprint of

TABLE 8

LINGUISTIC CLASSIFICATION OF ETHNIC GROUPS OF NORTHERN AND CENTRAL EAST AFRICA
(Mentioned in chapter 7)

Language phylum	Khoisan	Afroasiatic		Nilo-Saharan	Niger-Congo
Language family		Cushitic		Eastern Sudanic	Benue-Congo
Linguistic groups and sub-groups in East Africa		Southern Cushitic — Dahaloan, Rift	Eastern Cushitic	Nilotic → Southern (Datoga, Kalenjin) / Eastern (Ateker, Maa)	Bantu — Eastern Bantu
East African peoples	Sandawe, Hadza	Dahalo; Aramanik, Asa, Iraqw, Gorowa, Alagwa, Burunge	Yaaku, Dasenech, Arbore, El Molo, Somali, Rendille, Boni (Aweera), Oromo, Boran	Barabaig (Datog); Okiek, Pokot, Tugen, Nandi, Kipsigis, Keyo; Teso, Jie, Dodoth, Turkana, Karimojong; (Dorobo), Maasai, Arusha, Baraguyu, Samburu, Ongamo	Swahili, Pokomo, Gikuyu, Kamba, Sonjo, Haya, Luyia

previous contacts will be readily apparent, and a record of the groups that have surrounded the territory of a hunting group can be traced through time. Oral traditions in acephalous societies preserve a very limited time depth in comparison with loanword evidence. Indeed, unstratified tribal societies in East Africa are notorious for their historical amnesia. Although oral traditions may speak eloquently of recent contacts and local movements, loanword strata reveal contacts far beyond the reaches of human memory.

Linguistic Reconstructions and Regional Archaeological Successions

The origins of the present diversity of cultures and languages and their complex distributions are not amenable to simplistic explanations. The historical linguistic and archaeological evidence is equally complex, and circular reasoning is difficult to avoid. Thus separate reviews of historical linguists' reconstructions of population movements and archaeologists' reconstructions of industrial successions are needed before attempting correlations between the two (table 9).

Khoisan

It is widely assumed (but as yet unproven) that in the distant past most of eastern sub-Saharan Africa was populated by a "Bushmanoid" physical type, speaking Khoisan languages characterized by clicks (Murdock 1959: 44). Today in East Africa, evidence of this presumably formerly widespread autochthonous language phylum is found in three widely distant locations, the first in northern and central Tanzania, where the Sandawe and Hadza speak languages that, although graphically close to each other, are apparently quite distantly related. Sandawe is clearly related to Khoisan, while Hadza, although inadequately known, appears to be much more distantly related (Honken 1977). The second location showing evidence that a click language was formerly widely spoken is near the coast of Kenya in the Tana River area. Dahalo, a Southern Cushitic language, is spoken by people who were formerly hunters and gatherers. It contains words with a dental click, a feature unknown in any other Southern Cushitic language. Apparently the language spoken by these hunters before coming into contact with Southern Cushites was related to Sandawe, judging by the roots, especially with clicks shared between the two (Ehret 1974*b*:11). The third location where there is evidence that a

TABLE 9
DISTRIBUTION OF RADIOCARBON DATES IN EAST AFRICA, BY PHYSIOGRAPHIC-ECOLOGICAL PROVINCES

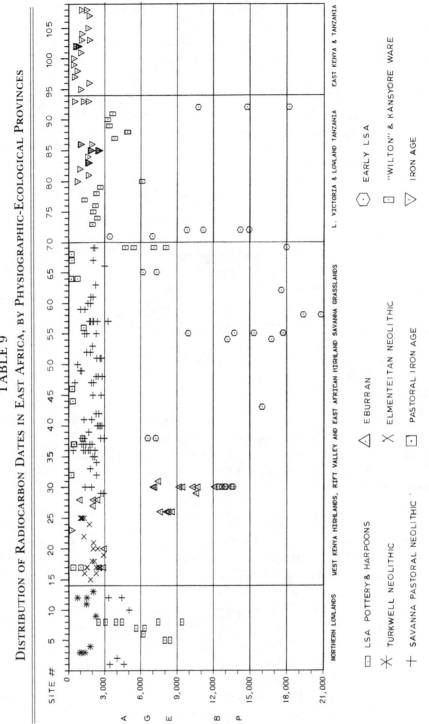

Khoisan language was formerly spoken is on Mt. Kenya, where Eastern Cushitic (Yaaku) speakers share some basic vocabulary, such as man, woman, and bone, with Hadza and Sandawe (Ehret 1974b:88). The sharings by these remote and isolated groups of features of the Khoisan language phylum imply that languages of the phylum were once spoken by hunter-gatherers over most of the region between the Somalia-Kenya border and central Tanzania.

Southern Cushitic

The first food-producing immigrants into East Africa are presumed to have been Southern Cushites, who originated in the fringe of the southern Ethiopian highlands. This movement into a territory previously occupied solely by hunter-gatherers and fishermen is estimated to have occurred between 3,000 and 5,000 years ago (Ehret 1974b:7). Modern speakers of this branch of Cushitic are found in eastern Kenya, represented by Dahalo, and in northern Tanzania, represented by an archipelago of isolated groups in a deep arc from the Mbulu Highlands to the Usambara Hills, including Asa, Aramanik, Iraqw, Gorowa, Alagwa, Burungi, and Ma'a. The occurrence of Southern Cushitic loanwords in almost every language between Lake Victoria and the Indian Ocean indicates prolonged and often intimate contacts with the Southern Nilotes, Eastern Cushites, and Eastern Bantu, all of whom came later than the Southern Cushites, displacing or absorbing them in many areas of Kenya and Tanzania. There is no linguistic evidence for food production in East Africa prior to the entrance of Southern Cushites. Moving into an unoccupied ecological niche, with domestic animals and the knowledge of agriculture, they must have spread rapidly in the absence of competition for essential resources.

Eastern Cushitic

The second series of movements to be documented was the expansion of Eastern Cushites into northeast Uganda, into northern and eastern Kenya as far south as Mt. Kenya, and to the coast of the Indian Ocean. Their modern representatives are the Yaaku hunters who live on the northern slopes of Mt. Kenya; Galaboid speakers, represented by the Arbore and Dasanech herders and cultivators in the Lake Turkana/Chew Bahir (Lake Stefanie) region; and the Elmolo fishermen of east Turkana. Their presence in the Turkana Basin is estimated to date to between 2,000 and 3,000 years ago (Heine et al. 1979). The Eastern Cushites must have displaced or absorbed the Southern Cushites who were previously in control of the Turkana Basin. The Eastern Cushites are also represented by the Rendille and Somali camel pastoralists, and the Oromo (including the Boran), but these populations derive from two later sets of movements (Fleming 1964).

Southern Nilotic

The next well-documented language group to enter East Africa is Southern Nilotic. From a nuclear area in the Uganda/Sudan/Ethiopia border region the Southern Nilotes moved south through eastern Uganda and the western highlands of Kenya, eventually as far south as Mt. Hanang and the Lake Eyasi area in northern Tanzania. Their influence appears to have been weak east of the Kenya Rift Valley. The modern representatives of Southern Nilotes are the Tatog or Barabaig pastoralists in Tanzania who are separated from their nearest relations, the Kalenjin speakers of western Kenya, by an intrusive wedge of Maasai in the Serengeti and Mara plains. Their movement from the Sudanic nuclear area appears to have begun prior to the entrance of Bantu groups into the Lake Victoria Basin, thus earlier than 2,000 years ago. An early, strong Eastern Cushitic loanword set in Southern Nilotic is indicative of enduring interactions in the region between northeast Uganda and southwest Ethiopia. Moving south, Southern Nilotic speakers probably displaced and absorbed most of the Southern Cushites in western Kenya, the Rift Valley, and northern Tanzania. There are, however, a few pockets of Southern Cushitic speakers in the area formerly occupied by Southern Nilotic speakers and now occupied by the Maasai. These are the Asa and Aramanik hunters who live in the area south of the Pare Mountains. Contacts with Southern Nilotes prior to the expansion of Maa speakers (Maasai, Samburu, Camus) is well attested in loanwords in Asa and Aramanic (Fleming 1969). Thus, although the original language of these hunters may have been completely replaced by a Southern Cushitic tongue, its overlays of Southern Nilotic and Maa loanword strata reflect their past and present contacts with dominant food-producing groups.

The Asa and Aramanik are an excellent example of the role that hunters and gatherers play in recording in their language the presence of groups that have been displaced from their former territories (Ehret 1971:56; Fleming 1969). At present they speak a Southern Cushitic language, indicating that they had prolonged and intensive interactions with the ancestors of the early Rift Southern Cushites. An overlay of

Southern Nilotic loanwords, rather than complete replacement by this language, suggests that interactions with the newcomers were either less intense or lasted a shorter period of time, or were caused by a combination of these and other factors. The area they inhabit is at present Maasai territory. The recent interactions of the hunters with the Maa-speaking pastoralists (Maasai) are reflected in a more recent stratum of Maasai loanwords (Fleming 1969).

Bantu

The radiation of Bantu-speaking populations from their West African homeland through the interlacustrine region occurred soon after the movements of Southern Nilotes. The presence of Nilotic and Cushitic food producers in Kenya and northern Tanzania, however, deflected their course south around their periphery, into areas that were probably not suitable for cattle. This movement took the Bantu speakers south to the southern highlands of Tanzania and beyond, and also east, and then north, parallel to the Indian Ocean as far north as Somalia and to the interior as far as the eastern edge of the Rift Valley in central Kenya. The presence of the Sonjo, Bantu cultivators, in the Lake Natron Basin of the northern Tanzania Rift Valley is an ecologically understandable exception to the distribution of Bantu speakers. Modern speakers of Bantu languages are predominantly mixed farmers like the Pokomo, Kikuyu, Kamba, Chaga, and Luhya. Domestic cattle play a far less significant role in their economic and social systems than in those of Nilotes and Cushites.

Eastern Nilotic

The final major population movements of concern here are the incursions of Eastern Nilotic speakers into central Kenya and northern Tanzania from their homeland in the Uganda/Sudan border area. The first movements of Eastern Nilotes from the Kenya/Uganda border area, represented by the divergence of the Teso-Turkana cluster from the Ongamo-Maa cluster, appear to have occurred early in the first millennium A.D. The proto-Ongamo-Maa division moved south into Kenya and northern Tanzania. The degree of difference between Ongamo and Maa, taken in conjunction with the present distribution of these languages, suggests that the split between them took place in the highlands between the Nyandarua Mountains of Kenya and Mt. Kilimanjaro, sometime in the middle of the first millennium A.D. (Ehret 1971:53; Vossen 1978). They would have abosrbed and displaced both Southern Nilotes and Southern Cushites during this radiation from their nuclear area. Modern Maa speakers, representing the most recent wave of Eastern Nilotic expansion, are the Maasai and Samburu pastoralists, who occupy the Rift Valley and adjacent highlands from Lake Turkana to the Pare hills of eastern Tanzania, and the Camus, with a mixed economy which includes fishing, in the Baringo Basin, Kenya. The Ongamo division is represented by the Ongamo, mixed farmers of Mount Kilimanjaro who are rapidly being absorbed by the Chaga.

A brief summary of this complex sequence of population expansions, migrations, replacements, and assimilations is needed before moving on to a consideration of the regional archaeological evidence.

The earliest evidence of significant contacts are those between Eastern Sudanic (but not Nilotic) and Eastern Cushitic speakers in the area of the Sudanese and Ethiopian border, dating to between 4,000 and 6,000 years ago. After these contacts, Southern Cushites radiated out from the fringes of the southern Ethiopian highlands between 3,000 and 5,000 years ago. Eventually they spread as far south as central Tanzania and the coast of the Indian Ocean in the Tana River area of Kenya. The next major movement was by Southern Nilotes from the Sudan/Uganda border region south along the Kenya/Uganda border area and through the higher parts of western Kenya, as far east as the Rift Valley, and eventually south as far as Lake Eyasi in northern Tanzania. On the way they displaced and absorbed most of the Southern Cushites who preceded them. Just prior to the movement of Southern Nilotes was the movement of Eastern Cushites into northeast Uganda, into northern Kenya as far south as Mt. Kenya, and east to the Indian Ocean. Eventually, in a later series of movements, Eastern Cushites radiated into Somalia probably from the headwaters of the Juba River in southern Ethiopia (Fleming 1964). Soon after the earliest Eastern Cushitic and Southern Nilotic movements Bantu expansion began, moving from the Victoria Basin south to central Tanzania and beyond, with a branch radiating east and then north around the high plains between the Indian Ocean and the Rift Valley as far north as the Somali border. The final major movement into East Africa was by Eastern Nilotic speakers. In the first millennium A.D. Ongamo-Maa speakers radiated out from the Kenya/Uganda/Sudan borderland south through central Kenya, along the Rift Valley and adjacent highlands to the highlands of northern Tanzania where they established themselves as agriculturalists in the Kilimanjaro area and as pastoralists in the savanna along the Rift Valley and adjacent highlands. No significant movements have been postulated for Khoisan speakers, but they appear to have occupied most of East Africa prior to the influx of food-producing societies. The modern distribution of these language families is outlined in map 11, and the intermediate stages in their expansions and migrations are charted in Ehret 1971 (maps 4–9) and 1974b (maps 5–8).

The series of population movements outlined above is but a small segment of a larger series of radiations and displacements which occurred throughout the broad belt of the Sahel and savanna zone between the tropical rain forest and the Sahara, from Ethiopia to the Atlantic Ocean. These movements appear to have taken place along a broad front, relatively synchronously in comparison with the scale of human movements and culture change in Africa prior to the Holocene. The relative contemporaneity of these movements implies that there was a powerful underlying causative factor which may account for the phenomenon. Perhaps it was linked to desiccation of the once verdant Sahara (Butzer et al. 1972; van Zinderen Bakker 1976), which may have forced the pastoralists and grain collectors out of the Sahara, compressing populations in the reduced Sahel and savanna zones.

Alternatively, the climatic and environmental link may have been indirect, and instead the broad population movements may have been set in motion by the widespread domestication of local plants in this zone (Harlan 1971). The availability of a potentially more abundant and reliable food source, along with domestic stock adopted from, or carried with, the pastoralists from the Sahara, may have been the impetus for an increase in population densities. The higher density must have led to competition, exclusion, and migrations of groups seeking new lands on which to establish food-producing economies. Also, the diffusion of concepts, techniques, and the paraphernalia of food production to the indigenous populations must have preceded the newcomers in some areas.

In Ethiopia, where indigenous agricultural systems may have great antiquity (Ehret 1979; Brandt, forthcoming), population pressures, perhaps in conjunction with mid-Holocene aridification, may have provided the impetus for the development of independent pastoral adaptations among poorly situated mixed farming groups, resulting in the expansion of Southern and Eastern Cushitic groups into the northern East African lowlands (Ambrose, forthcoming; Fleming 1964:90). Whatever the causes of these migrations, expansions, and assimilations, the result in East Africa is the complex mosaic of languages, cultures, and economies seen at present.

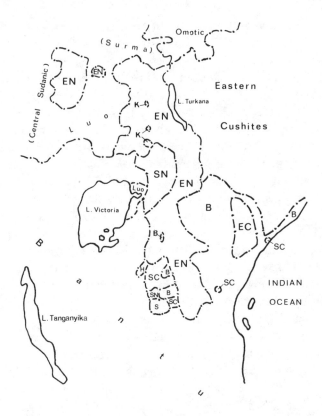

Map 11. Modern East African language groups. B—Bantu; EC—Eastern Cushites; EN—Eastern Nilotes; H—Hadza (Khoisan); K—Kuliak (Nilo-Saharan); S—Sandawe (Khoisan); SC—Southern Cushites; SN—Southern Nilotes.

Regional Archaeological Successions in East Africa

Because of its nature, the archaeological evidence is best outlined as a series of regional culture stratigraphic successions from the Turkana Basin in northern Kenya to the Eyasi area in Tanzania (table 10). The distribution of archaeological research is extremely limited in its regional coverage (table 7) in comparison with the broad regional surveys performed by historical linguists. Archaeology can therefore say very little about many areas where historical linguistic research has demonstrated prehistoric population movements.

Northern Lowland East Africa

Although some archaeological research has been carried out in northeastern Uganda (Nelson 1973; Posnansky and Nelson 1968; Robbins 1972; Robbins et al. 1977), most of it has been restricted to the Turkana area, a hot arid fault-bounded basin lying at an elevation between 1,230 and 3,000 feet. The vegetation varies at present from grassland to semidesert with riverine gallery forests. Rainfall is less than ten inches a year. East of the Turkana escarpment, which forms the Kenya-Uganda border, elevations are higher, as are precipitation and resource predictability.

The earliest Later Stone Age industries date to approximately 12,000 b.p. (Barthelme, personal communication). Their sites have yet to be described in print, and their relationship to succeeding industries are unknown. The better-documented part of the Later Stone Age sequence is characterized by a series of sites that have pottery, microlithic as well as heavy-duty stone tools, and bone harpoons. The ceramics are mainly undecorated, but there are some Wavy Line and Dotted Wavy Line sherds sparsely represented both in situ and on surface sites. The material culture has generalized affinities with the Early Khartoum Tradition, which is widely distributed throughout the Sahara and the Sahel from the Turkana Basin to the Atlantic Coast in Mauretania (Sutton 1974). The economy was based on hunting and fishing from small shoreline settlements. In the Turkana Basin these sites date to between 8,240 and 4,700 b.p. (Phillipson 1977c; Robbins 1972; Barthelme 1977).

Numerous burials have been recovered from shallow pits on these sites, but most of them are too poorly preserved to provide meaningful measurements (Rightmire 1977). A comparative study of the morphological characteristics of the burials associated with this early fishing economy would help us understand whether the huge area of the continent where this adaptation and tradition are found is a product of demic diffusion (Sutton 1974) or stimulus diffusion.

Immediately following the bone-harpoon occurrences are a series of sites with several new kinds of pottery, a new economy, and new microlithic tool kits. Until systematic studies are undertaken and a proper name for this complex is proposed it will be referred to as the Lowland Savanna Pastoral Neolithic Complex. These sites contain large quantities of obsidian for artifacts, a prized raw material whose closest sources are the Galla Lakes region of the Ethiopian Rift Valley and the Naivasha-Nakuru Basin in the Kenya Rift Valley. Thus the inhabitants of these sites must have been tied into a larger regional exchange network. The source of the glass is unknown, but it would be an excellent indicator of the direction of contacts and the homeland of the newcomers. Their economy was based in large part on domestic animals, although hunting and fishing may have been of equal economic importance. They made stone bowls of lava and a diverse range of pottery wares, including an internally scored type with an impressed or punctate exterior decoration called Nderit Ware (Bower et al. 1977:135; Barthelme 1977; Robbins 1972), originally called Gumban A pottery by Leakey (1931:199). Its distribution extends through the East African highlands as far south as Lake Eyasi in Tanzania (Smolla 1956; Bower 1973a). Another type, unnamed but equally widespread, has an incised or impressed herringbone design. These sites date possibly as early as 5,020 b.p. (Robins 1972), but more reliable age estimates fall between 4,600 and 3,300 b.p. (Barthelme 1977, and forthcoming; Phillipson 1977a; Maggs 1977:184). In the Chalbi Desert, a former lake east of Lake Turkana, David Phillipson has excavated a large site with domestic fauna, pottery, and stone bowls, dated to about 4,400 b.p. (Maggs 1977: 184). The site contains the herringbone-decorated ware as well as what may be the antecedent of Narosura Ware, which is widely distributed in the highlands to the south but at a later date. Thus these early pastoral sites represent an economic pattern, a system of obsidian trade, and three pottery wares which make their appearance in the East African highlands at a later date.

The next dated occurrences are again of a mixed pastoral, hunting, and fishing economy, with a microlithic industry. The ceramics, called Turkwel Ware (Robbins et al. 1977; Lynch and Robbins 1979), are rather different, being predominantly thin-walled bowls with closely spaced horizontal grooves and incisions. A large site with possibly related pottery, although lacking evidence of fishing, has been excavated by David Phillipson at North Horr, east of Lake Turkana (Phillipson 1976b). This site dates to 1,525 b.p. (Phillipson 1977b:236; Maggs 1977:184). Other reliable dates on the Turkwel Culture, between 1,800 and 950 b.p., are from sites in the Turkwel area of the Turkana Basin (Robbins 1972; Lynch and Robbins 1979). The earliest dates for the Turkwel Culture come from two Neolithic horizons at Ngenyn, Lake Baringo (Hivernel 1975, 1978). The upper horizon is dated to 2,080 b.p., indicating an earlier age for the ceramics of the lower horizon. The ceramics, tool kit, and economy of Ngenyn, and perhaps sites of the nearby Loboi Plain (Farrand et al. 1976), are very similar to the Turkwel pattern in the type area; both contain microlithic and heavy-duty stone tools, and both have an economy based on fishing, hunting, and herding.

The presence of this complex in the Baringo district extends the reported distribution throughout the arid regions of northern Kenya, northeast Uganda, and the Omo Valley of southern Ethiopia (Robbins 1972; Lynch and Robbins 1979).

There appears to have been a diversity of settlement types and economic adaptations at this time. In addition to the pastoral sites with thin-grooved and incised pottery, there are sites that have no domestic fauna but give evidence of hunting wild animals and of fishing. One of these sites, dominated by lava-backed blades, is dated to 1,100 b.p. (Robbins and Lynch 1978). Perhaps the harpoon-using fishermen persisted throughout the Neolithic era, coexisting with pastoralists as do the Elmolo fishermen today.

A unique burial complex has been discovered in south Turkana which may be extremely significant for determining ethnic and linguistic affinities. There are several stone pillar arrangements called Namoratunga (Lynch and Robbins 1979), one of which has been dated to 2,285 b.p. on the associated burials (Lynch and Robbins 1978). One site has an arrangement of nineteen basalt pillars oriented toward the same set of stars and constellations as those used by the Konso (Eastern Cushitic speakers) of southwest Ethiopia for calculating their calendar. This is the first archaeoastronomic megalithic site in sub-Saharan Africa. The burials at these pillar arrangements are associated wtih domestic cattle and ovicaprid teeth but unfortunately have no accompanying grave goods. Moreover, there are no habitation sites in the Turkana area which are known to be contemporary with them. Given the limited amount of research carried out in this region, the absence of such sites is not too surprising. The dated site closest in time to the burial sites is Ngenyn, near Lake Baringo, which dates to earlier than 2,080 b.p. Since the tenure of this ware in the northern East African lowlands comes very close to the age of the burial complex, these sites could represent the villages of those buried in the stone-circle graves. Lynch and Robbins (1979) have discounted the significance of their earlier dates on the Turkana Turkwel Tradition sites, disavowing connections between the habitation sites and the burials. This assumption puts them in the awkward position of lacking living sites for the residents of the Namoratunga Complex. However, the dated Baringo evidence resolves this dilemma.

Archaeological evidence relating to the earliest Iron Age inhabitants in the Turkana area is scarce. Robbins (1972:365) concluded that the Turkwel Tradition persisted well into the Iron Age, which he suggests begins at 1,500 b.p. The evidence he used—Turkwel Ware associated with iron tools in a totally disturbed site with inverted radiocarbon dates (Robbins et al. 1977)—cannot, however, serve as a basis for this conclusion. Throughout the region there are many stone burial cairns which, according to Robbins (1972), postdate the Later Stone Age. These burial cairns are still being constructed at present (Sutton 1973), although one cannot rule out the possibility that some of them were constructed during the Lowland Savanna Pastoral Neolithic era prior to 3,000 b.p., particularly since they are a consistent feature of the Highland Savanna PN and have been dated to earlier than 2,300 b.p. (Sassoon 1968). Since undisturbed, excavated Iron Age habitation site are few and recent (Robbins et al. 1977), one is forced to rely mainly upon oral traditions and historical linguistic studies to determine the sequence of recent events.

The Eastern Rift Valley and Highlands of East Africa

The central Rift Valley, situated in the central highlands of Kenya, contains a diverse range of floral communities and topographic features. Rainfall varies with elevation and the distribution of rain shadows. It is as low as less than 20 inches in the Naivasha Basin at 6,100 feet and 30 inches in the Nakuru Basin at an elevation of 5,700 feet. Only 20 miles to the west and east of the Naivasha Basin rainfall rises to more than 60 inches on the Mau Escarpment at 10,000 feet and to more than 70 inches in the Nyandarua Mountains at 13,000 feet. Floral zones correlate with elevation, temperature, slope, and precipitation. Going from open savanna at the lower elevations, the flora changes to bush on steeper slopes and at higher elevations. Montane forest is found on the higher mountain slopes, and the highest elevations are covered with a mosaic of open grassy moorlands, bamboo groves, and evergreen forests. Adjacent to the Rift Valley are the highlands, defined as regions above 4,500 feet and characterized by open grassland and lightly wooded savanna, with precipitation between 10 and 30 inches, divided into two discrete wet seasons in most areas. These high grassland stretch from the Loroghi Plateau near Maralal, Kenya, in the north to the Serengeti Plain of northern Tanzania.

As in the Turkana Basin, an unbroken composite stratified sequence of archaeological cultures is lacking, although the intensity of work here has been far greater. The pre-food-producing industry in the Naivasha-Nakuru Basin of Kenya is called the Eburran Industry (Ambrose et al.

1980); it was previously known as the Kenya Aurignacian (Leakey 1931) and later renamed the Kenya Capsian because its affinities were thought to be closer to the North African Industry (Leakey 1952). A combination of settlement pattern and climatic data and preliminary observations of the fauna indicate a broad-spectrum hunting and gathering adaptation. Unlike the early fishing sites in the Turkana Basin, fishing seems to have played an extremely minor role, if any, in the economy, and the evidence for early pottery (Leakey 1931:103) and bone-harpoon manufacture (Oakley 1961) is equally ambiguous and not confirmed by recent excavations (Ambrose et al. 1980, contra Sutton 1974). Eburran occurrences date to between approximately 12,000 to 6,000 b.p. The industry may have developed from any of several industries that were present in the central Rift between 16,000 and 13,000 b.p.

Outside the Rift Valley early highland sites, dated to between 21,000 and about 12,000 b.p., have been found at Lukenya Hill (Gramly 1976; Miller 1979; Merrick 1975) and on the Serengeti Plain near Olduvai Gorge (Leakey et al. 1972; Mehlman 1977). Although some authors have suggested genetic relationships between the Serengeti and Kenya Rift Valley industries (Leakey et al. 1972; Cole 1963:255), the differences between the assemblages in these regions are far broader than can be accounted for by differences in raw materials alone. The inferred similarities are as yet unproven, and close relationships seem unlikely.

The next well-documented phase of occupation in this area follows a rather intractable hiatus in the archaeological record between about 6,000 and 3,300 b.p. (tables 7, 10). In fact, there are no well-documented in situ habitation sites that date to these three millennia anywhere in the East African highlands at elevations above 4,500 feet, with the single possible exception of Nasera Rock, Tanzania (Mehlman 1977).

Following this hiatus is the extremely complex Neolithic era, which dates to between 3,300 and 1,300 b.p. There were at least three contemporary cultures, formerly identified as the Elmenteitan, Gumban A, and the Upper Kenya Capsian Phases C, D, and Capsian of Neolithic tradition (Leakey 1931; Cole 1963). Prior to the advent of radiometric dating they were assumed mainly to represent an evolutionary cultural succession. The dating evidence now, however, shows that they are contemporaneous (tables 7, 9, 10). For present purposes they are assumed to represent three ethnic/linguistic groups, each having distinct origins, socioeconomic adaptive systems, and material cultures, all living in adjacent ecological zones within the confines of the Rift Valley and adjoining highlands during most of this era.

One industry has most of the features that characterized the indigenous Eburran Industry, suggesting that the Eburran did persist through the gap in the succession and that sites dating to between 6,000 and 3,000 b.p. will eventually be found. This portion of the Eburran succession, called Phase 5 of the industry, is composed of two previously named entities called the Upper Kenya Capsian Phases C and D, and the Kenya Capsian of Neolithic tradition (Leakey 1931:109, 1942; M. D. Leakey 1945:301; Cole 1963).

Of the three contemporary Neolithic era cultures, phase 5 of the Eburran is the least well documented. The phase can be divided into two subphases on the basis of stone-tool typology, economic adaptation, and settlement patterns but one must bear in mind that this division may prove to be arbitrary—a function of poor chronological control on two activities facies of a single adaptive system. Phase 5A sites are located on the Rift Valley margins in a savanna/bush ecotone, a placement analagous to that of Phases 1−4 of the Eburran Complex (Ambrose et al. 1980). The three known sites are Layer 12, Gamble's Cave (Leakey 1931:93), Naivasha Railway Rock Shelter Layers 1−4 (Leakey 1942; Cole 1963: 256−258; Onyango-Abuje 1977*b*; Nelson 1973), and Masai Gorge Rock Shelter, lower Stratum 3 (Ambrose 1977). The lower horizon at Keringet Caves, as yet undescribed (M. Cohen 1970), may also belong to Phase 5A.

The faunal assemblage from Naivasha Railway Rock Shelter has low proportions of domestic stock and a wild fauna dominated by closed-environment species (Onyango-Abuje 1977*b*), and a similar pattern probably occurs at Masai Gorge Rock Shelter. The lithic assemblage shows only minor stylistic and type-frequency differences from the pre-Neolithic Industry, and the pottery includes a heterogeneous mix of Savanna PN wares and some unique forms. The settlement pattern and faunal composition of Eburran 5A sites suggest that these people were not constrained in their choice of site locations by the requirements of herding domestic animals. The ceramics do, however, indicate trade with adjacent pastoral groups. Radiometric dates from Masai Gorge Rock Shelter indicate that Phase 5A began prior to 2,865 b.p. (Ambrose 1977) and continued to well beyond 2,000 b.p. at Naivasha Railway Rock Shelter. Gamble's Cave Layer 12 is undated but lies almost four meters above layers dated to between 8,550 and 8,090 b.p. (Ambrose et al. 1980). On the basis of regional evidence for the age of the overlying Elmenteitan occurrence in Layer 6 (table 10), Layer 12 should date to between roughly 3,000 and 2,500 b.p. (contra Protsch 1978).

Phase 5B of the Eburran would correspond to the Upper Kenya

Capsian of Neolithic Tradition of M. D. Leakey (1945:276; Cole 1963: 282) and is known only from Hyrax Hill and the Causeway site near Crescent Island, Lake Naivasha (Onyango-Abuje 1977a). This subphase shares the eclectic mix of ceramics and a similar lithic industry with Phase 5A sites (e.g., M. D. Leakey 1945:311–312), but site location resembles that of the Highland Savanna PN, that is, in the middle of a grassland habitat, maximizing access to pasture (Ambrose, forthcoming). This implies that site locations were dictated by the pasturage and water requirements of domestic stock. These sites could be therefore be interpreted as evidence for a transition from a hunter-gatherer economy to a pastoral economy by indigenous groups, an ongoing process among Okiek hunter-gatherer groups today (Blackburn 1976). It is possible that Phase 5B started later than 5A since the Causeway site is dated to 2,380 b.p. (Ambrose, forthcoming), and the dominant ware at Hyrax Hill, Maringishu Ware, has been dated to 1,700 b.p. at the type site (Bower et al. 1977:137).

Another series of sites originally called the Gumban A branch of the Stone Bowl Culture (Leakey 1931:198) were considered to have developed out of the Eburran (M. D. Leakey 1945:301). There are features that link it to the aforementioned Lowland Savanna PN sites of northern Kenya, including domestic animals, stone bowls, at least two pottery wares, traded obsidian, and possibly cairn burials. This unified culture complex, which dates to between 3,300 and 1,250 b.p., appears abruptly in the highlands 1,600 years after its appearance in the lowlands (tables 7, 10). Because it seems to derive from the Lowland Complex it is called, for present purposes, the Highland Savanna Pastoral Neolithic.

Two of the wares associated with the Highland Savanna PN in central Kenya have exact correlates with those of the first lowland pastoralists of the Turkana Basin: Nderit Ware (Robbins 1972; Barthelme 1977) and the incised or impressed herringbone motif ware (John Barthelme, personal communication; Phillipson 1977a:72). Phillipson also sees connections between some of the ceramics from his excavations at North Horr I on the Chalbi Desert (Phillipson 1976b) and Narosura Ware (personal communication). Narosura Ware, the most widespread ware associated with these pastoral sites, is characterized by bands of comb stamping and incisions below the rim, in closely spaced vertical, oblique, or crosshatch designs, or pendant triangles (Odner 1972). In later-dated sites Narosura Ware is often associated with Akira Ware (originally called T.I.P. Ware by Bower (1973a) and Gramly (1975a)) as at Lukenya Hill, Nasera, and Laikipia (Bower et al. 1977:140; Mehlman 1977). Akira Ware is composed of very thin-walled, often flat-based, burnished vessels with incised and impressed decorations in panels which may cover most of the body. The last-named type found on Highland Savanna PN sites is called Maringishu Ware (Bower et al. 1977:137), first found at Hyrax Hill (M. D. Leakey 1945:302–305). This ware is characterized by ovoid beakers with a broad belt of deep oblique incisions, or a curvilinear trellis motif, or rows of deep punctations parallel to the rim. Several other minor wares exist but, like the herringbone motif pottery, there is as yet no suitable type site from which they can be named.

The Highland Savanna PN Complex is widely distributed throughout the highland savanna grasslands of Kenya and Tanzania at elevations between 4,500 and 7,000 feet. Obsidian, which has a localized distribution in the Naivasha-Nakuru area, was widely traded throughout the region and is always associated with one or several of its recognized pottery wares. At the Mumba-Höhle, Tanzania, however, the pottery is associated with a lithic assemblage totally unlike that at other Savanna PN sites (Smolla 1956; Mehlman 1979). At this site quartz dominates the lithic assemblage, obsidian is very rare, and the pottery is not associated with domestic fauna. The ecological context is tsetse-infested bush at an elevation of 3,200 feet near the edge of Lake Eyasi and is thus beyond the ecological range of the Highland Savanna PN adaptation. The indigenous stoneworking industry associated with Neolithic pottery indicates contacts between local hunter-gatherers and immigrant pastoralists along the southern border of Highland Savanna PN territory.

The mortuary practice of the Savanna PN Complex is fairly well known. Cairn burials, either single or multiple in the open (Leakey 1931; Sassoon 1968; M. D. Leakey 1945, 1966; Brown 1966; Siiriäinen 1977; Sutton 1973) or in crevices in rocky outcrops, are an integral feature of the landscape (Bower et al. 1977:140; Leakey 1931:200). These burials are usually asociated with a few large obsidian blades, stone bowls, pestle rubbers, and thin, flat palettes for grinding ocher. A date of 2,300 b.p. has been obtained on a cairn in Ngorongoro Crater, Tanzania (Sassoon 1968). Some cairns have proved to be cenotaphs or to contain only a part of the characteristic assemblage (Posnansky 1968a; Siiriäinen 1977; Sutton 1973). Cairn burials are also widely distributed throughout the northern lowlands and Ethiopia—another possible indication of highland-lowland Savanna PN connections. The ages of the northern cairns are, however, unknown (Sutton 1973).

The third Neolithic complex in the Rift Valley was originally known as the Elmenteitan Culture (Leakey 1931:172; Leakey and Leakey 1950), a name that is still valid today. This complex was previously thought to have developed out of the Upper Kenya Capsian Phase C (Eburran 5A). There is, however, no evidence for an intermediate stage between the two cultures; actually, they are, partly contemporaneous with each other and the "Gumban A" (Highland Savanna PN). Although the Elmenteitan shares some generalized features with the Highland Savanna PN, including domestic animals and similar mortuary paraphernalia, it is characterized by a different pattern of land use, settlement, economy, hunting and food-production practices, stylistically different lithic and ceramic assemblages, and a different mortuary pattern. No antecedents are known for the Elmenteitan either within or outside its known distribution.

The Elmenteitan Culture was described by Louis Leakey (1931:172–175) from Gamble's Cave, and later from Njoro River Cave (Leakey and Leakey 1950). The lithic industry and ceramic tradition have recently been described and redefined from newly excavated and radiometrically dated occurrences (Ambrose 1977, 1980; Wandibba 1980; Bower et al. 1977:131). The lithic industry is characterized by the production of large, broad two-edged blades. These were used unmodified, or they served as blanks that were often segmented in a distinctive way for the production of a wide variety of small tools and cores (Nelson 1980). The ceramics are mainly unburnished and undecorated semiglobular bowls; decoration is fairly idiosyncratic and rare. The only common motifs are irregular punctations and rim milling. Rims are usually slightly outturned, and at several sites some smaller bowls have horizontal lugs or handles with small holes (Leakey and Leakey 1950; Bower et al. 1977:136–139).

With this definition in hand, Neolithic sites previously attributed to the Elmenteitan Industrial Complex have been reexamined. Many have been excluded from membership (e.g., Narosura), falling into the broadly defined Savanna PN Complex or, more rarely, becoming a candidate for the final phases of the Eburran Industry. The occurrences that do conform to the definition of the Elmenteitan lithic industry and ceramic tradition have been found to form a discrete regional cluster on the western side of the central Rift Valley and, to the west, on the Mau Escarpment. Surface collections of pottery from three Later Stone Age sites in Kisii district seem partly to conform to the Elmenteitan pottery description (Bower 1973b:136, and personal communication) and thus may give an indication of the western extension of the Elmenteitan.

Located in the wetter regions of western Kenya, it is likely that Elmenteitan groups had a mixed pastoral-agricultural-hunting economy, Carbonized gourd fragments were found at Njoro River Cave (Leakey and Leakey 1950). Although gourds grow wild in parts of East Africa they are commonly cultivated along with sorghum and finger millet, suggesting that the indigenous agricultural systems of western Kenya have been practiced for at least 2,500 years.

Elmenteitan mortuary practices differ widely from those of the Highland Savanna PN. The dead were characteristically cremated in caves, as at Njoro River Cave, Keringet Caves, and possibly Egerton Cave (Leakey and Leakey 1950; M. Cohen 1970; Faugust and Sutton 1966). Lion Hill Cave (Bower et al. 1977:131) and Bromhead's site (Leakey 1931, 1935) may also have served as crematoriums, but they lack the characteristic grave goods. One cremation burial reported by Siiriäinen (1977) is far east of the known distribution of the Elmenteitan Culture. Most Elmenteitan burial sites share similar grave goods with the Highland Savanna PN: stone bowls, pestle rubbers, and palettes. The shared mortuary assemblage was a prime factor in preventing the acceptance of the Elmenteitan Industry as a unique archaeological and cultural entity.

The Elmenteitan Industrial Complex appears to have entered the western highlands of Kenya fully developed, at about 2,500 b.p. (Ambrose, forthcoming). It was thus contemporary with the Highland Savanna PN Complex from this time up to the end of the Neolithic era at 1,300 b.p. and also with Phase 5 of the Eburran Industry until the end of the Neolithic era.

The Highland Savanna PN sites are a major component of what has been commonly called the "Stone Bowl Neolithic" or the "Stone Bowl Culture" (M. Cohen 1970; Cole 1963). The use of a single artifact type— the stone bowl—to determine the affinities of a site that contained microlithic stone tools and pottery, however, served only to obscure an extremely basic division within the Stone Age food-producing cultures of the highlands of Kenya and Tanzania, a division that, as argued below, has significant correlations with ethnic and linguistic groups. Although the Leakeys were certain of the distinctive character of the Elmenteitan Culture, it was lumped with Highland Savanna PN sites by more recent workers on the basis of the presence of stone bowls, occasional large "two-edged" blades in the Savanna PN sites, and the presence of certain classes of shaped stone tools (Odner 1972; Onyango-Abuje 1977a:150; Siiriäinen 1977:172; M. Cohen 1970; Sutton 1966).

This relapse in the understanding of the classification of the Neolithic in East Africa was a direct result of Sutton's (1966:38) unfounded pronouncement that "Elmenteitan may remain a useful name for indicating two-edged blades of exaggerated length but not for describing tools of diverse types, pottery, or a culture at large" (also see Sutton 1973:79–80). The distinctions between the Elmenteitan and the Highland Savanna PN were further obscured by Sutton's pottery classification (1964; 1971:146, 1973:146–153) which lumped the distinctive Elmenteitan pottery with that of the Savanna pastoralists. Finally, unqualified application of the term "Pastoral Neolithic" to unrelated Later Stone Age sites with pottery and different economies (Bower et al. 1977) has done little to clarify the classification of highland sites. Fortunately recent excavations, analysis, and reviews of the literature and museum collections (Ambrose 1977, 1980, and forthcoming; Nelson, 1980; Wandibba 1980) have reaffirmed the Leakeys' interpretation, demonstrating that the Elmenteitan is a discrete coherent cultural entity with distinctive, covarying lithic and ceramic technologies, mortuary traditions, economy, settlement patterns, and a discrete geographic distribution.

With the introduction of an Iron Age technology to the central highlands, the use of obsidian tools and the quality of workmanship rapidly declined. At Deloraine Farm on the western side of the Rift Valley north of Lake Nakuru was found a degenerate industry, strongly reminiscent of the Elmenteitan. The faunal assemblage is wholly dominated by cattle. The presence of a carbonized finger millet seed (*Eleusine coracana*) and numerous large upper and lower grindstones are positive evidence of agriculture (Chittick 1978; Chittick and Ambrose, in preparation). This is the earliest Iron Age site in the Rift Valley, dating to between 1,300 and 1,100 b.p. (M. Cohen 1972). Similar pottery has been found only at the Makalia burial site (Leakey 1931:207) and the Gil-Gil River burial site where a "Gumban C" vessel was recovered (M. D. Leakey 1945:331; Brown 1966:68). Related wares may, however, be represented in Kisii district (Bower 1973*b*). On the basis of broad similarities in lithic industry, ceramic tradition, and site location, this poorly known Iron Age culture is the most likely candidate for the Iron Age transformation of the Elmenteitan Industry.

A more widespread pastoral Iron Age culture characterized by Lanet Ware (Posnansky 1967*b*) appears prior to 1,185 b.p. (Bower et al. 1977: 131–133; Bower and Nelson 1979). Few sites have been excavated, but the characteristic pottery is often associated with shallow depressions called Sirikwa Holes, which are a common feature of the highland Kenya landscape. Grossly similar features are, however, found in far-flung regions among unrelated groups from Ethiopia to Tanzania (Sutton 1973:143). This archaeological culture is distributed over the areas previously inhabited by both Elmenteitan and Savanna PN peoples (Bower et al. 1977:128); it is characterized by a degenerated lithic industry in the earlier phase, as at the Northeast Village at Hyrax Hill (M. D. Leakey 1945:354) and Salasun and Akira (Bower et al. 1977:144), which drops out almost entirely by 350 b.p., as at Hyrax Hill site I (M. D. Leakey 1945:276; Onyango-Abuje 1977a) and Lanet (Posnansky 1967b). The relationship between the Highland Savanna PN lithic industry and that of the pastoral Iron Age is presently uncertain. Trade goods, including glass beads and cowrie shells, are represented in the latest phase (Leakey 1945:373). The pottery, originally called Gumban B by Leakey (1931: 204), renamed Lanet Ware by Posnansky (1967b) and "Kenya Highlands Class C" by Sutton (1964; 1973:150–153), is characterized by elongated gourd- or bag-shaped vessels with handles and spouts and twisted-cord roulette decoration. Closely allied regional variants have been found at Mount Kadam in northeast Uganda (Robbins et al. 1977), Mt. Elgon (Chapman 1966), in the Rift Valley at Hyrax Hill, Lanet, Salasun, and Akira (M. D. Leakey 1945; Posnansky 1967b; Bower et al. 1977:130– 133), in the western highlands of Kenya (Sutton 1973), east of the Rift Valley at Lukenya Hill (Gramly 1975a, b), and in Tanzania at Seronera (Bower 1973a, 1976). Similarly decorated pottery is still being made by the Okiek (Blackburn 1973) and is widely used by the Maasai and other Eastern Nilotic groups (Sutton 1971:175; Gramly 1975a, b) and by some northern Kalenjin groups (Sutton 1973:152) who were previously in close contact with the Maasai. Lanet Ware is often associated with large, shallow depressions commonly called Sirikwa Holes, which have been interpreted as cattle enclosures (Sutton 1973:56) or house pits (M. D. Leakey 1945; Chapman 1966; Posnansky 1967b). Mainly distributed in higher, wetter regions of the Rift Valley and adjacent highlands, they may have been the work of settled peoples with a mixed pastoral/agricultural economy.

The Early Iron Age, which begins prior to 2,000 b.p. in the Lake Victoria region (Phillipson 1977b:108; Schmidt 1975) and by 1,700 b.p. to the east (Soper 1967a:3), is virtually unknown within the Rift Valley and adjacent high grasslands (map 12). It is represented by less than a handful of potsherds from widely separated locations.

Eastern Kenya and Northeastern Tanzania

Adjacent to the highland savanna grassland regions discussed above, in both the high forested regions east of the Rift Valley and the lower-lying regions of eastern Kenya and Tanzania, the archaeological record, although poorly documented, is patently different. Dated sites containing

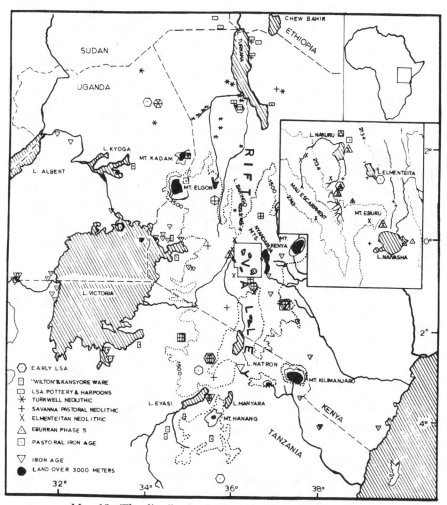

Map 12. The distribution of Later Stone Age and Iron Age
sites in East Africa.

Stone Age sequences which span the introduction of ceramics, food
production, or the Later Stone Age/Iron age transition are unknown.
The best-documented part of the archaeological sequence begins with
Early Iron Age sites containing Kwale Ware, which is dated to 1,700 b.p.
at the type site near the coast of Kenya (Soper 1967*a*:3) and slightly earlier
at a site in the Pare hills of Tanzania (Soper 1967*b*:24). This beautiful,
well-made ware is characterized by necked pots and open bowls, usually
with thickened rims which have multiple bevels or grooves. There may be
a band of oblique or crosshatch twisted-cord roulette or comb-stamp

impressions or incisions below the rim, and parallel grooves with chevrons on the shoulders. At Gatung'ang'a, west of Mt. Kenya, Siiriäinen (1971) has found a late variant of Kwale Ware dated to 820 b.p. It is contemporary with Maore Ware, which is characterized by walked zigzag impressions and has been dated to 1,080 b.p. at the type site in the Pare hills, Tanzania (Soper 1967*b*:24–26). These wares have also been found at two sites at Lukenya Hill, and several other sites in eastern Kenya (Siiriäinen 1971:220–221). The ceramics seem to evolve toward necked jars with a remarkable decrease through time in the amount of rim elaboration and decoration. Later sites, such as those in the Chyulu Hills in southeast Kenya (Soper 1976), may be linked to the Kwale-Maore developmental sequence, possibly providing a link between the Early Iron Age people and modern Bantu such as the Kamba (Soper 1976).

The Lake Victoria Region and Lowland Northern Tanzania

The Victoria Basin, at an elevation between 3,700 and 5,000 feet, has rainfall between 30 and 50 inches a year. The flora has been greatly modified by agricultural activities, but it may originally have been forest and woodland (Livingston 1976). An ecologically and archaeologically similar, though drier, zone stretches south and east around the Serengeti Plain, joining up with the low-lying areas of eastern Kenya and Tanzania discussed above. The topography is diverse and fragmented where the southern end of the Rift Valley fades out into a series of faulted half grabens, which produce spectacular fault scarps, and lakes such as Eyasi at 3,400 feet. The tsetse fly makes a pastoral economy untenable in this predominantly closed bush/savanna woodland mosaic, but a single long rainy season, rather than the two short ones in the high grasslands, permits shifting agriculture in most places.

The Later Stone Age sequence is sparsely documented here, starting at least as early as 17,000 b.p. at Buvuma Island (van Noten 1971). Most sites, however, are younger than 7,000 b.p. (Nelson 1973) and contain lithic assemblages made mainly on quartz. This material, unlike chert or obsidian, is not amenable to the production of formalized shaped tools; thus most assemblages take on a generalized "Wilton" character. The term "Wilton" is used only with extreme reservation since it has been proven inapplicable outside the type area in South Africa (Nelson and Posnansky 1970:159), although no suitable replacement name has been suggested. The poor flaking properties of the dominant raw material control the form of finished tools to a large degree and may thus mask significant regional cultural differences. The lithic assemblages of later sites are typically characterized by many bipolar cores, small-backed microliths, and occasional thumbnail scrapers and burins. Assemblages of this type are found in western Kenya (Gabel 1969), the Mwanza region of Tanzania (Soper and Golden 1969), southeastern Uganda (Chapman 1967; Nelson 1973; Nelson and Posnansky 1970), Nasera Rock, Serengeti (Mehlman 1977), Mumba-Höhle, Eyasi (Mehlman 1979), Lululam-pembele (Odner 1971a), and in the Dodoma and Singida regions of central Tanzania (Masao 1979).

A continuous sequence can be discerned from at least 8,000 b.p. to Early Iron Age. Indeed, six of the dozen or so dated sites in this region have dates between 5,000 and 3,000 b.p. No sites are conclusively dated to this period in the more intensively studied highlands. Possibly as early as 4,500 b.p., but no later than 2,600 b.p. ceramics were added to this assemblage throughout the area (Soper and Golden 1969; Mehlman 1979). The pottery is almost all of one type, called Kansyore Ware (Chapman 1967), characterized by small bowls with tapered rims. Decoration, which covers most of the body, is composed of closely set incisions or impressions, sometimes apparently made with a comb (Soper and Golden 1969:25). Kansyore Ware is said to bear striking resemblances to the early Khartoum pottery in the Sudan (Sutton 1971:157).

Kansyore Ware and the "Wilton" lithic industry persisted until quite recent times. The presence of Early Iron Age wares associated with stone tools and Kansyore Ware has often been attributed to a mechanical mixture, but it could also be interpreted as evidence of the persistence of the indigenous Stone Age way of life after settlement by Iron Age food-producing societies, as has been documented in southern central Africa (Miller 1969).

The distribution of Kansyore Ware and the lithic industry slightly overlaps that of the Highland Savanna PN. At Seronera, on the higher grasslands, Kansyore Ware is present in one shelter (Bower 1973a). At Nasera Rock, in a similar ecological context, the "Wilton" Industry beginning at 8,000 b.p. and Kansyore Ware at possibly 4,500 b.p. (the accuracy of the early dates on pottery are in question, Mehlman, personal communication) continue until about 2,000 b.p., when they are replaced by a Highland Savanna PN Industry with imported obsidian and Akira and Narosura wares.

Farther south, at the Mumba-Höhle, at an elevation below 3,400 feet, there is a slightly different sequence of events. The quartz-based "Wilton" Industry is at the base, and Kansyore Ware is present in the same chronological position as at Nasera (Mehlman 1979). In contrast with Nasera, however, this industry persists through the introduction of Savanna PN ceramics and Lelesu Ware, suggesting that the site was on the periphery of the territory of the Early Iron Age and Savanna PN food producers. In this case, the indigenous populations were probably not displaced; rather, they may have established exchange relationships with the adjacent food-producing cultures as in the Kenya Rift Valley.

Kansyore Ware is thus contemporary with and has a nearly mutually exclusive distribution with Savanna PN wares, but it has an overlapping distribution and is probably partly contemporary with Early Iron Age wares. It is almost always associated with a "Wilton" industry made on quartz, and a hunting-fishing-gathering economy, with burials often at habitation sites (Soper and Golden 1969; Mehlman 1979; Leakey 1935: 89; Chapman 1966; Masao 1979). The ecological context—low-elevation bush and savanna woodland—is also complementary to that of the Highland Savanna PN Culture. Kansyore Ware has, however, been reported from Salasun in the high central Rift Valley of Kenya (Bower et al. 1977:130, 139; Bower and Nelson 1979), although it bears little resemblance to that found in the type region and has a different ecological context with a different lithic industry and a pastoral economy. If Salasun is discounted, the boundary between these two cultures would roughly correspond with the ecotone between the high grasslands and lower-elevation tsetse-infested bush in northwest Tanzania (Soper and Golden 1969:41). Whereas the indigenous hunters may have been excluded from the high savanna grasslands by pastoralists, they seem to have coexisted with Iron Age agriculturalists; they may have achieved this compromise by retreating to more arid zones less favorable for agriculture (Twaddle 1975:154).

The Early Iron Age in the Lake Victoria region is represented by Urewe Ware, which occurs at numerous open sites and rock shelters (Soper 1969, 1971c). It was originally known as Dimple Based Pottery. Aside from this feature the ceramics are characterized by necked pots and shallow thick-walled bowls with externally thickened, fluted rims. Decoration includes incisions near the rim and sets of grooves in pendant loops and other elaborate motifs. Farther south and east are the closely related, though slightly later, variants called Lelesu Ware in central Tanzania and Kwale Ware in eastern Kenya. Urewe Ware is the earliest, dating to 2,400 b.p (Schmidt 1975). Lelesu and Kwale date to between 1,850 and 1,700 b.p. (Phillipson 1977b:104–109, 140). Posnansky (1968b) suggests the Early Iron Age pottery tradition persists in evolving forms on Lolui Island, Lake Victoria, at least until the middle of the second millennium A.D.

During the Later Iron Age regional differentiation of pottery traditions becomes apparent. This period also witnessed the rise of the inter-lacustrine chiefdoms and kingdoms (Sutton 1971:168–171). Many wares, such as Bigo Ware, retain general features of the Early Iron Age wares, like thickened rims and pot and bowl forms. As to the east, however, the elaborate decorations drop out and plaited or knotted roulette decoration (not to be confused with twisted-cord roulette decorations in the highlands) becomes the dominant motif and is still widely used throughout the region today.

In the hot, arid Rift Valley south of Lake Natron, Tanzania, there are several Later Iron Age village sites characterized by stone line–bounded terraced fields, complex irrigation canals, revetted walls, circular hut platforms cut into hillsides, and cairns. This fascinating complex, known from excavations at Engaruka (Sassoon 1966; Sutton 1978), has long fired speculation about the Azanian megalithic civilization of East Africa. The bulk of the radiocarbon dates cluster around 400 b.p., although earlier and later occupations, between 1,600 and 200 b.p., cannot be ruled out, given the wide range of dates (Sassoon 1966; Phillipson 1977*b*:245). The material culture seems uniform, however, and glass beads and cowrie shells indicate coastal trade and a late age for most of the remains. The relationships of this unique complex to other archaeological entities is presently uncertain, since the pottery has no obvious parallels, ante-cedents, or successors nearby. The settled irrigation agriculture system represented at Engaruka has strong and detailed parallels with that of the Sonjo who live farther north in this section of the Rift Valley, near Lake Natron. These similarities include overall village structure, house place-ment and construction, and ceremonial outdoor hearth design, indicating the Sonjo agricultural settlement system has a respectable antiquity.

A brief summary of these regional archaeological successions and their relationships is necessary to help digest the mass of data presented above (see map 12, tables 7, 9). The effects of past climatic shifts are then discussed, and an attempt is made to demonstrate how these may have affected movements of human populations.

In the Turkana Basin the relevant portion of the sequence begins with a microlithic Later Stone Age industry with bone harpoons and pottery; some of the pottery resembles that of the Early Khartoum Tradi-tion which is distributed throughout the Sahel. This industry dates to between 8,400 and 5,000 b.p. The hunters and fishers are succeeded by Lowland Savanna pastoralists between 5,000 and 3,300 b.p., who also fished and hunted. These were the first food-producing peoples in East Africa. Their microlithic industry was characterized by imported obsid-ian, stone bowls, and new pottery types. They were succeeded by a different group of pastoralists before 2,300 b.p., represented by the Turkwel Tradition. The ceramics were quite different, and stone bowls and obsidian were absent. This industry dates to about 1,800 b.p. in the Turkana area. A regional variant may be represented farther south in the Baringo Basin, dated to earlier than 2,080 b.p. The Turkwel Tradition may be associated with the archaeostronomic site on the west side of Lake Turkana, dated to 2,300 b.p. The date of the end of the Stone Age is uncertain, but it is probably late in the first millennium A.D. when cord-rouletted pottery became common.

In the central Rift Valley and adjacent highlands of Kenya and Tanzania the relevant sequence begins with the Eburran Industry in the Kenya Rift Valley, dated to between 12,000 and 6,000 b.p., and also unnamed early Later Stone Age industries at Lukenya Hill, Kenya, and the Serengeti Plain of Tanzania which date to roughly 17,000 b.p. After a hiatus in the Rift Valley sequence between 6,000 and 3,000 b.p., the Eburran Phase 5 industry may have persisted in a variety of forms until the end of the Later Stone Age.

At 3,300 b.p. the Highland Savanna PN Complex appears quite suddenly over the entire highlands, with sites distributed throughout the savanna zone at elevations between 4,800 and 7,000 feet, as far south as the Serengeti Plain in northern Tanzania. This complex includes domestic stock, stone bowls, and several pottery wares, of which two or three may have antecedents in the Turkana region. The Highland Savanna PN lasts until 1,250 b.p., coexisting with the Eburran and Elmenteitan industries in adjacent parts of the highlands.

At about 2,500 b.p. the Elmenteitan Culture appears in the sequence. It has a lithic and ceramic industry, a burial tradition, and a geographic distribution that differs radically from that of the Highland Savanna PN and the Eburran. The Elmenteitan Culture is distributed on the western side of the Rift Valley and the adjacent western highlands, at generally higher elevations than the Savanna PN Culture. The Elmenteitan Culture may have persisted briefly into the Iron Age at Deloraine Farm. The introduction of an Iron Age technology to the rest of the highlands of East Africa at 1,250 b.p. is represented by the overall degeneration of the quality of the lithic technology, accompanied by the spread of twisted-cord rouletted pottery known as Lanet Ware, which is often found on sites with Sirikwa Holes.

In eastern Kenya and northeastern Tanzania the Stone Age sequence is unknown. The Iron Age begins at 1,700 b.p. with Kwale Ware, supplanted by Maore Ware by 1,100 b.p. and by less distinctive wares antecedent to modern ceramics by the middle of the second millennium A.D.

In the Lake Victoria Basin and the adjacent low-lying areas below 4,500 feet in northern Tanzania, at least as far south as Dodoma and Singida, there is a quartz-based microlithic industry of "Wilton" aspect, with an economy based upon hunting, fishing, and snail and shellfish collecting. This industry dates to between 8,000 and 2,000 b.p. or later, with Kansyore Ware entering the sequence possibly as early as 4,500 b.p. but certainly as early as 2,600 b.p. In the higher savanna of the Serengeti Plain at Nasera Rock this industry is replaced by the Savanna PN complex at about 2,100 b.p. There are, however, Savanna PN occurrences elsewhere on the Serengeti which date to as early as 3,000 b.p. (Bower, personal communication, 1979). At lower elevations in the Victoria Basin and northern Tanzania the Iron Age is represented by the introduction of Urewe and Lelesu wares, followed by various rouletted forms. The "Wilton" Industry appears to persist long after the advent of the Iron Age, suggesting contemporaneity of hunter-gatherers and agriculturalists. In the higher plains Highland Savanna PN occurrences are followed by pastoral Iron Age occupations with Lanet Ware.

Prehistoric Climate

The beginning and ending of many parts of the dated archaeological succession seem to correlate with past climatic regimes and their transitions (table 7). Implicit in these correlations between the climatic and cultural succession is the notion that many of the population movements documented by historical linguists may have been in part climatically controlled or induced. Likewise, the primary cause of observed lacunae in the archaeological succession may have been the effects of climate on the abundance, distribution, and predictability of resources, which would in turn require adaptive shifts in patterns of mobility, group size, and site utilization (Dyson-Hudson and Smith 1978).

The climatic succession of the terminal Pleistocene and Holocene has been reconstructed from the dating of high lake levels, pollen cores, and diatom studies (Butzer et al. 1972; Richardson 1966; Richardson and Richardson 1972; Coetzee 1964, 1967). In the terminal Pleistocene between 17,000 and 13,000 b.p. there was a hyperarid period over most of the northeastern part of the continent. It was succeeded between 12,000 and 6,000 b.p. by an extremely moist period which turned the Sahara into a verdant lake-studded savanna and caused existing saline lakes like those in the Rift Valley to rise to overflow levels, sometimes hundreds of feet above their present elevations. This period of higher rainfall radically altered the distribution of floral communities. Montane forest expanded, descending to lower elevations, and the savanna of the highlands may have become woodlands. After 6,000 b.p. precipitation gradually tapered off to nearly modern levels. By 4,000 b.p. the Sahara had turned back to desert, Rift lakes had fallen, montane forests had receded, and savanna had expanded. In central Kenya, however, there are indications that between 5,600 and 3,000 b.p. the climate became more arid than at present. This arid phase is not consistently documented in East Africa, but a hyperarid period dating between 5,500 and 3,000 b.p. has been noted in the Sahelian zone (Dumont 1978). This period may have turned the open savanna into tsetse-infested bush. From about 3,000 b.p. to the present the climate has been variable, although essentially similar to that recorded since the turn of the century.

The terminal Pleistocene hyperarid interval appears to correlate with a widespread hiatus in the archaeological succession throughout East Africa, suggesting a climate so severe that human populations, living at very low densities, were so mobile as to be invisible in the archaeological record. The bone-harpoon fishing tradition would not, of course, have been distributed over so large a portion of the Sahara between 8,600 and 5,000 b.p. had it not been for the period of increased precipitation which followed. The brief hiatus in the archaeological succession in the East African highlands during the middle Holocene may be linked with the short drier phase documented between 5,600 and 3,000 b.p. The appearance of the Savanna PN Complex in the highlands of Kenya and Tanzania apparently did not occur until the modern climatic regime was attained. The late arrival of the first pastoralists to the highlands may have been related to the short arid period between 5,600 and 3,000 b.p. Otherwise it is difficult to see why the pastoralists remained in the Turkana region for close to 2,000 years, from 5,000 to 3,300 b.p., before using the abundant resources of the highland savanna grasslands.

Correlations of Linguistic Groups and Archaeological Cultures

The East African stage has been set, with its lakes, mountains, forests, savannas, and desert as the props, seasonal rhythms providing ambience, archaeological cultures serving as the actors, with lines provided by lin-

guists, and the timing of acts and intermissions determined by the vaga-
ries of climatic change, population pressure thresholds, and migrations.
At present it is a story whose plot is unknown. Pages are still missing from
the script and some of the actors may have the wrong lines. An attempt is
made here to review some previously held ideas about roles played by
selected cultures, but some actors are cast in new parts, new roles are
introduced, and the timing of some acts is changed. The first and last
well-documented movements are by far the easiest to correlate; it is within
the middle ranges of the succession where there is the greatest probability
of error, although by following the rigorous procedures described above
such mistakes should become obvious.

Khoisan speakers have often been correlated with the early Later
Stone Age "Wilton" industries in East Africa (Murdock 1959). The evidence of the human skeletal populations does not at present contradict
this view (Cole 1963:218). The "Wilton" Industry may have persisted
until recent times in northern and central Tanzania where the Khoisan-
speaking Hadza hunter-gatherers and Sandawe farmers and hunters are
still found.

In the Victoria Basin, Kansyore Ware was introduced at an early
date. This ware has parallels with the ceramics of the Early Khartoum
Tradition, but other aspects of the material culture, particularly bone
harpoons, are lacking. The lithic industry does not show drastic change
when ceramics are introduced; thus it is possible that the appearance of
ceramics is not accompanied by population replacement but represents
diffusion of techniques and ideas from a Sudanic source area and adoption by Khoisan speakers.

In the Turkana Basin the early Holocene fishing adaptation may
have appeared fully formed, containing bone harpoons and Wavy Line
pottery. Since the relationships, if any, to local antecedent industries are as
yet unknown it is possible that there are genetic connections with the
Khartoum Mesolithic Industry. Sutton (1974) has argued, on the basis of
the modern distribution of speakers of the Nilo-Saharan languages (including Nilotic), that they can be correlated with this archaeological
entity. The linguistic evidence for the position of early Eastern Sudanic
speakers places them in the Ethiopia-Sudan border region, near Lake
Turkana, between 4,000 and 6,000 b.p. (Ehret 1974*b*:48). Thus, although the archaeological and linguistic dates do not quite agree, it is
possible that Sutton's (1974) interpretation may be correct for the
Turkana Basin. If so, Eastern Sudanic speakers would have been in East
Africa as early as 8,000 b.p. Since linguistic evidence in support of this

conclusion is very slim, however, and the relationships between the harpoon makers and their local predecessors are unknown, I would not
wholeheartedly support this correlation.

On the basis of an unconfirmed association of pottery and bone
harpoons with the Eburran Industry (Kenya Capsian), however, Sutton
has extended the range of this early "Chari-Nile" substrate and fishing
adaptation into the central Rift Valley of Kenya. Sutton supports his
conclusions using modern distribution of Eastern and Southern Nilotic
speakers. The arrival of Nilotic speakers in highland East Africa, however, is demonstrably later (Ehret 1971, 1974*b*, Vossen 1977).

The poorly understood Eburran Industry has misled other people
on the basis of a spurious, misinterpreted association of "Mediterranean
Caucasoid" skeletons (Leakey 1931; Protsch 1975, 1978), which are more
likely to be of Highland Savanna PN origin. This association has led some
people to postulate an early center of Cushitic speech in central Kenya
(Fleming 1964, 1969, 1976:265; Murdock 1959:197). Since there are no
skeletons that can actually be attributed to pre-Neolithic industries, it is
more likely that the makers of this industry originated from a local
population with great antiquity. Given the evidence for the formerly
widespread distribution of Khoisan languages throughout East Africa, it
is more likely to have been spoken by Eburran hunter-gatherers and
other pre-Neolithic East African populations than an Afroasiatic
language.

Correlation of the Savanna PN "Stone Bowl Culture" with Southern
Cushitic groups has been the orthodox interpretation for many years
(Sutton 1966, 1971, 1973; Odner 1972; Phillipson 1977*a*). Southern
Cushitic speakers are theorized to have been the earliest food producers
in East Africa, possessing cattle, sheep, and goats and probably cultivating
grain. They would correlate with the Lowland Savanna PN, the first
pastoralists, who made stone bowls and Nderit Ware in the Turkana
region between 5,000 to 3,300 b.p. and later, at 3,300 b.p., spread to the
highlands of Kenya and northern Tanzania.

This interpretation is not controverted by the skeletal evidence
amassed by Rightmire (1975), which shows that many of the Neolithic
peoples of the Rift Valley have their closest affinities with Egyptian
populations. The skeletal evidence, however, also demonstrates the
presence of peoples whose closest affinities were with modern Negroid
populations and who were not "Mediterranean Caucasoids," as Leakey
proposed (1935). Thus two groups of people, of different racial and
geographic origins, were present in the Rift Valley. As noted above,

ethnic boundaries may persist despite the exchange of goods and individuals across such boundaries. Linguistic evidence indicates that the history of Nilo-Saharan/Afroasiatic contacts has considerable antiquity in the Sudan/Ethiopia region as well as in the Kenya/Uganda region. Thus it is highly unlikely that there would have been a one-to-one correlation among language, race, and material culture in East Africa. Intergroup membership exchange resulting in genetic mixture between these contemporary populations has probably obscured the original magnitude of racial differences and makes it unlikely that one skeletal type will always be associated with one culture even if two races may have been present.

Archaeological evidence, in the form of the Elmenteitan Culture which was contemporary with the Highland Savanna PN Complex for 1,200 years, supports the conclusion that Neolithic groups in the Rift Valley had different origins. Until the Elmenteitan Culture was reaffirmed as a discrete coherent cultural entity, there was a degree of incongruence in the correlation of language groups and cultures. Phillipson (1977b:242) recognized some discordance between the archaeological record and the sequence of population movements: "Virtually no archaeological remains have been located which may be reasonably attributed to the early phases of Southern Nilotic settlement in the Western Highlands; and such are urgently needed to support or modify the complex patterns of developments and migrations which have been proposed from linguistic sources by Christopher Ehret." It is proposed here that the Elmenteitan Culture represents the remains of the earliest Southern Nilotes in the western highlands and the western edge of the central Rift Valley. Most workers have tended to correlate the Southern Nilotes with the Iron Age Lanet Ware makers (Sutton 1973; Phillipson 1977b:241). But Lanet Ware dates to around 1,200 b.p. (Bower et al. 1977:133), far later than the linguistic evidence allows. Moreover, only some Kalenjin groups—those that were in close contact with Maasai and other Eastern Nilotic groups—use this type of pottery (Sutton 1973:152). Since this ware is distributed far beyond the range of present and prehistoric Southern Nilotic groups but closely corresponds with that of Eastern Nilotic speakers, the correlation seems rather weak. Once again there is strong support for the Elmenteitan linkage from the skeletal evidence. The practice of extraction of the central incisors, a widespread Nilotic trait, is found among tribes as far apart as the Barabaig of northern Tanzania and the Anywak and related groups of the southern Sudan (Murdock 1959:173; Klima 1970:8). This practice is well represented among many of the skulls found on the western side of the Rift Valley of

Kenya, particularly at Njoro River Cave and the Makalia burial site (Leakey 1935; Leakey and Leakey 1950), attributable to Elmenteitan and thus to the early Southern Nilotes.

Before returning to the Turkana Basin, I bring the more complete and well-documented succession of the highland areas of Kenya and Tanzania up to recent times.

The next group to enter the highland areas of Kenya and Tanzania is represented by the Iron Age tradition, characterized by Lanet Ware and later by Sirikwa Holes. The correlation, usually made with the Southern Nilotes (Phillipson 1977*b*:241; Sutton 1973), is based mainly upon Maasai and Kalenjin oral tradition which has a shallow time depth and provides no accurate indication of the duration of their tenure in East Africa. It has been demonstrated above that the second food-producing culture to enter the highlands, the Elmenteitan Culture, is in the correct geographic location and the right time for this correlation. The Lanet Culture dates to earlier than 1,180 b.p. (Bower et al. 1977:133), which is the approximate date given for the presence of the Ongamo-Maa cluster of Eastern Nilotic in the highland areas. This ceramic tradition is associated at present mainly with Eastern rather than Southern Nilotic speakers. The earliest Maa speakers, the Ongamo agriculturalists who lived near Mount Kilimanjaro in Tanzania, represented the first wave of Eastern Nilotes in the highlands. They may have absorbed the Southern Cushites and made the smaller and more extensive settlements seen in the Rift Valley. They would also have displaced and absorbed Southern Nilotic groups on the west side of the Rift Valley, pushing them back to their present distribution in the western highlands.

The evidence of oral history is not clear regarding the identity of the Sirikwa. Blackburn (1974) recorded from one reliable Okiek informant that the Sirikwa, the makers of these sites and pottery, were Maasai. Sutton, however, has associated these features with the antecedents of Southern Nilotes, although the oral traditions on which he bases his conclusions give equal weight to a Maasai origin (Sutton 1973:26–32). The evidence outlined above for the geographic, temporal, and ethnic affiliation of Lanet Ware, in addition to the early age of about 1,250 b.p. postulated for the presence of Eastern Nilotes on linguistic grounds (Vossen 1978; Ehret 1974*b*), and dates of 1,150–1,250 b.p. for the archaeology argue for correlation of the Lanet Culture with Eastern Nilotes. If this correlation does not hold, then the early passage of Maa speakers south to Tanzania, and their long tenure in the region between the Nyandarua Mountains of Kenya and Mount Kilimanjaro in Tanzania, have left no recognizable traces in the archaeological record.

Returning to the lowlands of northern Kenya, the whole region east of Lake Turkana is presently inhabited by Eastern Cushites. Their presence in the Turkana Basin is estimated on linguistic grounds to date to between 3,000 and 2,000 b.p. (Heine et al. 1979). The archaeoastronomic site on the western shore of Lake Turkana, which dates to 2,300 b.p., is designed according to the principles of the Konso, an Eastern Cushitic group in southwest Ethiopia (Lynch and Robbins 1978). This correlation is so obvious that the point does not require elaboration. Habitation sites that are closely contemporary with the monuments are those that contain the thin-walled grooved pottery of the Turkwel Tradition with a microlithic industry dated to earlier than 2,080 b.p. (Hivernel 1975, 1978). Recently it has been argued by Lynch and Robbins (1979) that the Turkwel Tradition represents Eastern or Southern Nilotic settlement of the northern East African lowlands. They discount the earlier dates from these sites (1,800 b.p.) and are unaware of the dated evidence at Lake Baringo. Moreover, another weak point in their proposed reconstruction is the absence of Eastern Cushitic habitation sites and the pronounced discordance between the early dates for the habitation sites and the late linguistic dating and geographic distribution of Eastern and Southern Nilotic occupation in the lowlands of East Africa.

The last linguistic group that remains in East Africa is Bantu. They have consistently been associated with the Iron Age Urewe, Lelesu, Kwale, and Maore wares, which date to between approximately 2,250 and 600 b.p. and are found in areas that are almost all presently inhabited by Bantu speakers (Phillipson 1977*b*:212–225). Schmidt (1975) has demonstrated that the tenure of the Haya in their present location in western Tanzania can be traced to 2,400 b.p. through excavations at sites that play a mnemonic role in their myths and oral history.

In the Lake Victoria region, unlike the northeast Uganda region, the archaeological evidence for prior occupation by food producers is very weak, as it is for eastern Kenya and northeastern Tanzania. Since the appearance of the Early Iron Age is abrupt and obviously intrusive, and since it appears possible to trace the evolution of this culture to recent times and to modern Bantu groups, its correlation with the Bantu intrusion seems inevitable.

The Later Iron Age Engaruka Complex has intimate links with modern Sonjo irrigation agriculturalists (Sassoon 1966; Sutton 1978). Unfortunately, Sutton (1978:68) has attributed this complex to Southern Cushitic farmers and Phillipson (1977*b*:245), to Southern Nilotic speakers. Both authors reason that since the Sonjo have no recollection of living at these sites, or in the vicinity, they could not have been responsible for them. The weak point in this argument is that no Southern Cushitic or Southern Nilotic group has any recollection of living there either. Thus, like Maa speakers, the Sonjo have been denied a pre- and protohistoric existence merely because of the vagueness and shallow depth of oral tradition and their historical amnesia.

The correlations between archaeological cultures and linguistic groups outlined above may be summarized as follows (see also table 7). Khoisan would equate with earlier Later Stone Age hunting groups represented by the makers of the Eburran Industry in the Rift Valley and the "Wilton" Industry and Kansyore Ware in lowland Tanzania. The earliest Eastern Sudanic speakers may, as Sutton has argued (1974), correlate with the harpoon fishermen in the Turkana Basin. However, the absence of information about the relationships between the harpoon sites and any antecedent industries in the Turkana region, together with the absence of solid linguistic data, makes correlations here rather tenuous. The Southern Cushites probably correlate with the Lowland Savanna PN in the Turkana Basin and the Highland Savanna PN Culture in the highlands of Kenya and Tanzania. Southern Nilotes probably correspond to the Elmenteitan Culture and later, after the introduction of iron, with the industry represented at Deloraine Farm. The Eastern Cushites almost certainly correlate with the Namoratunga archaeoastronomic site and burials, and they may correlate with the makers of the Turkwel Tradition in the northern lowlands. (See David chap. 6, above, who favors the correlation of the latter tradition with early Eastern Nilotes.) The Maa-Ongamo may correspond to the Lanet Culture throughout the East African highlands. Finally, Bantu speakers can be linked with the early Iron Age Urewe, Lelesu, Kwale, and Maore wares and with the Engaruka Complex, which are distributed around the fringes of the highlands of East Africa.

Concluding Remarks

The mass of archaeological, climatological, and linguistic data outlined above has been tentatively integrated into a coherent scenario of prehistoric population movements which is congruent with the modern and prehistoric distribution of language families as well as the archaeological data. Many of the archaeological data on which this conclusion is based are new or unpublished and have not previously been integrated on this scale or in the form presented above. Incorporation of this information into the extant data base using a rigorous methodology with explicit assumptions sheds new light on the later pre- and protohistory of East Africa, raising questions about some previously held assumptions and rendering untenable some uncritically accepted correlations such as Lanet:Southern Nilotic (Kalenjin), Elmenteitan:Southern Cushitic, and Turkwel:Eastern or Southern Nilotic. If the correlations proposed above can stand the test of future research, then the radiometrically dated archaeological succession may become a valuable asset to historical linguists by calibrating the age estimates of the relative dates for the movements and contacts of prehistoric peoples. Conversely, the linguistic data can provide valuable information about the age and origin of artifacts, domestic food sources, and cultural practices which may be represented in or affect the interpretation of economy, settlement patterns, and adaptations of prehistoric cultures. Determination of the antiquity of modern rituals and customs through linguistic research may, in addition, provide the elusive social dimension for the pottery, stones, and bones found in prehistoric middens.

Archaeologists today draw heavily upon the ethnographic record for analogies that may be used as interpretive aids (e.g., Gifford 1978). For example, among the Maasai, Samburu, and Dasanech the timing of slaughter of domestic stock, the distribution of different parts of animals to different age and sex groups, and the places at which these specified cuts of the animal are eaten are subject to strong ritual and cultural controls (Spencer 1973:128–131). Many parts of the slaughtered animals cannot be eaten on the habitation site. Since each of the ceremonial occasions and cuts of meat is named, the antiquity of these kinds of practices may be determined by historical linguistic methods. Warrior age-grade meat feasting, an Eastern Cushitic and Eastern Nilotic practice, induces a strong bias into the faunal assemblage on Maasai, Samburu, and Dasanech settlements. Meat eaten by warriors cannot be seen by women and thus must be eaten away from the homestead. As often as not such feasting takes place in a rock shelter, creating a different kind of faunal assemblage than that found on open sites (Gramly 1975*b*). One can predict that on pastoral sites that predate the introduction of these practices a rather different distribution of midden debris would be found. Ethnographic analogies about this aspect of site formation drawn from Maasai and Samburu sites would thus prove misleading when one is interpreting older Savanna PN bone assemblages. Historical linguistic research has already demonstrated the antiquity of many cultural practices that have been, or have the potential to be, detected in the archaeological record. Among them are the presence of domestic plants and animals and, with some ingenuity, the practice of milking cattle (Gramly 1972). Other culturally determined behaviors that may affect the archaeological record are fish taboos and the practice of manuring fields. For these kinds of cultural practices, and surely many others, historical linguistic evidence offers invaluable interpretive tools.

The ultimate goals of archaeological research are no longer only the construction of continuous cultural and developmental successions. Archaeology is not simply a means of extending the reach of history further into the past; it involves the reconstruction of past ways of life—economic, settlement, and land-use systems. Historical problems should not, however, be abandoned by archaeologists. Knowledge of the historical, cultural-stratigraphic context of an archaeological site is a basic prerequisite for regional analysis of human behavior and reconstruction of past life-styles. Collaboration with linguists as well as ethnographers in these pursuits would be mutually rewarding, providing indications of which groups would prove most relevant for drawing analogies, leading to an intimate understanding of prehistoric life.

I would like to close with a plea to linguists to intensify their search of ethnographic documents for cultural practices, such as the division of meat mentioned above, which can be traced back in time by linguistic methods. Such practices can be extremely useful for archaeological interpretations and can, if the predicted features, objects, and behaviors are found, provide empirical evidence to support historical linguistic methods.

Acknowledgments

I am grateful to my wife Nicki for introducing me to the historical linguistic evidence which made this paper possible and for advice and editorial assistance. I also extend my thanks to Charles Nelson, J. Desmond Clark, and Robert Soper for critical advice, comments, and corrections on an earlier draft of this paper.

TABLE 10

Radiometric Dates for Archaeological Sites in East Africa

Abbreviations: LSA = Later Stone Age; MSA = Middle Stone Age; SPN = Savanna Pastoral Neolithic; PN = Pastoral Neolithic; IA = Iron Age; PIA = Pastoral Iron Age; UP = Unnamed Pottery Tradition; KSW = Kisii Soft Ware; BNP = Botton Necked Pottery Numbers at left refer to figure 8.

a. Dates for the pre-Neolithic sites of northern Kenya. Linguistic affinities uncertain.

7	LOTHAGAM	5610 ± 1000 UCLA1247E	LSA POTTERY/HARPOONS (Robbins 1972)
7	LOTHAGAM	6300 ± 800 UCLA2124A	LSA POTTERY/HARPOONS (Robbins 1972)
8	LOWASERA	2520 ± 150 GX4345-A	LSA POTTERY/HARPOONS (Phillipson 1977c)
8	LOWASERA	3070 ± 135 GX4347-A	LSA POTTERY/HARPOONS (Phillipson 1977c)
8	LOWASERA	3920 ± 120 GX4348-A	LSA POTTERY/HARPOONS (Phillipson 1977c)
8	LOWASERA	4410 ± 110 GX4349-A	LSA POTTERY/HARPOONS (Phillipson 1977c)
8	LOWASERA	7435 ± 150 GX4346-A	LSA POTTERY/HARPOONS (Phillipson 1977c)
8	LOWASERA	9420 ± 200 HEL867	LSA POTTERY/HARPOONS (Phillipson 1977c)
6	ZU-10 TURKANA	6200 ± 125 N-812	LSA POTTERY/HARPOONS (Robbins 1972)
5	ZU-4 TURKANA	8420 ± 165 N-1100	LSA POTTERY/HARPOONS (Robbins 1972)
5	ZU-6 TURKANA	7960 ± 140 N-813	LSA POTTERY/HARPOONS (Robbins 1972)

b. Dates for "Wilton" sites in the Lake Victoria Basin and northern Tanzania. Assumed to represent Khoisan speakers.

69	APIS ROCK SERENGETI	8100 ± 120 ISGS427-G	LSA (Mehlman 1977)
69	APIS ROCK SERENGETI	7100 ± 75 ISGS427	LSA (Mehlman 1977)
69	APIS ROCK SERENGETI	5400 ± 150	LSA KANSYORE (Mehlman, pers. comm.)
69	APIS ROCK SERENGETI	4720 ± 150	LSA KANSYORE (Mehlman, pers. comm.)
73	ABINDU, KISIMU	1980 ± 240 GX1099	LSA UP (Gabel 1969)

TABLE 10—*Continued*

74 AGORO, KISUMU	2375 ± 320 GX1097	LSA UP (Gabel 1969)
75 JAWUOYO, KISUMU	2040 ± 110 GX1096	LSA UP (Gabel 1969)
76 NYAIDA, KISUMU	2230 ± 320 GX1098	LSA UP (Gabel 1969)
77 RANDHORE, KISIMU	1310 ± 95 GX1152	LSA UP (Gabel 1969)
78 RANGONG, KISUMU	2315 ± 185 GX1100	LSA KANSYORE? (Gabel 1969)
79 NYANG'OMA, MWANZA	2640 ± 120 N-493	LSA KANSYORE (Soper & Golden 1969)
80 MAGOSI II	6080 ± 130 SR-64	LSA (Posnansky & Nelson 1968:57)
87 LULULAMPEMBELE	3830 ± 180 N-787	LSA (Odner 1971*a*)
88 MUMBA-HOHLE	4890 ± 70 FRA-1-C	LSA KANSYORE (Mehlman, pers. comm.)
88 MUMBA-HOHLE	4860 ± 100 UCLA1913	LSA KANSYORE (Mehlman, pers. comm.)
89 KANDAGA RS	3375 ± 180 GX3677	LSA (Masao 1979:37)
90 KWA MWANGO-ISANZU	3270 ± 110 GX3679	LSA (Masao 1979:69)
91 KIRUMI ISUMBIRIRA	3665 ± 140 GX3681	LSA (Masao 1979:80)

c. Dates for the Lowland and Highland Savanna Pastoral Neolithic. Assumed to represent Southern Cushitic speakers.

1 GAJI4 ILERET	3405 ± 130 GX4642-IA	SPN NDERIT (Barthelme, forthcoming)
1 GAJI4 ILERET	4580 ± 170 GX4642IIA	SPN NDERIT (Barthelme, forthcoming)
2 FWJJ5 ILERET	4000 ± 140 GX4643-A	SPN UP (Barthelme, forthcoming)
10 BB-14 KANGATOTHA	5020 ± 220 N-814	SPN NDERIT? (Robbins 1972)
12 NORTH HORR I	4405 ± 130 GX3705	SPN NAROSURA? (Maggs 1977:184)
12 NORTH HORR I	3330 ± 130 GX3706	SPN NAROSURA? (Maggs 1977:184)
29 PROSPECT FARM	2690 ± 80 UCLA1234	SPN UP (Cohen 1970)
29 PROSPECT FARM	2910 ± 110 N-651	SPN UP (Cohen 1970)
30 GSJI2 NDERIT DRIFT	1370 ± 140 GX4320	SPN UP (Bower et al. 1977)
30 GSJI2 NDERIT DRIFT	1925 ± 160 GX4318I-C	SPN UP (Bower et al. 1977)
32 GSJI23 NDERIT DRIFT	2360 ± 155 GX4503-A	SPN NDERIT (Bower et al. 1977)
33 GRJI22 L. ELMENTEITA	1830 ± 130 GX4216	SPN UP (Nelson, pers. comm.)
34 GRJJ5 COLE'S BURIAL	2355 ± 150 GX4714-A	SPN? (Nelson, pers. comm.)

No.	Site	Date	Lab No.	Source
35	GSJJ44 GIL GIL	2200 ± 130	GX4323-C	SPN UP (Bower et al. 1977)
35	GSJJ44 GIL GIL	2040 ± 155	GX4323-A	SPN UP (Bower et al. 1977)
36	GTJI3 NDIBIBI	1665 ± 145	GX4463-A	SPN NAROSURA (Bower et al. 1977)
36	GTJI3 NDIBIBI	1815 ± 120	GX4465-A	SPN NAROSURA (Bower et al. 1977)
36	GTJI3 NDIBIBI	1415 ± 150	GX4464-G	SPN NAROSURA (Bower et al. 1977)
36	GTJI3 NDIBIBI	2225 ± 155	GX4465-G	SPN NAROSURA (Bower et al. 1977)
36	GTJI3 NDIBIBI	1255 ± 125	GX4463-G	SPN NAROSURA (Bower et al. 1977)
36	GTJI3 NDIBIBI	410 ± 110	GX4464-A	SPN NAROSURA (Bower et al. 1977)
37	GUJJ2 AKIRA	1965 ± 140	GX4386-G	SPN AKIRA (Bower et al. 1977)
37	GUJJ2 AKIRA	1255 ± 140	GX4384	SPN AKIRA (Bower et al. 1977)
37	GUJJ2 AKIRA	1775 ± 115	GX4385-G	SPN AKIRA (Bower et al. 1977)
37	GUJJ2 AKIRA	1440 ± 120	GX4386-A	SPN AKIRA (Bower et al. 1977)
37	GUJJ2 AKIRA	1090 ± 150	GX4383-A	SPN AKIRA (Bower et al. 1977)
38	GUJJ13 SALASUN	1315 ± 135	GX4421-G	SPN NAROSURA (Bower et al. 1977)
38	GUJJ13 SALASUN	2990 ± 170	GX4468-A	SPN UP (Bower et al. 1977)
38	GUJJ13 SALASUN	1110 ± 115	GX4468-G	SPN UP (Bower et al. 1977)
38	GUJJ13 SALASUN	2680 ± 150	GX4421-A	SPN NAROSURA (Bower et al. 1977)
39	GQJI6 MARINGISHU	1695 ± 105	GX 4466-A	SPN MARINGISHU (Bower et al. 1977)
40	CRESCENT ISLAND	2660 ± 120	GX4585-A	SPN NAROSURA (Onyango-Abuje 1977b)
40	CRESCENT ISLAND	2405 ± 150	GX4588-A	SPN NAROSURA (Onyango-Abuje 1977b)
40	CRESCENT ISLAND	2660 ± 160	GX4589-G	SPN NAROSURA (Onyango-Abuje 1977b)
40	CRESCENT ISLAND	2535 ± 140	GX4586-G	SPN NAROSURA (Onyango-Abuje 1977b)
40	CRESCENT ISLAND	2795 ± 155	GX4587-G	SPN NAROSURA (Onyango-Abuje 1977b)
41	GRJI25 HYRAX HILL	1295 ± 105	GX4582-A	SPN CAIRN (Onyango-Abuje 1977a)
41	GRJI25 HYRAX HILL	1955 ± 125	GX4582-G	SPN CAIRN (Onyango-Abuje 1977a)
42	GRJI1 PROLONGED DRIFT	2315 ± 150	GX5735-A	SPN UP & NAROSURA (Gifford et al., in press)
42	GRJI1 PROLONGED DRIFT	2530 ± 160	GX5735-G	SPN UP & NAROSURA (Gifford et al., in press)
45	TUNNEL ROCK	2050 ± 60	Y-1396	SPN UP (Sutton 1966:54)
45	TUNNEL ROCK	2730 ± 60	Y-1398	SPN UP (Sutton 1966:54)

TABLE 10—Continued

47	KFR-A4 TERRACE RS	530 ± 100 HEL-531	SPN UP? (Siiriäinen 1977)
47	KFR-A4 TERRACE RS	2100 ± 110 HEL-530	SPN UP? (Siiriäinen 1977)
47	KFR-A4 TERRACE RS	1900 ± 90 HEL-533	SPN UP (Siiriäinen 1977)
48	KFR-A5 PORCUPINE CAVE	2320 ± 160 HEL-852	SPN AKIRA? (Siiriäinen 1977)
48	KFR-A5 PORCUPINE CAVE	2830 ± 120 HEL-871	SPN AKIRA? (Siiriäinen 1977)
48	KFR-A5 PORCUPINE CAVE	2490 ± 110 HEL-851	SPN AKIRA? (Siiriäinen 1977)
49	KFR-A12 RIVER RS	980 ± 100 HEL-532	SPN UP (Siiriäinen 1977)
49	KFR-A12 RIVER RS	1100 ± 120 HEL-534	SPN UP (Siiriäinen 1977)
50	KFR-C4 KISIMA FARM	760 ± 90 HEL-853	SPN UP (Siiriäinen 1977)
51	NAROSURA	2640 ± 115 N-703	SPN NAROSURA (Odner 1972)
51	NAROSURA	2660 ± 115 N-701	SPN NAROSURA (Odner 1972)
51	NAROSURA	2360 ± 110 N-700	SPN NAROSURA (Odner 1972)
51	NAROSURA	2760 ± 115 N-702	SPN NAROSURA (Odner 1972)
52	GVJM3 LUKENYA	1804 ± 119 GX3539	SPN NDERIT (Gramly 1975a)
52	GVJM3 LUKENYA	1501 ± 170 N-1827	SPN NDERIT (Gramly 1975a)
53	GVJM14 LUKENYA	1991 ± 133 N-1884	SPN AKIRA (Gramly 1975a)
55	GVJM22 LUKENYA	1490 ± 131 UCLA1709D	SPN AKIRA (Gramly 1975a)
55	GVJM22 LUKENYA	2311 ± 127 UCLA 1709C	SPN NAROSURA (Gramly 1975a)
55	GVJM22 LUKENYA	1307 ± 122 N-1076	SPN AKIRA (Gramly 1975a)
57	GVJM44 LUKENYA	2085 ± 135 GX4160-A	SPN NAROSURA (Bower & Nelson 1979)
57	GVJM44 LUKENYA	1710 ± 135 GX4160-C	SPN NAROSURA (Bower & Nelson 1979)
57	GVJM44 LUKENYA	2030 ± 125 GX4507-A	SPN AKIRA (Bower & Nelson 1979)
57	GVJM44 LUKENYA	2070 ± 155 GX5638-G	SPN AKIRA (Nelson, pers. comm.)
57	GVJM44 LUKENYA	1775 ± 150 GX4507-G	SPN AKIRA (Bower & Nelson 1979)
57	GVJM44 LUKENYA	2415 ± 155 GX5138	SPN NAROSURA (Nelson, pers. comm.)
57	GVJM44 LUKENYA	3290 ± 145 GX5348	SPN NDERIT (Nelson, pers. comm.)
57	GVJM44 LUKENYA	1820 ± 200 GX5638-A	SPN AKIRA (Nelson, pers. comm.)

59	GVJM47 LUKENYA	1340 ± 145 GX4161-A	SPN UP (Bower & Nelson 1979)
59	GVJM47 LUKENYA	970 ± 130 GX4161-C	SPN UP (Bower & Nelson 1979)
60	GVJM48 LUKENYA	1810 ± 135 GX5347-G	SPN NAROSURA (Nelson, pers. comm.)
60	GVJM48 LUKENYA	1600 ± 130 GX5347-A	SPN NAROSURA (Nelson, pers. comm.)
61	GVJM52 LUKENYA	1855 ± 180 GX5692-A	SPN NAROSURA (Nelson, pers. comm.)
61	GVJM52 LUKENYA	2050 ± 115 GX5692-G	SPN NAROSURA (Nelson, pers. comm.)
63	NGORONGORO BURIAL	2260 ± 180 GX 1243	SPN (Sassoon 1968)
66	HBJD3 SERENGETI	3000 ± 140 GX5640	SPN UP (Bower, pers. comm.)
67	SE-3 SERONERA	2020 ± 115 N-1067	SPN NDERIT (Bower 1973a)
69	APIS ROCK SERENGETI	2060 ± 100 ISGS438	SPN AKIRA (King & Bada 1979)
69	APIS ROCK SERENGETI	2180 ± 200 ISGS438	SPN AKIRA (King & Bada 1979)

d. Dates for the Turkwel Tradition of northern lowland East Africa. Assumed to represent Eastern Cushitic speakers.

3	LOPOY	1080 ± 80 UCLA2124G	PN TURKWEL (Lynch & Robbins 1979:325)
3	LOPOY	950 ± 80 UCLA2124J	PN TURKWEL (Lynch & Robbins 1979:235)
3	LOPOY	1100 ± 80 UCLA2124H	PN TURKWEL (Lynch & Robbins 1979:325)
3	LOPOY	1375 ± 125 GX5041	PN TURKWEL (Lynch & Robbins 1979:325)
4	APAGET I	1800 ± 300 UCLA 2124K	PN TURKWEL (Lynch & Robbins 1979:325)
9	NAMORATUNGA	2285 ± 165 GX5042-A	PN ?TURKWEL (Lynch & Robbins 1979)
11	TURKWEL SCHEME	1500 ± 100 N 909	PN TURKWEL (Robbins 1972)
12	NORTH HORR II	1525 ± 155 GX3707	PN TURKWEL? (Maggs 1977:184)
12	NORTH HORR II	748 ± 140 GX3708	PN TURKWEL? (Maggs 1977:184)
13	NGENYN BARINGO	2080 ± 130 UCLA1322-C	PN TURKWEL (Hivernel 1978)

e. Dates for the Eburran (Kenya Capsian) Industry in the central Rift Valley of Kenya. Phases 1–4 possibly representing Khoisan speakers.

17	GSJJ25 MASAI GORGE RS	2595 ± 135 GX5346	EBURRAN 5 (Nelson, pers. comm.)
17	GSJJ25 MASAI GORGE RS	2865 ± 150 GX4462-A	EBURRAN 5a UP (Ambrose 1977)
20	KERINGET CAVES	2910 ± 115 N-635	EBURRAN 5a? UP (Cohen 1970)

TABLE 10—Continued

26 GSJI1 GAMBLE'S CAVE	8095 ± 190 GX0290	EBURRAN 3 (Ambrose et al. 1980)	
26 GSJI1 GAMBLE'S CAVE	8245 ± 175 GX0289	EBURRAN 3 (Ambrose et al. 1980)	
26 GSJI1 GAMBLE'S CAVE	8540 ± 180 GX0283	EBURRAN 3 (Ambrose et al 1980)	
26 GSJI1 GAMBLE'S CAVE	7555 ± 190 GX0499	EBURRAN 3 (Ambrose et al. 1980)	
27 GTJK21 NAIVASHA RWY	2000 ± 135 GX4583-G	EBURRAN 5a Narosura & UP (Onyango-Abuje 1977a)	
28 GTJJ3 CAUSEWAY	895 ± 105 GX4319-C	EBURRAN 5b (Bower & Nelson 1979)	
28 GTJJ3 CAUSEWAY	2380 ± 140 GX5639-A	EBURRAN 5b (Bower & Nelson 1979)	
28 GTJJ3 CAUSEWAY	2045 ± 125 GX4319-A	EBURRAN 5b (Bower & Nelson 1979)	
29 PROSPECT FARM	10560 ± 1650 GX0244	EBURRAN 2/3 (Anthony 1973)	
30 GSJI2 NDERIT DRIFT	7105 ± 180 GX4315	EBURRAN (Bower et al. 1977)	
30 GSJI2 NDERIT DRIFT	7005 ± 175 GX4317	EBURRAN (Bower et al. 1977)	
30 GSJI2 NDERIT DRIFT	10685 ± 270 GX4214	EBURRAN 2 (Bower et al. 1977)	
30 GSJI2 NDERIT DRIFT	9425 ± 160 GX4313-A	EBURRAN 2 (Bower & Nelson 1979)	
30 GSJI2 NDERIT DRIFT	9135 ± 235 GX4417	EBURRAN (Nelson, pers. comm.)	
30 GSJI2 NDERIT DRIFT	12065 ± 365 GX4215	EBURRAN 2 (Bower et al. 1977)	
30 GSJI2 NDERIT DRIFT	10280 ± 270 GX5136	EBURRAN 1 (Nelson, pers. comm.)	
31 GSJI29 NDERIT DRIFT	7415 ± 200 GX4505-A	EBURRAN (Bower & Nelson 1979)	

f. Dates for the Elmenteitan Neolithic and descendant Iron Age variants in the western highlands of Kenya. Assumed to represent Southern Nilotic speakers.

15 GRJI60 LION HILL	1850 ± 130 GX4715	ELMENTEITAN (Bower & Nelson 1979)	
16 GSJH1 REMNANT	1355 ± 145 GX4634	ELMENTEITAN (Bower et al. 1977)	
16 GSJH1 REMNANT	2315 ± 150 GX4324	ELMENTEITAN (Bower et al. 1977)	
17 GSJJ25 MASAI GORGE RS	1545 ± 135 GX4312	ELMENTEITAN (Ambrose 1977)	
17 GSJJ25 MASAI GORGE RS	2515 ± 140 GX4471-A	ELMENTEITAN (Nelson, pers. comm.)	

No.	Site	Date	Lab no.	Category (Reference)
17	GSJJ25 MASAI GORGE RS	1560 ± 135	GX4311-C	ELMENTEITAN (Ambrose 1977)
17	GSJJ25 MASAI GORGE RS	2495 ± 150	GX4345-A	ELMENTEITAN (Ambrose 1977)
17	GSJJ25 MASAI GORGE RS	2325 ± 145	GX5344	ELMENTEITAN (Nelson, pers. comm.)
18	GUJH4 ROTIAN	2155 ± 140	GX5135-G	ELMENTEITAN (Ambrose 1980)
18	GUJH4 ROTIAN	1965 ± 150	GX5135-A	ELMENTEITAN (Ambrose 1980)
19	NJORÒ RIVER CAVE	2920 ± 80	Y 91	ELMENTEITAN (Cole 1963)
20	KERINGET CAVES	2430 ± 110	N-654	ELMENTEITAN (Cohen 1970)
20	KERINGET CAVES	2055 ± 110	N-655	ELMENTEITAN (Cohen 1970)
21	KISII GSJD6	2090 ± 170	N-1234	IA "KSW" (Bower 1973b:140)
22	KISII GSJD21	1290 ± 75	N-1235	IA "KSW" (Bower 1973b:140)
24	KISII GTJC9	1750 ± 90	N-1237	LSA POTTERY (Bower 1973b:140)
25	DELORAINE FARM	1070 ± 110	N-652	IA UP (Cohen 1972)
25	DELORAINE FARM	1150 ± 135	GX5542-A	IA UP (Chittick & Ambrose, in prep.)
25	DELORAINE FARM	985 ± 130	GX5542-G	IA UP (Chittick & Ambrose, in prep.)
25	DELORAINE FARM	1110 ± 120	GX5541-G	IA UP (Chittick & Ambrose, in prep.)
25	DELORAINE FARM	1000 ± 115	GX5541-A	IA UP (Chittick & Ambrose, in prep.)
25	DELORAINE FARM	1300 ± 140	GX5543	IA UP (Chittick & Ambrose, in prep.)

g. Dates for the "Pastoral Iron Age" Lanet Tradition of the East African highlands. Assumed to represent Eastern Nilotic speakers.

No.	Site	Date	Lab no.	Category (Reference)
17	GSJJ25 MASAI GORGE RS	1025 ± 130	GX4310	PIA OKIEK (Ambrose 1977)
17	GSJJ25 MASAI GORGE RS	405 ± 120	GX4309	PIA OKIEK (Ambrose 1977)
32	GSJI23 NDERIT DRIFT	260 ± 120	GX4504	PIA LANET (Bower et al. 1977)
32	GSJI23 NDERIT DRIFT	260 ± 105	GX4502-A	PIA LANET (Bower et al. 1977)
37	GUJJ2 AKIRA	485 ± 135	GX4382-G	PIA LANET (Bower et al. 1977)
37	GUJJ2 AKIRA	445 ± 120	GX4381	PIA LANET (Bower et al. 1977)
38	GUJJ13 SALASUN	1185 ± 140	GX4420-A	PIA LANET (Bower et al. 1977)
44	LANET	365 ± 100	Y-570	PIA LANET (Posnansky 1967b)
46	MURINGA	300 ± 80	Y-1395	PIA LANET (Sutton 1973)

TABLE 10—*Continued*

46 MURINGA	300 ± 60 Y-1396	PIA LANET (Sutton 1973)
56 GVJM41E LUKENYA	1250 ± 115 GX4506-G	PIA CAIRN (Bower & Nelson 1979)
56 GVJM41E LUKENYA	1240 ± 145 GX4506-A	PIA CAIRN (Bower & Nelson 1979)
64 HPKD12 SERENGETI	260 ± 100 GX5687	PIA? (Bower, pers. comm.)
64 HPKD12 SERENGETI	755 ± 135 GX5690	PIA? (Bower, pers. comm.)
64 HPKD12 SERENGETI	225 ± 105 GX5688	PIA? (Bower, pers. comm.)
64 HPKD12 SERENGETI	205 ± 120 GX5689	PIA? (Bower, pers. comm.)
67 SE-3 SERONERA	265 ± 100 N-1068	PIA LANET (Bower 1973*a*)
68 SE-4 SERENGETI	250 ± 100 N-1158	PIA LANET (Bower 1973*a*)

h. Dates for sites of the Iron Age of the Lake Victoria Basin, lowland northern Tanzania, eastern Tanzania, and eastern Kenya. Assumed to represent Bantu speakers.

23 KISII GTJC7	267 ± 80 N-1236	IA "BNP" (Bower 1973*b*:140)
80 MAGOSI II	700 ± 100 SR-80	IA UREWE? (Posnansky & Nelson 1968:57)
81 CHOBE 14A	1640 ± 125 N-125	IA UREWE (Soper 1971c:81)
82 NSONGEZI	925 ± 150 M-113	IA UREWE (Soper 1969:152)
83 ULORE II	1560 ± 95 GX1186	IA UREWE (Soper 1969:152)
83 ULORE II	1680 ± 110 N-435	IA UREWE (Soper 1969:152)
83 ULORE II	1630 ± 110 N-436	IA UREWE (Soper 1969:152)
84 YALA ALEGO	1550 ± 235 N-437	IA UREWE (Soper 1969:149)
85 RUGAMORA MAHE	2470 ± 110 RL-406	IA UREWE (Schmidt 1975:132)
85 RUGAMORA MAHE	1830 ± 110 N-892	IA UREWE (Schmidt 1975:132)
85 RUGAMORA MAHE	1780 ± 150 N-898	IA UREWE (Schmidt 1975:132)
85 RUGAMORA MAHE	2560 ± 100 RL-405	IA UREWE (Schmidt 1975:132)
85 RUGAMORA MAHE	2500 ± 115 N-895	IA UREWE (Schmidt 1975:132)

Site	Date	Classification
85 RUGAMORA MAHE	2400 ± 115 N-890	IA UREWE (Schmidt 1975:132)
85 RUGAMORA MAHE	1890 ± 115 N-891	IA UREWE (Schmidt 1975:132)
86 MAKONGO	965 ± 100 N-900	IA UREWE (Schmidt 1975:132)
86 MAKONGO	1910 ± 100 N-902	IA UREWE (Schmidt 1975:132)
86 MAKONGO	1040 ± 100 N-901	IA UREWE (Schmidt 1975:132)
93 ENGARUKA	1230 ± 120 GX-0347	IA (Sassoon 1966:90)
93 ENGARUKA	1620 ± 90 GX-0348	IA (Sassoon 1966:90)
93 ENGARUKA	490 ± 90 GX-0247	IA (Sassoon 1966:90)
95 MWANGA IIIA	990 ± 105 N-649	IA GROUP B (Odner 1971c:114)
96 MWIKA IV (4)	1700 ± 330 N-883	IA KWALE/MAORE (Odner 1971b:139)
97 MATUNDA (32)	510 ± 190 N-885	IA GROUP C (Odner 1971b:143)
98 MARANGU T.C.	725 ± 180 N-882	IA (Odner 1971b:145)
99 CHYULU HCJP3	430 ± 75 N-1317	IA (Soper 1976:89)
100 CHYULU HCJP1	435 ± 105 N-1290	IA (Soper 1976:91)
101 CHYULU HCJP2	985 ± 75 N-1317	IA (Soper 1976:98)
102 GATUNG'ANG'A	850 ± 150 HEL-224	IA KWALE (Siiriäinen 1971)
102 GATUNG'ANG'A	810 ± 130 HEL-222	IA KWALE (Siiriäinen 1971)
102 GATUNG'ANG'A	690 ± 100 HEL-225	IA MAORE (Siiriäinen 1971)
102 GATUNG'ANG'A	600 ± 80 HEL-226	IA MAORE (Siiriäinen 1971)
102 GATUNG'ANG'A	820 ± 130 HEL-223	IA KWALE (Siiriäinen 1971)
103 BOMBO KABURI	1060 ± 110 N-348	IA GROUP B (Soper 1967b:28)
103 BOMBO KABURI	1730 ± 115 N-347	IA KWALE (Soper 1967b:24)
104 GONGA MAORE	1080 ± 115 N-257	IA MAORE (Soper 1967b:26)
105 AMBONI CAVE	1590 ± 130 N-349	IA GROUP C (Soper 1967b:31)
107 KWALE	1690 ± 115 N-297	IA KWALE (Soper 1967a:3)
107 KWALE	1680 ± 115 N-291	IA KWALE (Soper 1967a:3)
108 USANGI HOSPITAL	1060 ± 135 N-646	IA KWALE/MAORE (Odner 1971c:107)
108 USANGI HOSPITAL	1470 ± 280 N-648	IA KWALE/MAORE (Odner 1971c:107)

TABLE 10—*Continued*

i. Dates for early Later Stone Age sites in East Africa. Assumed to represent Khoisan speakers.

30	GSJi2 NDERIT DRIFT	13025 ± 375 GX4467	EARLY LSA (Bower et al. 1977)
30	GSJi2 NDERIT DRIFT	12475 ± 320 GX4418	EARLY LSA (Bower et al. 1977)
30	GSJi2 NDERIT DRIFT	13485 ± 365 GX4316	EARLY LSA (Bower et al. 1977)
30	GSJi2 NDERIT DRIFT	13610 ± 395 GX4321	EARLY LSA (Bower et al. 1977)
30	GSJi2 NDERIT DRIFT	12710 ± 310 GX4314	EARLY LSA (Bower et al. 1977)
30	GSJi2 NDERIT DRIFT	12935 ± 310 GX4322	EARLY LSA (Bower et al. 1977)
38	GUJJi3 SALASUN	6595 ± 235 GX4469-A	LSA (Bower et al. 1977)
38	GUJJi3 SALASUN	7255 ± 225 GX4422-A	LSA ?POTTERY? (Bower et al. 1977).
43	GRJi21 KARIANDUSI	15990 ± 365 GX4717-A	EARLY LSA (Nelson, pers. comm.)
54	GVJM16 LUKENYA	16750 ± 200 UCLA1747D	EARLY LSA (Merrick 1975)
54	GVJM16 LUKENYA	13150 ± 200 UCLA1747B	EARLY LSA (Merrick 1975)
55	GVJM22 LUKENYA	17680 ± 800 UCLA1709A	EARLY LSA (Gramly 1976)
55	GVJM22 LUKENYA	9910 ± 300 HEL-535	EARLY LSA (Gramly 1976)
55	GVJM22 LUKENYA	13730 ± 430 GX3698-A	EARLY LSA (Gramly 1976)
55	GVJM22 LUKENYA	17700 ± 760 UCLA1709B	EARLY LSA (Gramly 1976)
55	GVJM22 LUKENYA	15320 ± 450 GX3699-A	EARLY LSA (Gramly 1976)
58	GVJM46 LUKENYA	20780 ± 920 GX5349-A	EARLY LSA (Miller 1979)
58	GVJM46 LUKENYA	19330 ± 1000 GX5350-A	EARLY LSA (Miller 1979)
62	OLDUVAI, NAISIUSIU	17550 ± 1000 UCLA 1695	EARLY LSA (M. D. Leakey et al. 1972)
65	HCJE1 SERENGETI	7310 ± 190 GX5642-A	LSA (Bower, pers. comm.)
65	HCJE1 SERENGETI	6185 ± 165 GX5641-A	LSA (Bower, pers. comm.)
69	APIS ROCK SERENGETI	22600 ± 400 ISGS425	MSA/LSA (King & Bada 1979)
69	APIS ROCK SERENGETI	21600 ± 400 ISGS445	MSA/LSA (King & Bada 1979)
69	APIS ROCK SERENGETI	18000	EARLY LSA (Mehlman 1977)
71	KALOKUROK	6925 ± 190 GX4218-A	LSA (Nelson 1973)

71	KALOKUROK	3415 ± 175 GX4218-C	LSA (Nelson 1973)
72	MUNYAMA CAVE	11145 ± 90 GrN-5707	EARLY LSA (van Noten 1971)
72	MUNYAMA CAVE	9780 ± 160 GrN-5851	EARLY LSA (van Noten 1971)
72	MUNYAMA CAVE	14925 ± 80 GrN-5850	EARLY LSA (van Noten 1971)
72	MUNYAMA CAVE	14180 ± 130 GrN-5708	EARLY LSA (van Noten 1971)
92	KISESE II	10720 ± 132 NPL-36	EARLY LSA (Inskeep 1962)
92	KISESE II	14760 ± 202 NPL-35	EARLY LSA (Inskeep 1962)
92	KISESE II	18190 ± 306 NPL-37	EARLY LSA (Inskeep 1962)

8 | The First Spread of Food Production to Southern Africa

CHRISTOPHER EHRET

ONE OF THE MORE important scholarly achievements of the past decade for African history was the discovery of the presence of Stone Age food-producing peoples at the southern edge of the continent. By the very beginning of the first millennium A.D. sheep were already being raised in considerable numbers all along the southern littoral of the Cape, and before the mid-first millennium cattle were being kept along with the sheep. Sheepherding was also known in central Namibia by the fourth century A.D. To have reached the far south coast of Africa by no later than the turn of the eras, livestock raising must already have penetrated south of the Zambezi at least two or three centuries earlier, that is, by 200 or 300 B.C. or earlier. Hence the linguistic inference made in the 1960s (Ehret 1967, 1968) that stock keeping in southern Africa preceded the arrival of the Bantu was confirmed in the 1970s by archaeology.

There are two hypotheses about the means of spread of Stone Age stock raising as far as the Cape of Good Hope, and two hypotheses as to the route of spread. Some scholars have suggested that sheep raising diffused ahead of the movement of the Khoikhoi, the peoples who were the sixteenth- and seventeenth-century inheritors of the Stone Age pastoral tradition throughout the Cape; the alternate solution is that the Khoikhoi spread itself brought sheep (and later cattle). The choice of initial route of spread is between a southward access through Namibia and the exceedingly dry lands of the lower Orange to the western Cape, and an alternative access via far eastern Botswana and the lands of the Orange-Vaal confluence to the eastern Cape. The linguistic evidence suggests that population movements adequately account for the spread of pastoralism, but that these movements were more complicated than either hypothesis of the direction of spread allows. Two Khoisan-speaking peoples, the Khoikhoi (formerly "Hottentot") and the Kwadi, followed pastoral ways of life at the time of the first written records of each. The Khoikhoi of the Cape and nearby regions raised both cattle and sheep; the Kwadi of far southwestern Angola kept small stock. It is from their languages and those of their nearest relatives that the evidence of a spread of stock raising in Stone Age times can be extracted.

The Khoikhoi Evidence

The first step that must be taken is to work out the internal linguistic relationships of the several Khoikhoi dialects and languages. The assumption of almost every historian of South Africa is that the Khoikhoi communities at the time of contact with Europeans in the seventeenth century all spoke dialects of a common language. But what rather seems to have been the case was that two Khoikhoi languages existed in that century, each with wide internal dialect diversity. One language, which may be called Orange River Khoi, consisted of two primary dialects— Nama, spoken in the regions about the mouth of the Orange River, and !Kora, spoken even then in the confluence zone of the Vaal and Orange rivers. The idea that the !Kora came from the Cape in the seventeenth or eighteenth century—a historian's myth based on a single unsubstantiated claim recorded by a nineteenth-century observer—is contradicted by other evidence (Harinck 1969) and is out of accord with the linguistic indications. The other language, Cape Khoi, spread in a long dialect chain from the area right around the Cape of Good Hope eastward to the !Gona beyond the Fish River. Other Khoikhoi dialects had formerly been spoken as far east as the modern Transkei. The existence of this dialect chain is clearly attested in seventeenth-century references which describe the understanding of local Khoi speech as becoming progressively more difficult for a western Cape Khoi interpreter as one traveled eastward, until by the time the farthest east Khoikhoi were reached the dialect differences were beginning to approach the point of nonintelligibility. The distinction between the two languages, though demonstrable on linguistic grounds, can also be inferred from the early written sources (as perceptively demonstrated by Elphick 1977:21).

Because of the nature of the extant data, the relative closeness of the relationship between the two Khoi languages can now be approximated only through the means of partial core vocabulary counts. Nama and !Kora continued to be spoken in the twentieth century, and each has been recorded and studied in some detail. It is thus possible to collect a full core vocabulary for Nama and an almost complete list for !Kora. Cape Khoi dialects variously died out during the eighteenth and early nineteenth centuries, but fortunately a number of short vocabularies were recorded, usually in poor phonetic transcription, before that happened. The fullest data are for Khoikhoi as it was spoken in and about the Cape Town region at the far west of the dialect chain. Several different writers, particularly in the second half of the seventeenth century and the beginning of the eighteenth, preserved useful materials from that area. Vocabularies for eastern Cape Khoi tend to be more fragmentary and cannot be attributed in the same way to one dialect. So, whereas more than two-thirds of the core vocabulary list can be constructed for Western Cape Khoi, lists safely attributable to a single eastern Cape dialect tend to be still shorter. The Nama, !Kora, and Western Cape lists, along with one particular collection of an eastern Cape vocabulary, chosen as representative of the eastern dialects, are reproduced in table 11.

To overcome the problem of incommensurate lists, three counts were made of cognation, each restricted to the portion of basic vocabulary for which all the dialects included in that count had an attested item. The fewer the items to be counted, the more likely it was that two things might happen. One was that smaller vocabularies would tend to consist of more retentive words from the core list and so percentages of cognation would be distorted upward in shorter lists. Second, random perturbations in retention not balanced out by fuller collections of data might produce inconsistent patterns of cognation. As it happened, the first expectation was borne out; the second was not, and the internal consistency of percentages and therefore the usefulness of the counts were maintained.

Counting the short list of thirty-seven items attested for all four languages/dialects gives the following percentages of apparent cognation,

NAMA

86	!KORA		
68	73	WESTERN CAPE	
72	72	80	EASTERN CAPE

and therefore the tree of relationship shown in the accompanying diagram.

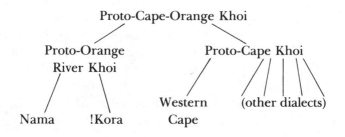

Despite the paucity of data available, this grouping is confirmed by another kind of linguistic evidence. At least two lexical innovations turn up in the core lists, distinguishing not only Cape from Orange River Khoi, but Cape from the wider grouping of Khoisan languages of which Khoi-khoi is a subgroup. One of these is the word for "head"; the other, the word for "belly." The latter root, although not noted in the particular eastern Cape Khoi source used here, can be found in other eastern Cape collections.

The two other cognate-counting exercises were undertaken to establish correction factors to bring the percentages from the short count into line with those obtained from more nearly complete counts. First Nama, !Kora, and Western Cape percentages of cognation were calculated for the seventy-item set of core vocabulary which could be found for all three, with the following result:

NAMA

84	!KORA	
68	69	WESTERN CAPE

The short list counted for the four dialects above and the seventy-item set show approximately, therefore, the same overall rate of change. In cognate counting a linguistic relationship twice as distant as another is represented by a figure that is the square of the figure for the closer affinity. The square of the 84–86 percent internal cognation of Orange River Khoi in the two shorter lists would be 71–74 percent; hence the distance of relationship between the Orange River dialects and Western Cape Khoi, for which the better evidence exists, is in the general range of somewhat more than twice that between Nama and !Kora.

The last of the three counts, of cognation between Nama and !Kora for which ninety-eight of the hundred words could be compared, yielded a figure of 77 percent, whereas the shorter lists, apparently containing high proportions of the core items most resistant to change, gave higher Nama-!Kora cognations of 84 and 86 percent. The percentages obtained for the Cape Khoi dialects on the shorter lists had thus to be considered also inflated and had to be lowered accordingly. Since Cape Khoi dialects appear to have been slightly more than twice as distantly related to Nama and !Kora as those two are to each other, and since twice as distant a relationship as that represented by 77 percent would be .77 squared, or 59 percent, the Cape Khoi percentages of cognation with Orange River Khoi

in the preceding two charts may be considered approximately equivalent
to a percentage range in the 50 percents for the 100-word list. The
Western Cape figure of 80 percent with the eastern Cape dialect, obtained
from the 37-word count, falls somewhat closer to the Orange River depth
of relationship than to that between Orange River and Cape dialects and
so would fit on the high side of midway between 77 percent and the 50
percents, or roughly the high 60 percents. The projected approximate
figures of core vocabulary cognation would have the following overall
appearance:

NAMA

77	!KORA		
50's	50's	WESTERN CAPE	
50's	50's	65−70	EASTERN CAPE

From these data it is possible, using the glottochronological hypothesis, to propose what sorts of time depth of divergence the percentages
represent. However ill formulated and, to some, improbable sounding
glottochronology may be, it responds to a real phenomenon of lexical
change in languages and can be used as long as the dates it gives are
understood as center points along ranges of possible dates. The standard
glottochronological figure, representing 1,000 years of approximate
divergence of two languages before the base date of collection, is 74
percent. The base date is the mean date of the collection of evidence from
the two languages being compared. The Orange River Khoi, with 77
percent cognation, therefore split at a date perhaps just slightly more
recent than 1,000 years before the early twentieth century, or sometime
close to 1000 A.D. Western Cape Khoi data were gathered at dates mostly
in the later seventeenth century, so that the base date for their cognation
with Orange River Khoi would lie between then and the early twentieth
century, or about 1800. Since cognation in the 50 percents is indicative of
a split of about 2,000 years, the divergence of Orange River from Cape
Khoi should be placed toward the end of the last millennium B.C., conceivably around 100 to 200 B.C.

The beginning of divergence within the Cape Khoi dialect chain,
with cognation just below 70 percent, would be put at 1,300 or 1,400 years
before the Cape Khoi base date of the early eighteenth century, that date
being the mean between the mostly late seventeenth-century collection of
Western Cape Khoi and the mostly eighteenth-century collection of east-

ern Cape materials—except for two things. For one, the Cape versions of Khoi continued to be the dialects of a chain of cooperating and interacting communities right down to their collapse in the eighteenth century, and in that kind of situation rates of linguistic divergence are damped by the diffusion of changes through parts of the chain. For another, the eastern Cape data do not come from one of the easternmost dialects, which can be expected to have been still more divergent, by reason of distance, from Western Cape Khoi. Hence the beginnings of divergence within Cape Khoi probably go back considerably before the 400 or 500 A.D. date the percentages might seem to indicate, perhaps to the start of the first millennium A.D.

In addition to the Khoikhoi societies which lasted down to recent centuries, at least one other major grouping, the Limpopo Khoikhoi, must be postulated. Their existence is known so far only from loanwords in Bantu languages, especially in proto-Southeast Bantu ancestral to the modern Nguni, Sotho, Tsonga, Nyambane, and Venda languages. Since proto-Southeast Bantu is best sited on linguistic-geographical grounds somewhere in eastern Transvaal and/or southern Mozambique (Ehret et al. 1972) and its speakers were therefore quite possibly the makers of the Early Iron Age Matola Culture of those areas (Ehret and Kinsman 1981), the territory of the Limpopo Khoi should also be sought in or about the same region. A further Khoikhoi presence in northern or central Transvaal by the beginning of the Iron Age may be attested by a set of loanwords in proto-Shona which includes such basic vocabulary as the word for "breast" (Ehret et al. 1972). The spread of the Shona language in Zimbabwe can be attributed to Bantu settlers coming from the Transvaal at the end of the Early Iron Age (Huffman 1978), and so the contact with Khoi speakers which preceded this expansion of Shona would again have to be placed in areas of the Limpopo watershed. But whether this Khoikhoi tongue which influenced early Shona was the same as that of the Limpopo Khoi remains to be determined.

What the Limpopo Khoi word borrowings in Southeast Bantu show is that their source language was either ancestral to proto-Cape-Orange Khoi or a sister Khoikhoi dialect coordinate with and contemporary with it. The key piece of evidence for this conclusion is the proto-Khoikhoi word for "cow," *komo-, which maintains original final *o in the Southeast Bantu loan form *-komo. Cape-Orange Khoi languages show instead a reconstructible shape *koma-, in which the earlier final *o became *a (see Beach 1938 for discussion of constraints in Nama disallowing occurrence of stem-final /o/ in such a consonantal environment). The occurrence of a shape *kuma- in eastern Cape Khoi shows that this phonological condition goes back to proto-Cape-Orange speech. In view of the previous placement of the proto-Cape-Orange language at least as early in time as the Limpopo Khoi interaction, at the beginning of the Iron Age, with the proto-Southeast Bantu, the better solution seems to be that proto-Cape-Orange and early Limpopo Khoi were sister languages or, more correctly, sister dialects of an already diverging proto-Khoikhoi language.

Proto-Khoikhoi itself began as one of a group of languages frequently called "Central Khoisan." A less unwieldy and more precisely applicable name Khwe, first proposed by Professor Oswin Köhler of Cologne in the form *Khoe*, from the reconstructible word for "person," is used here. The alternative spelling Khwe has been chosen to avoid confusion with the terms *Khoikhoi* and *Khoi*. In one form or another, the genetic relationship of the Khwe languages has been recognized by all investigators. What distinguished the proto-Khoikhoi culturally from the rest of the group was their adoption of livestock raising; what distinguishes them linguistically is not so clear, although a partial subclassification of their position in the Khwe group may be proposed at this point.

The Khwe language group is a relatively tightly related one, its greatest time depth probably not reaching back much more than a millennium before the Khoikhoi adoption of food-production practices. A cognate count for Orange River Khoi and the two best known Khwe languages spoken by hunter-gatherers, Naro and Hietsho, yields the following pattern (see table 11):

NAMA			
77	!KORA		
47	50	NARO	
38	37	51	HIETSHO

On the surface this cognation pattern would seem to describe an early dialect network, with proto-Khoikhoi and pre-Hietsho at the respective extremes and Naro centrally located. The Naro evidence, drawn from Baucom (1974), is suspect, however, for including too many instances of multiple synonyms for particular entries, probably because of Baucom's collation of material actually from different Naro dialects, and his inclusion of all possible words for a meaning, in order to facilitate reconstruction of cognate phonology. Naro data collected by another scholar (Westphal 1965) tend to drop the percentages derived from Baucom's listing, but too few of those data were available to bring the Naro count into full comparability with the others. Thus it seems probable that Naro percentages of cognation as reckoned here are overly high and actually run nearer those of Hietsho with Nama and !Kora. Most of the rest of the Khwe languages for which there is diagnostic evidence can be attributed to one of the three subdivisions defined by this count, on grounds either of shared phonological or shared lexical innovations.

Hence the indication of the small cognation chart above that the lowest percentages, and therefore the greatest distance of relationship, within Khwe fall in the very high 30 percent range is probably not far off the mark. Assuming a rough validity for the time depth of Khoikhoi history projected so far, the ancestral Khwe tongue would have to be dated to around 1000 B.C. An overall scheme of Khoikhoi history is proposed in figure 3.

Correlating the Linguistics and the Archaeology

The area of origin of the Khoikhoi can be fairly narrowly located from this evidence of relationship. The Naro and Hietsho groupings cover various parts of central and northeastern Botswana, respectively. The Khoikhoi subgroup at its farthest extent spread over a much larger expanse of southern Africa—well to the east of Botswana, to its southeast, and all along the southern coastal belt of the Cape. But the narrower location of the two other identified subgroups requires that the third subgroup, Khoikhoi, be traced also back to the same general region of origin, somewhere in or about northeastern Botswana or the immediately adjoining regions.

The successive splits in Khoikhoi project a pattern of progressive southward movement down the middle of southern Africa. The first split of the proto-Khoikhoi resulted in the emergence of one Khoi population best placed in parts of the Limpopo watershed and of a second group, proto-Cape-Orange, whose descendants all lived much farther south. The second split, probably following close on the first and suggested above to date possibly just before the end of the pre-Christian era, divided the latter group into an Orange River community, presumably living in the region of the Orange-Vaal confluence, and a proto-Cape Khoi set of communities which settled in the eastern Cape, perhaps in the Sundays River areas, and expanded east and west from there. At a later time, which could be early in the present millennium, a group of Orange River

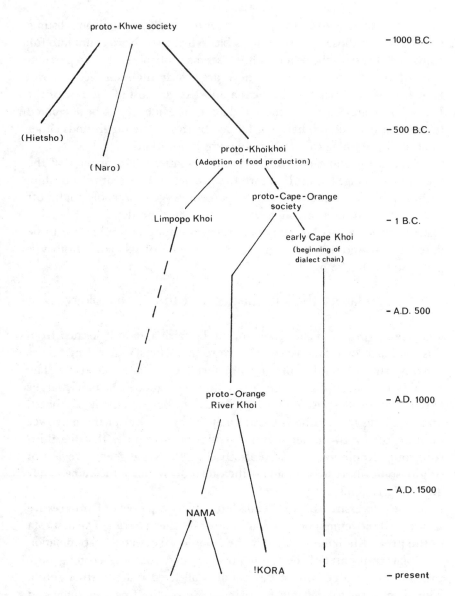

Fig. 3. Linguistic scheme of Khoikhoi history, with suggested approximate dating.

Khoi moved downriver to settle in the northwestern Cape and become the
nucleus of the later Nama people. According to oral tradition, some of the
Nama at about the seventeenth century spread northward into central
and even north-central Namibia (Vedder 1934:129–132), there linguistically assimilating the still today ethnically distinct Damara and then in

the eighteenth century beginning to face the countervailing pressure of the spread of the Herero, a Southwest Bantu people, from the north.

Such an overall Khoikhoi history fits the indications of earliest oral tradition of both Cape and Orange River Khoi (Elphick 1977: 20, 21). It also accounts very well indeed, in both the projected times and the inferred locations of population movements, for the archaeological evidence of early sheep raising in the Cape. Even the archaeological indications that the first Stone Age herders kept principally sheep and only subsequently began to put more reliance on cattle may be paralleled in the linguistic indications. Whereas Khoikhoi words for "ram," "young ram," and "ewe" can all be shown to be probable loanwords from a non-Khoikhoi language, for cattle only the generic term *komo- is an apparent loan (table 12). Although the earliest Khoikhoi therefore knew of cattle, it is for sheep that a clear breeding terminology is indicated. The Khoikhoi coinage of most of their specifically bovine breeding terms thus may well betoken a more gradual growth of acquaintance with cattle, at least among the more southerly of the Khoikhoi of the turn of the eras. By that time, however, the Limpopo Khoi were not only herding cattle but milking them as well, for in no other way can the adoption by the earliest Southeast Bantu of such Limpopo Khoi words as those for "cow" and for "(sour) milk" (Ehret et al. 1972) be explained.

What the Khoikhoi expansions do not account for, however, are the archaeological attestation of early first millennium A.D. sheep raising in Namibia and the occurrence of rather Khoikhoi-like approaches to livestock keeping among Southwest Bantu societies—Herero, Kwanyama, Ndonga, Nyaneka, and others—of southern Angola and northern Namibia (see esp. Murdock 1959:370–373), along with the adoption of some livestock terms, derived from roots seen also in Khoikhoi (table 13), into the proto-Southwest Bantu language spoken probably a bit more than a thousand years ago in those regions (Papstein 1979: chap. 2). Apparently some of the Khwe communities which took up pastoral pursuits in the latter half of the last millennium B.C. spread across the northern edges of the Kalahari westward toward the Atlantic.

There is no good reason to attribute this particular spread to a Khoikhoi people. The probable candidates for bringing animal husbandry to southern Angola and Namibia were instead another Khwe people, speaking a language ancestral to that of the recent Kwadi pastoralists of coastal southern Angola. The Kwadi, raisers of small stock, had a language that appears to share several fundamental sound shifts with, and so belongs to, the Hietsho subgroup of Khwe. The proto-Kwadi, it may be proposed, participated in the same developments of the northeastern Botswana regions which produced the Khoikhoi adoption of livestock, but they expanded westward 2,000 years ago even as the ancestors of the Khoikhoi advanced southward. The modern Kwadi would be the last remnants, persisting in declining numbers in marginal grazing lands, of once wider-spread herding populations elsewhere generally absorbed into the Southwest Bantu societies, in the process contributing to the physical makeup of Southwest Bantu populations and to the ideas and practices of livestock keeping. On this view the Damara, who also keep small stock and physically resemble the Kwadi, would be descendants of a southern offshoot of the proto-Kwadi expansion. Their adoption of the Nama language would be a reflection of the more recent Nama predominance in Namibia. The Mirabib site of central western Namibia, with its evidence of fourth-century sheepherding (Sandelowsky 1974; Sandelowsky et al. 1979), would be the remains of the southern proto-Kwadi settlement, whereas Kapako, an Early Iron Age Site of the later first millennium in far northern Namibia (Sandelowsky 1973), is a candidate for a settlement of the early Southwest Bantu who succeeded the proto-Kwadi farther north.

No need arises therefore to postulate an improbably roundabout route for the introduction of the sheep raising which is attested all across the southern Cape by the turn of the eras. The linguistic evidence allows for one introduction of livestock into northern or northeastern Botswana after 500 B.C., with two separate groups of former hunter-gatherers, both speaking languages of the Khwe branch of South African Khoisan, taking up aspects of the new way of life, and with each society expanding, because of the advantages conferred and the requirements imposed by the subsistence adoptions, in different directions outward from the region of adoption (map 13). The pattern and timing of Khoikhoi expansion fit well with those of the Cape finds; the proto-Kwadi spread appears a sufficient mechanism for the appearance of sheep in fourth-century Namibia. The visible physical anthropological differences between recent Khoikhoi and Kwadi peoples are also explained by the double expansion. The Khoikhoi, spreading southward through the middle of southern Africa, would by incorporation of preceding groups have reinforced their genetic resemblance to the hunter-gatherers of those regions. The Kwadi presumably intruded on hunter-gatherers of different genetic background and so, as incorporation proceeded, shifted genetically in the direction of the modern range of physical variation among Kwadi and Damara, the latter of which were suggested above as formerly Kwadi-related in language.

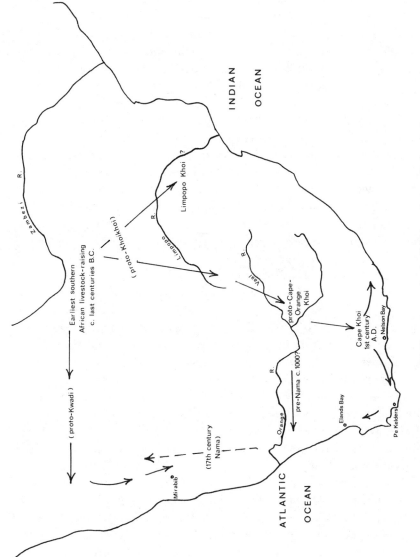

Map 13. Proposed directions of Khoikhoi and Kwadi expansions.

It is still quite possible, since no direct evidence of the earlier Damara language apparently remains, that the sheep keepers of Namibia in the first half of the first millennium A.D. were a linguistically unconnected group which adopted their animals from the proto-Kwadi to the north. The simpler solution, making the Damara a southern offshoot of the Kwadi, is available, however. It is also possible that the Khoikhoi settlement of the southern Cape coincided with the appearance of cattle in the region by or before the mid-first millennium and so followed by a few centuries the initial spread of sheep keeping there. But the presently known archaeology better accords with the postulated expansion of sheep-raising Khoikhoi people, to whom cattle diffused subsequently. The first spread of sheep, if as rapid as it now seems, would require population movement as its mechanism; the diffusion of subsistence animals from people to people over such long distances would, in contrast, proceed through a succession of periods of accommodation along the route of diffusion. The delayed appearance of cattle in the southern Cape thus fits with diffusionary expectations, whereas the spread of sheep, sudden on present indications, would better be attributed to incoming people.

What has been left aside is the question of where the Khoikhoi and Kwadi word borrowings, and hence their livestock, came from in the first place. The apparent source of the loanwords was a Central Sudanic language. The loans appear limited to food-production vocabulary; hence the Central Sudanic contact seems to have had no deep general cultural impact on the two societies that adopted the sheep raising. The ancestors of the Khoikhoi and Kwadi therefore appear to have had contact with but to have lived outside the actual sphere of settlement of those from whom they got their animals. In Khoikhoi the borrowed words included at least two terms for cultivated food and one for a kind of food (broth) made in a pot and probably also the word for "pot" (table 12). The cultivation-related terms require only that the Khoikhoi knew of and had at least occasional contacts with people who did cultivate, whereas the livestock terms they adopted require actual keeping and breeding of at least sheep. The evidence also makes it highly probable that they took up pottery making at that time. The inclusion of subgeneric livestock terminology among the borrowings is best explained if the words entered the Khwe languages through direct encounter with Central Sudanic speakers. The reason is that while generic terms can spread widely with the diffusion of the concrete items they name, subcategorizations tend to be displaced frequently by new coinages as items spread. Conceivably an intermediate language might have transmitted the terms to proto-Khoikhoi, but even that minor degree of mediation is less plausible than direct transference.

The traceability of both the proto-Kwadi and the proto-Khoikhoi back to northern or northeastern Botswana homelands suggests a Central Sudanic settlement somewhere nearby, possibly as far off as southern Zambia, in the last millennium B.C. But the missing links in the transmission of livestock from northern East Africa to the north edge of Botswana, and the proposed Central Sudanic contribution to the process, have yet to be found in the archaeology.

TABLE 11
Khwe and Khoikhoi Core Vocabularies

Meaning	Nama	!Kora	Western Cape	Eastern Cape	Naro	Hietsho
1. I	tita	tire (m.) tita (f.)	tiri	--	tira tida	tšira
2. you (sing.)	sats (m.) sas (f.)	sats (m.) sas (f.)	t?aats	--	-tsa -sa	-tsa -ša
3. we	sikxum sam sase (etc.)	-kham sam sase (etc.)	sikhim	--	//ka (m.) sise (f.)	//kae (m.) sisee (f.)
4. who	taripa	dabi	--	--	dii	nare
5. what	tare, tae	tae-	--	--	du	nate
6. all	hoa-	hoa-	--	--	waxa	ihe
7. many	≠kui-	/xoa-	côassa (*/oa-)	xkwaesa (*/wa-)	kei	tsao
8. one	/kui	/ui	q'kui (*/ui)	xeu (*/oi)	/kui	kwi
9. two	/kam	/am	k'kam (*/am)	x-ām (/am)	/kam	/kam
10. three	!nona	!nona	k¯ouna (*!una)	xgonang (*!gona)	!nona	ngonawe
11. four	haka	haka	hakka	hakka	haka	haka
12. five	koro	koro	koro	gisi (*xisi?)	--	--

TABLE 11—*Continued*

Meaning	Nama	!Kora	Western Cape	Eastern Cape	Naro	Hietsho
13. big	kai	kai	bei	--	//go, kei, //kao	/gowe, /koo
14. little	≠kari	/a	gemech	xorae (*Core)	/kari-, /kwa, /ka	//kwa
15. long	kaxu	kaxu	--	--	kei	kxau
16. hot	/kam-sa	≠kxumi	--	--	ša	≠kee
17. cold	!xai	!xai	toucai (*tukai)	--	≠xei	haii
18. new	/asa	/'a-sa	--	--	/asa, kaba	!kao, /kxaie
19. good	!kãi	!aĩ, ≠hanu	--	xk'iinsi	!ãĩ	khaa
20. dry	≠nãsa	/'o (v.)	--	--	--	--
21. black	≠nu	≠nu	--	--	≠nuu	dzu-
22. white	!uri	xati	--	--	!u	/'ie
23. red	/apa	--	kaba (*/aba)	--	/noa	/geya
24. green	!am	!kxam	k'aa (*Caa), tama (*!ama?)	--	!am, tsã	čã, barati
25. yellow	!huni	/hai	--	--	/kore	/a sethas

TABLE 11—Continued

Meaning	Nama	!Kora	Western Cape	Eastern Cape	Naro	Hietsho
26. round	!kupu	!um	--	--	dwerere, !gubu	!gubu, dweree
27. full	/oa-sa, /ãsa	/kxoa	--	--	/oe	!gwea, /kweha
28. this	ne-	he	--	--	/ne	/ne
29. that	nau	//na	ha	--	//na	a, ho
30. to eat	≠ū	≠'ū	ôung (*ū?)	x'ung (*≠ū)	≠'ū	ka
31. to drink	a	kxa	k⁻aa (*kxaa)	--	kx'a	≠kha
32. to bite	nã	ba	--	--	taa	ka, pha
33. to see	mū	mū	k'mon (*Cmõ)	--	mū	mõõ
34. to hear	//nãu	//nau	k'nom (*//nõ)	--	kum	tšom
35. to know	≠an	≠'an	--	--	≠ana	≠en
36. to sleep	//om	//'um	k'komma (*//om-), quee (*//oe)	x-omn (*//om)	//kx'om	//gom
37. to lie	//koe	//oe	k'quee (*//oe), k⁻obi (*kxobi?)	--	//gwe	//gweae

38. to die	//o	//ʔo	k⁻hro (*//o)	xgʼa (*Ca)	//o	oo
39. to kill	!kam	!am	—	—	/kū	/goo
40. to go	!kū, ʼï	ï, si, !ü	k'on (*!õ)	xg'ung (*!ü)	!kū	kho
41. to come	ha	ha	ha, see	ha	ha, ši	ya
42. to sit	≠nõa	≠nu	nõuw (*nõuʔ)	—	≠nu	nyo
43. to stand	mã	mã	mãa (*mã)	—	te	te
44. to give	ma	ma	maa	—	ma, au	ma, thee, t'ii
45. to say	mĩ	mĩ	—	—	mĩ	me
46. to burn	tãu, kxau	≠hubi	—	—	dau	dhau
47. sun	sore-s	sore-b	sore	soeroe (*suru)	kam	/kam
48. moon	//xã-p	//kxã-s	tchâ (*//khã)	xka (*//ka)	//nwe	!kowe
49. star	kamiro-p	amoro-b	k⁻uanehou (*≠uanehu) t'enhouw (*Cêhau)	sxgoro (*Coro)	≠gaunu	//kala
50. water	//kam-i	//am-i	kamma (*//kama)	x-gamma (*//kama)	čai	tsa

TABLE 11—Continued

Meaning	Nama	!Kora	Western Cape	Eastern Cape	Naro	Hietsho
51. rain	/api-p	tu-s	touquy (*tukai) onk¯ui (*okxaiʔ)	--	--	--
52. cloud	/nanu-p	/hum-a	--	--	/hom	nyaa
53. night	tsuxu-p	!xai-b	thoughou (*thuxu)	--	≠nou	haie
54. smoke	/an-i	/kxan-i	--	--	/kan, !ko	tsene
55. fire	/ae-s	/ʔae-b	ecy (*e-kiʔ)	xei (*/ai)	/ai	/ʔe
56. ash	tsao-p	thao-b	--	--	tou	dzoo
57. path	tao-p	dao-b	doudou	--	dau	dḥau
58. mountain	!hom /ui-p	!are-b	kˉhu (*Cu)	xkoago (*!oa-koʔ)	!gabi	!goa
59. stone	/ui-p	/ʔui-b	hip (*hi-p)	xeu (*/oi)	//nwa	//gwa
60. earth	!hu-p	!hu-b	kʔchou (*!xu)	xkhu (*!hu)	!hu	--
61. sand	//xae-p	//xae-b	--	--	xom	hom
62. tree	hai-s	hei-s	ay	hi	yi	hii
63. root	!noma-p	!nomā-b	--	--	--	--
64. bark	soro-p	soro-b	--	--	čora	dzoree
65. fish	//ʔau-p	//ʔau-b	k'auw (//au)	--	--	--

66. bird	ani-p	kxani-s	k¯anniqua (*kxani-)	xgani (kxani)	tsera	zera
67. dog	ari-p	'ari-b	likh¯anee (*likxani)	tu	agu	aba
68. to fly	//ana	--	--	--	!xwe	hwee
69. louse	uri-p	kxuri-b	hh¯oussi	--	/na	//gam
70. person	kxoe-p	khoe-b	k'koe (*kxoe)	--	kwe	čwa
71. man	ao-p	'ao-b	q¯uiebes (*kxoi-b-es)	xkoago (*kxoa-ko)	kx'aa	khao
72. woman	tara-s	tara-s	kq¯uiquis (*kxoikxoi-s) zobee	xkeukoe (*kxoi-ku)	//gai	//gai
73. egg	!upu-s	!ubu-b	ganep (*xane- or *Cane-)	--	ubi	ibi
74. meat	//kan-i	kxo-b	k?oô (*kxo-)	xo (*Co)	/xa	koho
75. skin	kxo-p	kho-b	gwummey	--	kuu	čo
76. bone	≠ko-p	--	--	--	oa	/ngwa
77. fat	//nui-p	//nui-b	ou¯nwie (*u//nui)	--	//nui	!gwi
78. horn	//nã-p	//na-b	nam (*na-?)	--	/na	//ngaa
79. tail	≠are-p	sao-b	--	--	čau	tsau
80. feather	!am-s	!'am-a	hamo (*!amo)	--	//ua	/go

TABLE 11—*Continued*

Meaning	Nama	!Kora	Western Cape	Eastern Cape	Naro	Hietsho
81. hair	/ū-p	/'ū-b	n⁻uqua-an (*/ū-)	xungxa (*/ū-)	/ū	/ʰoo nan
82. head	tana-s	!ā-b	biqua (*bi-)	binxk'a (*bi-Ca)	≠u	mʰa
83. ear	≠kai-s	!nau-b	nouw (*nau)	xn'aunka (*!naū-)	≠e	čee
84. eye	mū-s	mū-b	moe, mon (mū)	mung (*mū)	≠xai	čai
85. nose	≠kui-s	≠ui-b	ture, q⁻uoi (*≠oi)	xk'eu (≠oi)	≠wi	čui
86. mouth	am-s	kx'am-s	k⁻oamqua (*kxwam-)	xgamm (*kxam)	kx'am	/kxam
87. tooth	//kū-p	//u-b	k⁻ou (*//ku)	xkung (*//kū)	//kōō	//gōō
88. tongue	nam-s	tam-a	tamma	tamm	dam	dʰam
89. nail	//koro-p	//oro-p	clo' (*Clo)	— —	//kx'oro	/garo, !kxole
90. foot	≠ai-s	≠'ai-b	y, iqua (*i)	xei (*≠ai)	//nare	karee
91. knee	//koa-p	//oa-b	q⁻ua (*//oa)	— —	!kuru	kukuru
92. hand	!om-s	!um-s	omma	xoenn (!un)	čou	tsau

93. belly	!nã-p	!na-b	chomma (*ǂaoma)	—	/naa	/khoree
94. neck	!ao-p	!'ao-b	qˈuaö (*!wao?)	—	!kau	dǂhom
95. breast	sam-s	//xai-b	samme	samkˈa (*sam-)	bii	sam
96. heart	ǂkao-p	ǂao-b	qˈuau (*ǂwauʔ)	—	ǂao	čoo
97. liver	ãi-s	kxaĩ-b	quˈein (*kxai-)	—	kxˈai	čě
98. blood	/au-p	/au-b	—	—	/au	thaka
99. name	/on-s	/'on-i	kˈouna (*/un-)	—	/kwi	/kun
100. to swim	tsã	thã	—	—	!kha	!kha

NOTE: Nama data are rendered according to the spelling scheme suggested in D. M. Beach, *The Phonetics of the Hottentot Language* (London: Cambridge University Press, 1938). Cape Khoi words are given as recorded, but when possible a suggested corrected shape has been offered in parentheses; C in such renderings indicates an undetermined click.

TABLE 12
CENTRAL SUDANIC LOANWORDS IN KHWE LANGUAGES

Abbreviations: PKh = proto-Khoisan; PtÇ-O = proto-Cape-Orange Khoi; PCS = proto-Central Sudanic; MM = Moru-Madi (branch of Central Sudanic).

Khwe attestation	Central Sudanic attestation
PKh 'gu "sheep," Kwadi *guu-* "sheep," *gœ-* "cow"; also Naro *guu* "sheep," *gwe* "cow," etc.	PCS *g^cu "body, living thing"; with common semantic shift first to "animal," then to "livestock," with semantic specification by addition of PCS -V noun suffixes (*guu, *gue).
Nama *paira-* "ram"	MM *bilɔ "sheep," Bagirmi *bal* "ram"
Nama *kuro-* "young ram"	Probably root seen in Shona *kutukutu "young she-goat," apparently from Central Sudanic root for "young animal" seen with metathesis in Lugbara (MM) *tukutuku* "puppy" (stem medial *t > r in Khoikhoi).
Nama *oro-* "milk ewe"	MM *aro- "young female domestic animal"
PKh *komo "cow" (PtC-O *koma-)	PCS *-bi in form with movable k- prefix: *kobi > *kombi > *kombe > *kombo (for sound shifts, see Ehret (1967, 1973); *mb* automatically goes to *m* in Khoikhoi, which has no NC clusters.
PtC-O *bere- "grain, food from grain, bread"	MM *be "ear of grain" plus -1V noun suffix (see also Ehret 1973).
Nama topo- "porridge"	PCS *pa plus movable t- prefix (see Ehret 1973 for sound shifts): *tapa > *topo.
Nama *suro-* "broth"	PCS *siu plus -rV noun suffix
PtC-O *sa- "hunter-gatherer, person without livestock"	Lendu *ša "stranger, foreigner" (no *š in Khoikhoi, hence > *s).
!Kora *semi-* "sorghum"	PCS *sa "flour" plus *-me noun suffix: *same, with presumed vowel assimilation yielding *seme, and later shift of final *e to /i/.
PtC-O *sou- "pot" (Orange River Khoi *su- but Western Cape *sou-* with each vowel separately pronounced)	PCS *ša "pot" plus -V (*-u) noun suffix: *šau, with rounding of *a in environment of following *u; lack of [š] in Khoihoi causes shift to /s/.

TABLE 13
Southwest Bantu Words from a Khwe Source Language

Abbreviations: PtSW-B = proto-Southwest Bantu; PKh = proto-Khoikhoi.

Southwest Bantu root/word	Khwe attestation (see also table 12)
PtSW-B *-gu/*-gui "sheep"	Kwadi *guu-*, PKh *gu-, etc.
Kwanyama *-pedi* "ram" (*-peli or *-pelu)	Nama *paira-*
PtSW-B *-gu in *-tuegu "bull"?	Kwadi *goe-* "cow," Naro *gwe* "cow," etc.
PtSW-B *-guingui "female of cattle"	Kwadi *goe-* "cow," etc.
Herero *onduombe* "ox" (*-gu-gombe: *-gombe "cow")	Kwadi *goe-* "cow," *guu-* "sheep," etc.

9 | Models of the Spread of the Early Iron Age

D. P. COLLETT

THE EARLY IRON AGE COMPLEX in much of eastern and in southern Africa is associated with the first appearance of an agricultural economy which supported settled villages with metallurgical and potting industries. Two lines of evidence are used to support a migration model for the spread of the Early Iron Age: (1) the sudden appearance of the technocomplex as a fully formed entity; (2) the stylistic similarity among many of the pottery assemblages. Research has focused on the genetic links between cultures with the aim of providing a culture-historic framework. Numerous culture-historical reconstructions have been proposed (Fagan 1965; Huffman 1970, 1978; Oliver 1966; Phillipson 1977b; Soper 1971a, b), but so far no model has been widely accepted. The existence of competing models is explained by two factors: the different methods used to compare pottery assemblages and the failure by some workers to integrate cultural and chronological data (e.g., Oliver 1966). In addition to historical reconstruction, pottery analyses and comparisons have been used to infer the mechanisms of dispersal underlying the movement of Early Iron Age peoples into the subcontinent.

Only two mechanisms of dispersal have been proposed, a continuous wave-of-advance model (Soper 1971b) and a cataclysmic discontinuous-spread model (Huffman 1970). In both instances pottery comparisons isolated similar cultural groupings and the major difference was the structure of ceramic similarity in space. Soper (1971b) found that neighboring pairs of assemblages were the most similar and that similarity was a function of distance. The clinal variation was explained by a model in which the daughter settlements that resulted from village fission moved forward a short distance into previously uncolonized territory. These moves were associated with small changes in the ceramic assemblage and the movement of the Early Iron Age/Stone Age boundary was associated with a continual change in the pottery. The movement was conceptualized as a self-regenerating wave moving over the subcontinent. In contrast, Huffman (1970) assumed that cultures were homogeneous in space and that movement was not a stimulus for culture change. Because there was no evidence for a divergent evolution within the culture groups, he suggested that Early Iron Age cultures left the nuclear area as preformed entities, moved a considerable distance, and settled in the areas where their remains are now found. The movement was described as spreading "like pellets from a shotgun" (Huffman 1970).

One of the most important characteristics of the spread of the Early Iron Age was the rapidity of the migration. Early attempts to find a chronological ordering either failed (Soper 1971*b*) or did not examine the genetic links between cultures (Oliver 1966; Posnansky 1968*b*). The shotgun model (Huffman 1970) can explain the lack of temporal ordering and therefore does not contradict the available radiocarbon chronology. A more recent analysis of the radiocarbon chronology using dispersion diagrams has indicated a north-to-south spread (Phillipson 1975). The analysis may, however, be criticized on two counts, the choice of dates and the failure to examine critically the distribution of dates. Radiocarbon dates with a dubious association were included in the analysis (e.g., Rutare and Katuruka dates) and linked dates were given the same weight as single dates from a site. Dispersion diagrams use percentile ranges and are sensitive to differences in the skew and kurtosis of distributions. No attempt was made to check for differences in these parameters of the distribution of radiocarbon dates in different areas. Because of these problems the north-to-south temporal ordering should not be accepted, although the recognition of a north-to-south seriation in the Bambata Complex (Huffman 1978) suggests that a temporal ordering should exist.

The north-to-south seriation contradicts the shotgun model which has therefore been rejected. The wave-of-advance model can accommodate the spatial seriation, but this model is associated with two further problems. First, pottery assemblages were compared by a technique taxonomy, and, as a recent analysis of ethnographic assemblages has shown, this technique did not discriminate well even when assemblages were known to be different (Huffman 1980). The second problem was the rate of expansion associated with the spread of the Early Iron Age. The wave-of-advance model was a random-walk model similar to the model proposed for the spread of the Neolithic in Europe. Computer simulations of the latter model have produced rates of spread of about one kilometer a year (Ammerman and Cavalli-Sforza 1973). With this rate of spread the Early Iron Age people would have taken two millennia to reach South Africa. The Early Iron Age radiocarbon chronology indicates that the spread took less than a thousand years, (Phillipson 1975) and random-walk models would therefore appear to be too slow to account for the spread of the Early Iron Age.

In the present paper two simple ecological models are described, one a continuous spread and the second a discontinuous spread with sequential colonization of new areas. Computer models of both mechanisms are shown to produce different rates of expansion. By comparing these rates of spread with the Early Iron Age radiocarbon chronology it is shown that a discontinuous-spread model gives more realistic rates of expansion.

Ecological Models of Dispersal Mechanisms

Continuous Spread

In ecological models dispersal processes that give rise to continuous spreading have been linked to two variables, population growth and home ranges (Emlen 1973). A group territory or home range, a site territory in archaeology (Higgs and Vita-Finzi 1972), has a fixed carrying capacity under a specific system of exploitation. Two determinants of carrying capacity have been suggested: lack of a critical resource (Lack 1954; Chitty 1960) and social stress (Snyder 1968). The social-stress theory of population control has not been generally accepted by biologists (Emlen 1973), although research on laboratory animals has shown that increased population density is associated with increased stress and decreased fertility (Snyder 1968). The social-stress theory is used in the present model because it is felt that social stress would be associated with increased friction in human communities and a higher probability of settlement fission. In the present model carrying capacity is thought to be socially defined and not a result of population pressure on resources.

At the start of the Early Iron Age, population pressure would have increased until the social carrying capacity was approached. Once it was reached a village would have split into two or more groups and all but one of these would have moved into adjacent unoccupied areas. An imaginary boundary enclosing the site territories would have moved outward (fig. 4). If the population continued to grow, the boundary would have continued to move outward and unoccupied site territories in the center would have become more scarce. Once all the central site territories were occupied, population in this area would have stabilized by natural mechanisms.

In order to simulate this model, data on the factors affecting settlement location were essential but unfortunately not available. The model therefore had to be simplified, and population growth expressed as

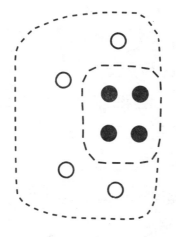

Fig. 4. Boundary expansion after village fission. Initial border is indicated by heavy dash line; border after fission, by light dashes; black circles show parent settlements, while circles with light centers represent daughter settlements.

changes in density was used instead of villages and village fission. A further simplification was made by assuming that all areas in the subcontinent could be occupied at a density equal to the social carrying capacity. A flow chart of the relationship among population growth, carrying capacity, and the boundary enclosing the colonized area (fig. 5) formed the basis of the computer simulation presented here (table 14).

Discontinuous Spread

In this model, as in the continuous-spread model, carrying capacity is defined by social tolerance. Similarly, the concept of an outward-moving boundary as a result of population increase remains the same. The assumption of natural population stabilization in the center of the group area was relaxed, and the assumption that only short-distance moves occurred was no longer maintained. Instead it was assumed that short-distance moves occurred when unoccupied territories were available. Once these were all filled, population would have continued to grow and friction would have increased. Social friction would no longer be confined to a single village but would have spread through the community. In this event the community may be treated in the same way as a single village; it would split into two or more subgroups, all but one of which would have left the natal area. These groups would not have moved to the periphery

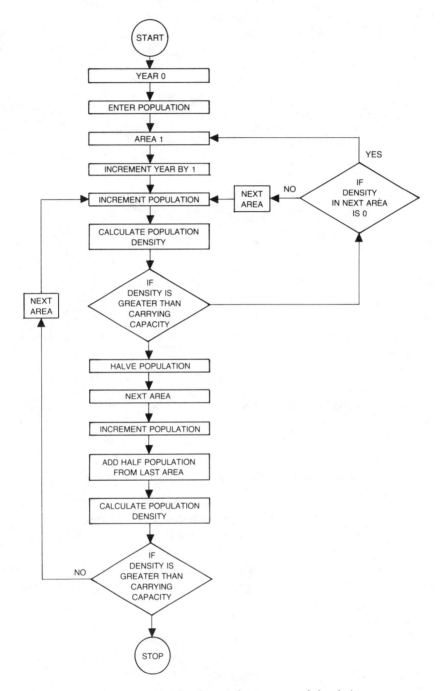

Fig. 5. Flow diagram for the continuous-spread simulation.

of the expanding boundary because in a relatively short time they would have been in an area with fairly high population density. Rather, they moved some distance from occupied areas before settling. The sub-groups would then act as nuclei from which further expansion could take place. A flow diagram and a computer simulation of the discontinuous-spread model were prepared (fig. 6; table 14).

Data

Quantitative Data

The rates of population growth used in the simulations were 2, 3.5, and 4 percent each year. The values are similar to those quoted by Birdsell (1957) for human groups colonizing uninhabited areas. Four values for carrying capacity were used: one, five, ten, and fifteen people a square kilometer. A value of five people per square kilometer has been used as the carrying capacity in a previous simulation of the spread of subsistence agriculturalists (Ammerman and Cavalli-Sforza 1973). The values coincide with population densities known from African ethnography (Tew 1950), but the possibility remains that the ethnographic values are too high because European medical attention may have lowered the death rate.

Both models were simulated with three different, arbitrarily chosen, input populations: 100, 500, and 1,000 people. In the simulations space was conceptualized as a series of concentric rings. The perimeter of each circle was set at 10 kilometers from the preceding ring.

Cultural Considerations

In the discontinuous-spread model it is essential to know the number of steps taken in the course of the expansion. The eastern stream has three steps in East Africa, Urewe to Lelesu to Kwale (Soper 1971*a*, *b*). It has been suggested that the spread then continued through Nkope to Ziwa/Gokomere areas and the Transvaal Early Iron Age groups (Robinson 1976; Phillipson 1977*b*; see also Soper, chap. 11, below). The use of the Nkope Culture as a link between the East African and South African Early Iron Age was probably incorrect, and the data should be critically evaluated before they are used as the basis for the simulation.

In the initial description of Nkope the material was placed as typologically intermediate between the East African and Zimbabwean Early Iron ages (Robinson 1970:117). The proportion of fluting and beveling was

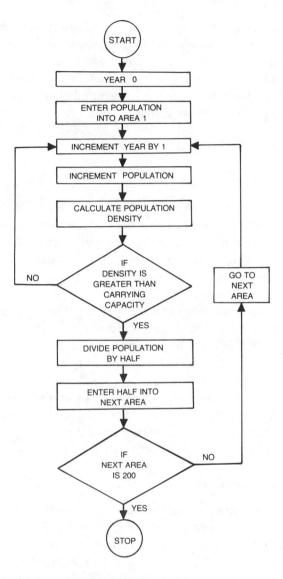

Fig. 6. Flow diagram for the discontinuous spread model.

fairly high in the type-site assemblage, which comes from the edge of Lake Malawi (Robinson 1970). The Nkope variants from the Shire Valley have a much lower proportion of these attributes (Robinson 1973: tables 1, 3), and the rapid decrease in fluting and beveling as one moves away from the lakeshore suggests that the assemblage from the type site may be atypical. In particular, the type site has Kwale-like jars which were absent from all other sites. The Ziwa/Gokomere-like jars found in Nkope variant sites cannot be derived from Kwale jars because their decoration concepts are completely different (fig. 7).

The high incidence of Kwale-like jars in the type-site assemblage may have been the result of the site's proximity to the lakeshore. Trade or migration would have been facilitated by the easily crossed lake and cultural mixing may be a feature of lakeside sites. The more "typical" Nkope sites away from the lake appear to have a strong generic link with Ziwa/Gokomere sites, and Nkope may be a regional variant of this tradition. This, coupled with the low similarity between Gokomere and Silver Leaves (Huffman 1978), suggests that the Nkope material should not be used as a step between Kwale and Silver Leaves. The simulation was, therefore, carried out in the following steps: Urewe → Lelesu → Kwale → Silver Leaves.

Results

The discontinuous-spread model produced a faster rate of expansion than the wave-of-advance model. Rates of less than one kilometer per year were generated by the wave-of-advance model (table 14*a*), and these were of an order of magnitude lower than the rates from the discontinuous-spread model (table 14*b*). The rate of spread for a culture in the discontinuous-spread model was similar to the rate generated by the wave-of-advance model (table 14*c*). Different input populations had little effect on the rates for the wave-of-advance model (table 14*d*) but did affect the internal culture expansion rates for the discontinuous-spread model (table 14*e*). The difference in the rates of spread within a culture for the discontinuous-spread model resulted from high population inputs being spread over a large area. Only a relatively small area was colonized before fission occurred. Therefore the time taken to reach the critical population density was short and thus the rates of expansion were fast.

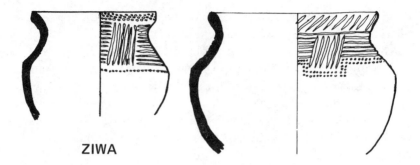

ZIWA

NKOPE

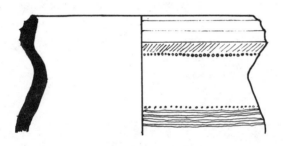

KWALE

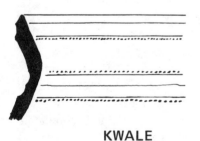

‒‒	flutes
�	broad line incision
⁄ ⁄ ⁄	incision
○ ● ●○	comb stamping
♭	punctates

KWALE

Fig. 7. Comparison of jar types from Kwale (after Soper 1967), Nkope (after Robinson 1973), and Ziwa (after Summers 1958).

The Radiocarbon Chronology

The rates derived from the simulations have shown that the discontinuous-spread model produced the faster rate of expansion. This model was also characterized by a slower rate of expansion for a single culture than for the whole tradition. A comparison of their rates of expansion derived from the models, with the values derived from the radiocarbon chronology, should provide a test of the appropriateness of the two models.

Method

Early Iron Age radiocarbon dates provide an estimate of the period during which a site was occupied. Since radiocarbon dates have an estimate of variability associated with them, it was decided that the rates of spread could not be calculated directly from the dates. By using populations of dates the problems of indeterminancy can be partly overcome. A least-squares method, linear regression, was used to describe the relationship between distance and dates. This technique is designed for use in situations where uncontrolled variables may give rise to variation in one or both of the dependent variables, and it is therefore appropriate for radiocarbon dates.

Where more than one date was associated with a single component of a site, a weighted average (Huffman 1977) was used to provide the best estimate. The weighted average was used only when dates clustered and were unlikely to be associated with pre−Iron Age events. If dates were obviously more recent than the earliest occurrence of the Early Iron Age in an area, they were not used because the analysis was an attempt to measure only the rate of spread of the Early Iron Age. After these procedures had been carried out the sample sizes left for the regression analysis were very small, possibly too small to yield a good estimate of the population variance. This problem has been common in earlier studies, however, and until more systematically collected radiocarbon dates are available, the archaeologist will have to work with inadequate data.

Data

Regressions of earliest dates against distance from the earliest date were calculated for the expansion of the Urewe Culture and for the Urewe to Silver Leaves route. The sites and associated dates used in the present study are shown in table 14 (*f* and *g*). In each instance the earliest date was set at a distance of zero, and the straight-line distance between this site and other early sites was measured. Rates of expansion were derived from the regression.

Results

The regression line for the Urewe Culture had a slope of 0.54 with the origin at ninety-two years (fig. 8). This gave a rate of expansion of just over half a kilometer a year (0.57 km/year). The slope derived from the regression of dates from Urewe to Silver Leaves was 0.116 with the origin at thirty-four years (fig. 8). This gave an overall expansion rate of just under ten kilometers a year (9.6 km/year). This value corresponds to the values obtained from the simulation of the discontinuous-spread model with moderate to high rates of population growth (see table 14*b*).

The values derived from the radiocarbon chronology were much faster than the values obtained from the wave-of-advance model. This datum, coupled with the evidence for a difference between the rate of expansion for a single culture and the rate for the whole tradition, provided support for the discontinuous-spread model for the movement of Early Iron Age peoples.

Discussion

The slow rate of expansion generated by the simulation of the wave-of-advance model demonstrates that this model cannot explain the spread of Early Iron Age peoples. The discontinuous-spread model produced rates of spread similar to those derived from the Early Iron Age radiocarbon chronology. Analysis of the chronology indicates that the rate of spread for an individual culture was slower than for the whole tradition. This pattern was predicted by the discontinuous-spread model, which would therefore seem to fit the available data.

A simplifying assumption was made in the simulations, and as a result the simulations may be criticized for a lack of realism. It was assumed that space was homogeneous and that environmental variation would not have affected the population density at which fission occurred or the rate of population growth. The first problem can be dealt with because the rate of expansion in the wave-of-advance model had almost no effect on the rate of spread (table 14*a*). Rates of population growth, however, are known to be affected by environmental variation (Emlen

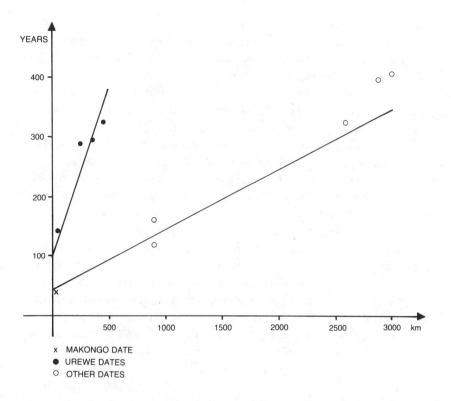

Fig. 8. Regression lines for Urewe Culture and for the fluted
and beveled complex.

1973). Simulation with rapid population growth rates resulted in the wave
of advance spreading at a rate that was two orders of magnitude lower
than the rates derived from the radiocarbon chronology (table 14*a*). The
problem of environmental variation may be at least partly ignored.
Another problem with the use of a homogeneous space was the failure to
incorporate ecological and geographical barriers such as deserts and
mountain ranges. This simplification can be accommodated by the model
because it assumed that population was stabilized behind the expanding
frontier. Such barriers would cause the boundary to stop but would not
affect the rate of expansion in other areas.

The simulation assumed that all areas in a concentric circle should be
occupied before the next circle was used. This meant that only short
moves would have occurred after village fission. Longer moves would be
expected to increase the rate of spread in a random-walk model. Move-

ment is controlled, however, by two factors: (1) the desire to move away from the natal village; (2) the desire to remain close to other members of one's own culture. The moving boundary would probably have taken the form of a sigmoidal curve (Ammerman and Cavalli-Sforza 1973). If longer moves occurred the slope of this curve would change, but the rate of spread would still be related to the rate of population growth. Longer moves would not have affected rates of spread.

In the analysis of the radiocarbon chronology it is pointed out that sample sizes were very small and that they may not be a true estimate of the earliest dates. This problem can be solved only by additional fieldwork and the processing of more dates. One of the major problems with the present radiocarbon chronology is the absence of columns of dates for each phase in the sequence from a restricted area. Archaeologists therefore cannot assess how stable the earliest date for a phase will be when the sample size increases. This problem is particularly acute when sample sizes are small. An additional problem is the lack of knowledge about the distribution of the radiocarbon estimates of a single event (Campbell, Baxter, and Alcock 1979). Regression analysis assumes that the dependent variable, in this case dates, is normally distributed (Snedecor and Cochran 1967). In the present study this factor is not important because the only estimate used was the slope, which should not be affected by the normality of the distribution. The origin is affected by the normality of the distribution, and the regression analysis cannot be used as an estimate of the absolute chronology of the spread.

The problems with the radiocarbon chronology will not be solved for a considerable time, and a conclusive test will probably not be possible for a number of years. Additional support for the discontinuous-spread model can be found, however, in African oral traditions. Long migrations after group fission are frequently mentioned in these traditions (Kimambo 1974; Legassick 1969; Monnig 1967; Turner 1954; Were 1974). In addition, fission is often said to have been a result of conflict. The discontinuous-spread model mimics dispersal processes recorded in oral tradition.

Mechanisms of dispersal have normally been based on pottery studies which have examined the similarities among assemblages as a function of distance (Huffman 1970; Soper 1971b). The process is reversed in the present study, and a model for the distribution of ceramic types in both space and time is derived from the mechanism of dispersal. Ceramics have been the most commonly used material for the definition of Iron Age cultural entities. Since decoration and form of pottery vessels cannot be directly related to function, they must be stylistic. Particular styles are thought to be associated with particular groups, as has been shown to be true for dress and stool types in the Baringo district of Kenya (Hodder 1978). In the absence of long-distance trade it is also probably true for pottery types. Different communities in southern Africa have different ceramic types (Lawton 1967; Schofield 1948), which would support a model in which ceramic style is related to group identity. Group fission would have produced two or more separate groups, and each group would have had a separate identity. Long-distance movements should have resulted in a rapid change in ceramic style. A boundary between different ceramic styles produced by different groups would be expected. Totemic change after fission and movement may be a weak analogy for this process; totems appear to have been changed after fission and movement among the Sotho (Legassick 1969; Monnig 1967). Totems may be changed, however, for a number of reasons, many of which have nothing to do with group identity.

Only one pottery analysis has been detailed enough to find boundaries (Soper 1971a); the results show that assemblage similarity was a function of distance. The absence of clear-cut boundaries indicates that the discontinuous model may be incorrect, but it has recently been shown that the technique taxonomy used by Soper is capable of producing false associations (Huffman 1980). The clinal variation was therefore probably a result of the technique and not of the spatial structure of ceramic types. The discovery of boundaries between related first-phase Early Iron Age entities would provide support for the discontinuous-spread model.

Acknowledgments

An earlier version of this paper was read at the biennial conference of the Southern African Association of Archaeologists at the University of Capetown in 1979. I would like to thank Dr. J. Alexander, Mr. T. M. Evers, Dr. I. Hodder, and Professor T. N. Huffman for comments on earlier drafts of the paper. Dr. D. S. Wilson helped to debug the programs and introduced me to evolutionary ecology. To him I owe special thanks.

TABLE 14
DATA AND ASSUMPTIONS FOR MODELS OF BANTU EXPANSION

Growth	Population density			
	1	5	10	15
0.020	0.43	0.43	0.43	0.42
0.035	0.76	0.76	0.75	0.75
0.040	0.87	0.86	0.86	0.85

a. Rates of spread for the fluted and beveled complex derived from the wave-of-advance model

Growth	Population density			
	1	5	10	15
0.020	7.60	6.27	5.36	5.12
0.035	18.13	9.20	9.20	7.43
0.040	17.52	11.29	13.19	25.73

b. Rates of spread for the fluted and beveled complex derived from the discontinuous-spread model

Growth	Population density			
	1	5	10	15
0.020	0.83	0.34	0.29	0.28
0.035	1.13	0.93	0.48	0.75
0.040	1.23	0.87	0.49	2.60

c. Rates of spread for individual cultures in the discontinuous-spread model

Growth	Input Population		
	100	500	1000
0.035	0.43	0.44	0.45

d. Effect of different input populations on rates of spread in the wave-front model (social carrying capacity was five people per square kilometer)

Growth	Input Population		
	100	500	1000
0.035	0.48	0.70	1.03

e. Effect of different input populations on rates of spread in the discontinuous-spread model (carrying capacity was ten people per square kilometer)

TABLE 14—*Continued*

Date	Site
40 ± 100	Makongo
120 ± 115	Kwale forest site
160 ± 115	Kwale ditch site
297 ± 40	Silver Leaves
325 ± 40	Eiland
400 ± 60	Castle Peak
411 ± 40	Castle Cavern

f. Dates used to calculate the regression for the fluted and beveled complex

Date	Site
40 ± 100	Makongo
141 ± 60	Katuruka
295 ± 60	Rutare
290 ± 125	Chobi
325 ± 65	Urewe

g. Dates used to calculate the regression for the Urewe Culture

h. Computer programs written in Texas Basic and run on a Texas 980B Mini Computer

```
10   PRINT "WAVE-FRONT EXPANSION MODEL"
20   DIM P(1000), D(1000), Q(1000)
30   PRINT "ENTER R,G,L"
40   INPUT R,G,L
50   PRINT "ENTER P1"
60   INPUT P(1)
70   S=22/7
80   C=0
90   N=0
95   N=N+1
96   IF N=200 GOTO250
100  C=C+1
120  P(N)=P(N)+P(N)xG
130  D(N)=P(N)/(SxNxRxNxR-(N-1)xRx(N-1)xR
140  D(N+1)=P(N+1)xRx(N+1)xR-SxNxRxNxR)
145  IF D(N)> L GOTO 200
150  GOTO100
200  P(N)=P(N)/2
210  PRINT "N"N; "C"C';
215  P(N+1)=P(N)
220  GOTO 95
250  END
```

```
10   PRINT "POPULATION FISSION MODEL"
20   DIM P(1000), D(1000), 0(1000)
```

TABLE 14—*Continued*

```
30   PRINT "ENTER R, G, L"
40   INPUT R,G,L
50   PRINT "ENTER P1"
60   INPUT P(1)
70   S=22/7
73   F=L−(0.03xL)
80   C=0
90   N=0
100  C=C+1
105  PRINT "C"C';
106  GOTO400
110  N=N+1
111  IF N=35 GOTO 500
120  P(N)=P(N)+P(N)xG
130  D(N)=P(N)/(SxNxRxNxR−Sx(N−1)xRx(N−1)xR
140  D(N+1)=P(N+L)/(Sx(N+1)xRx(N+1)xR−SxNxRxNxR)
150  IF D(N)> L GOTO 600
160  IF D(N+1)=0 GOTO 90
170  GOTO 110
200  If D(N+1)> L GOTO 300
210  Y=P(N)x0.5x(D(N)−D(N−1))/D(N)
220  P(N)=P(N)−Y
230  P(N+1)=P(N+1)+Y
240  GOTO 110
300  P(N)=P(N)/2
305  X=P((N))
310  Z=N
320  N=N+1
330  If P(N)> 0 GOTO320
340  P(N)=X
350  N=Z
360  GOTO110
400  N=N+1
410  If P(N)=0 GOTO450
420  GOTO 400
450  Print "N"N−1;
460  N=0
470  GOTO 110
600  D(N+1)=P(N+1)/(Sx(N+1)xRx(N+1)xR−SxNxRxNxR)
610  D(N+2)=P(N+2)/(Sx(N+2)xRx(N+2)xR−Sx(N+1)xRx(N+1)xR)
620  If D(N+1)< F GOTO 210
630  If D(N+2)<F GOTO 200
640  Print "FISSION" C;N;
1000 END
```

10

Bantu Expansion into East Africa: Linguistic Evidence

DEREK NURSE

1. Introduction

OF THE MAIN TOOLS available to the historian for the reconstruction of history in East Africa, one, archaeology, is discussed in the parallel study by Soper (chap. 11, below), and one, oral tradition, does not reach back far enough into the past to deal accurately with the events in which we are interested. These events took place, as far as we know, between 2,500 and 2,000 years ago, with lesser movements of people continuing up to perhaps 500 years ago. Comparative linguistics can tell us something of events at that range.

It is not my purpose to examine who was already present in East Africa when the first Bantu speakers arrived, or to suggest patterns of contact. Nor do I propose to examine through vocabulary the culture of the first Bantu migrants.

The purpose of this study is to suggest the relationships among the present-day Bantu languages of East Africa. From these patterns of relationship certain historical interpretations can be made. If the interpretations are put together with evidence from archaeology, we may be able to arrive at an outline of Bantu expansion into East Africa.

2. Types of Linguistic Evidence

Two main types of linguistic evidence are used here: lexicostatistics and phonology.

2a. Lexicostatistics

As languages pass through time, some communities split up while others come together. Individuals and groups move out of their original language community and join others. Communities are constantly in contact in a variety of ways. Many individuals are multilingual under these circumstances. This type of situation has obtained in East Africa for at least the last 2,000 or 3,000 years.

Languages can change considerably over so long a time span. The more obvious synchronic side of this change is that languages adopt new words; the less obvious converse, but the one in which we are equally interested, is that many words are lost. Loss of words happens all the time in all languages. While the processes by which, and the various circumstances under which, these vocabulary changes take place are well worth considering, I am here primarily concerned with the statistical end results.

Let us suppose a language community splits into three, B, C, D, which either may still be adjacent or may be physically separate. At this early point in time the linguistic differences among the three are negligible, but as time passes slight differences start to develop, for a variety of reasons. The speakers of B, C, and D may wish to stress their new differentness, their allegiance to their own group, and one way of doing so is by exaggerating and emphasizing small differences in pronunciation, or by deliberately preferring certain lexical items over others. At the same time social, economic, political, or ideological differences among the three may lead to certain vocabulary items being more in use in one community than in the others, with new words being coined, or new meanings given to old words, or old words falling into disuse. Present-day Tanzanian and Kenyan usage of Swahili provides a good example of such changes. The process is strengthened by the differing contacts that the three communities make with outside societies and cultures. Each community may absorb different loanwords from outside.

If at this early stage we extract word lists for a fixed number of "basic" meanings from the vocabularies of B, C, and D, we find some differences in vocabulary and pronunciation, but they are still few in number. The differences may be compared with those among British and American and Australian English, which have taken but a few centuries to develop. At this point we may use the term "dialect" for the relationship among B, C, and D. The terms "dialect" and "language," which are hard to define in a strict linguistic sense, are therefore largely useless in East Africa today. They are used here because they are useful labels.[1]

[1]Vocabulary may be divided into basic and cultural words. The former refer to natural phenomena, basic objects, and activities, etc.; the latter, to things and activities having to do with culture in a broad sense. The latter are comparatively easily borrowed between languages, whereas the former pass less easily and are more "stable."

If we were to return to B, C, and D after the passage of one or two millennia we would find a radically altered situation (compare Old and modern English). Speakers of B, C, and D, most likely no longer able to understand one another, must consciously learn the languages of the others. The languages have diverged on many levels, phonological, morphological, syntactic, and of course lexical. If we reapplied our word list, we would find that the percentage of common vocabulary has dropped appreciably, to 70 or 50 percent; there are Bantu languages in East and southern Africa which have been separated for so long, and have been subject to such widely different experiences, that their percentage of cognate[2] vocabulary is even lower.

In practice, therefore, comparison of the vocabulary of any two languages or dialects by use of a standard word list would produce a percentage of similarity between zero and 100. If genetically unrelated languages—say Swahili and Maasai or Somali and Chinese—are compared, the percentage would theoretically be zero, but if members of the same language family are used—Swahili and Herero or French and Polish—we would find a middling figure. The exact point on the scale depends on how long ago the compared languages parted from their ancestral community (and on subsequent events). If the split is recent, the percentage of common vocabulary should be relatively high, whereas if the two or more languages diverged long ago their lexical similarity will be lower.

2b. Phonology

Consider the British and American pronunciations of *water*. Everyone who has heard them knows that the British version has a *t*-sound in the middle, whereas the American one has a *d*-like element. On reflection, many more examples of the same phenomenon can be adduced, as in the words *lighter, hitting, waited, hotter*, and so on.

Two principles are involved. First, such divergencies in pronunciation develop over time and in all languages. Not easy to perceive over a short period of time, they become much more audible after centuries, as, for example, the three centuries or so that separate British from American English. Second, the changes are regular and statable. That is, they do

---

[2]In linguistics two or more words are said to be cognate if it can be shown that they are derived by direct oral transmission from a single item in a hypothetical ancestral language. Thus English *finger* and German *finger* are cognate, as are Swahili *mtu* and Gikuyu *mundu*. Less obvious are the cognates English *head*, German *Haupt*, and Latin *caput*, and Swahili *tapika* and Pokomo *hapfika* ("to vomit").

not occur in a haphazard way, in isolated words, or in nouns and not verbs, or vice versa, but throughout the whole vocabulary of a language. They occur in describable positions within words: for instance, the change above could be stated as "Original *t* changes to *d* between vowels." A change is assumed to start normally in the speech of one or a few individuals and then spread (or not spread) throughout a community.

Similar regular sound changes and correspondences occur between all related languages, for example:

English	*German*
b*o*ne	b*ei*n
h*o*me	h*ei*m
h*o*t	h*ei*ss
p*o*le	pf*ei*l
gh*o*st	g*ei*st

Standard Swahili	*Lower Pokomo*
m*t*i	mu*h*i
wa*t*a*t*u	a*h*a*h*u
ku*t*apika	ku*h*apfika
m*t*o*t*o	mu*h*o*h*o

Given that such changes arise in a frequent and regular way which is amenable to systemization, we can use them to draw certain conclusions about the historical relatedness of languages and also, to a lesser extent, about outside influences on languages.

Consider again languages B, C, and D. If we find that in many cognate words, where B and C have the same sound /x/, language D has a different sound /y/, we tend to assume that D has innovated /y/ rather than that B and C innovated /x/, on the principle that it is simpler to assume the majority retention of the older sound, with a minority innovating, rather than vice versa. We may further assume that the ancestral language A, from which B, C, and D are descended, also had the (original, majority) sound /x/ rather than /y/. There are exceptions to this principle, but it holds true in most instances. If we then find that B and C have common innovations different from D's, the case for thinking that B and C developed together for some time before splitting up, while D had gone its own way earlier, is strengthened. We may represent this situation as in the first of the two accompanying diagrams. If we add another offspring E

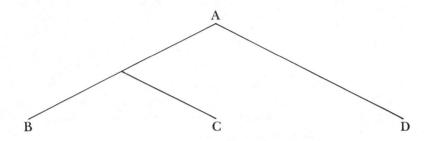

which shows the same changes as D, we may represent the similarity of B to C and of D to E as in the second diagram. This reconstruction implies

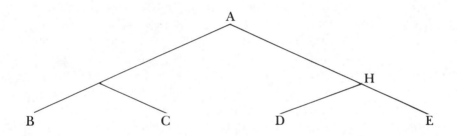

that the changes particular to D and E developed during their common period separate from B/C (the line A to H), and that the changes were then carried into D and E after they diverged from each other.

Another hypotheses is possible: only D (or E) developed the sound changes, but then it influenced E (or D) to such an extent that the changes also appeared in the latter. Although this case is less frequent than the cases of similarity through inheritance, it nevertheless occurs often enough for linguists to have to bear it in mind when considering phonological similarities.

This kind of innovation in sounds thus provides a further basis for subclassifying language families into groups. If two or more languages show identical or similar innovations in sound, the major hypothesis is that they form a related subgroup having a shared period of historical development. A minor hypothesis is that they are not members of the same subgroup but have been contiguous long enough for one to have influenced the other. Such evidence may be used together with the vocabulary similarities in order to subclassify language families—to isolate subgroups of related languages and therefore to posit a period of common historical development. Phonology has been used in this manner in the past decade for East African Bantu languages by several historical linguists, notably T. J. Hinnebusch, whose work is cited later.

2c. Loanwords

Besides lexicostatistics and sound change, a third method used by linguists to uncover the past is the analysis of loanwords. A loanword is a word taken from a source language into one or more other languages and thereafter used regularly in the latter. The material in the preceding two sections aims at providing a basis for classification of languages and therefore for statements about historical relatedness and development. Loanwords have also been used for this purpose (e.g., see Ehret 1973). The method is to plot the distribution of loanwords on a map, assuming that the recipient languages must have had a period of common development during which they absorbed the words.

More commonly, however, loanwords are used for learning something about the interaction of languages, either Bantu and Bantu, or Bantu and non-Bantu. If we trace the occurrence of certain words in the Bantu languages of East Africa, we find that some are widespread whereas others are limited in their geographical distribution. If we then concentrate on the words of limited Bantu distribution and examine neighboring non-Bantu languages, we find some of the same items occurring with the same or similar meaning and form. If they occur widely in the non-Bantu languages we may assume them to have been inherited by those languages and "borrowed" into the Bantu languages. This conclusion presupposes contact historically among at least some members of the two (or more) language families. If we look further at the exact distribution of the items and at the cultural areas in which they occur, we can draw conclusions about the type of contact that took place. Examples of such words are Swahili *baridi* "cold," *farasi* "horse," *fedha* "money," all the result of known contact with Arabic; *pesa* "money" from contact with Hindi; *meza* "table" from known contact with Portuguese; *mtasa* "barren," *kobe* "tortoise," *ndama* "calf," all from some South Cushitic language(s); *mori* "heifer" indirectly from Nilotic; and North Swahili *kugura* "move house" from Somali. These all attest some form of historical contact between speakers of Swahili and the other language communities. Although central to historical work, loanwords are not further considered here because they relate less to the actual movement of Bantu-speaking peoples into East Africa and more to the people they encountered when moving.

3. The Current Research

3a. Results

The classification here is based on lexicostatistical work, using a 400-word list of core vocabulary, with support from comparative phonology. It is not proposed to discuss the method since it is technical and is dealt with elsewhere. Discussions in varying degrees of detail of the lexicostatistical approach used may be found in Bender (1971), Henrici (1973), and Nurse and Philippson (1980). The phonology is treated in Hinnebusch (1973, 1976*b*), Nurse (1979*a*), Nurse and Philippson (1980), and Hinnebusch, Nurse, and Mould (forthcoming).

Nurse and Philippson (1980) deal lexicostatistically with the languages of Kenya, Uganda, and north and central Tanzania. The present statement goes further in that (*a*) it also covers the rest of Tanzania (and part of northeast Zambia) and (*b*) it includes more phonological considerations. It also differs in some details from Nurse and Philippson and, where it differs, should be considered a further step. It is by no means the ultimate statement, as much more work has still to be done.

The languages of the area under consideration fall into certain immediate and obvious subgroups, as follows. Guthrie's (1967–1972) numbers follow our names, and languages in brackets are related, but less closely than the other members. (For Guthrie's classification, see 6*a* below.)

Central Kenya [E50]:	(Thagicu): Gikuyu, Embu, Meru, Tharaka, Kamba, [Daiso]. A homogeneous group.
Chaga-Taita [E60, E74a,b]:	West Kilimanjaro, Central Kilimanjaro, Rombo, Gweno, [Daβida], [Saghala]. Chaga is less homogeneous than Central Kenya, although the Chaga varieties are normally referred to as dialects, whereas the Central varieties are usually labeled languages. Daβida, separate from Chaga for at least 1,000 years, and Saghala, for even longer, are therefore the outside members of the group (Ehret and Nurse, in press).
West Tanzania [F]:	[Bonde, Tongwe], Sumbwa, Sukuma, Nyamwezi, Nyaturu, Nilyamba,

	Kimbu, [Langi, Mbugwe]. A slightly less homogeneous group than Chaga, with Langi/Mbugwe peripheral.
Pare [G20, 21]:	Asu, Taveta. Asu (Pare) and Taveta are closely related dialects of one language.
Sabaki [G40, E71–73]:	Swahili, Pokomo, Mijikenda. A group intermediate in homogeneity between Central Kenya and Chaga groups.
Seuta [G20, G30]:	Shambala, Bondei, Zigula, Ngulu. Homogeneous group.
Ruvu [G30]:	Doe, Kwele, Zalamo, Kami, Kutu, Sagala, Lugulu, Kagulu, Gogo. Not so homogeneous as Seuta; Gogo appears peripheral because of intensive Njombe influence.
Njombe [G60, N11]:	(Southern Highlands): Bena, Hehe, Pangwa, Kinga, Wanji, Kisi, Sangu, Manda. Similar in homogeneity to Chaga and West Tanzania (less Langi-Mbugwe).
Corridor [M10, M20]:	Pimbwe, Rungwa, Fipa, Rungu, Mambwe, Wanda, Namwanga, Nyiha, Malila, Safwa, [Iwa, Tambo in Zambia], Bungu.
Nyakyusa [M30]:	Nyakyusa, Ndali. Ndali, not mentioned by Guthrie, is very similar to Nyakyusa.
Kilombero [G50 + Mbunga]:	Pogolu, Ndamba, Mbunga. Less homogeneous than core West Tanzania; much outside influence on this group from neighboring Bantu languages.
Tanzanian Ngoni [N10]:	Ngoni, Matengo, Mpoto (and others such as Ndendeule, etc.).
Rufiji [P10]:	Ndengeleko, Ruihi, Matumbi, Ngindo.
Ruvuma [P20]:	Yao, Mwera 1, Makonde, Maβiha.

Luyia [E30, E41]:	All Uganda and Kenya dialects, including Gisu and Logooli. Homogeneity similar to that of West Tanzania.
East Nyanza [E40]:	[Gusii], Kuria, Nguruimi, Zanaki, Shashi, Ikizu, Nata, and others. A compact group, but Gusii is peripheral.
Suguti [E20]:	Jita, Kwaya, Ruri, Regi. Very homogeneous small group.
Kitara [E10, E20]:	Nyore, Tooro, Nyankore, Chiga, Nyambo, Zinza, Haya, Kerewe. Ladefoged et al. (1971) indicate that Sese, Nabuddu, Kooki, and Naziba also belong here. Slightly less homogeneous than Central Kenya.
North Nyanza [E10]:	Ganda, Soga, Gwere. Ladefoged et al. (1971) add Lamogi, Siki, Diope, Vuma, Kenyi. Internal homogeneity similar to that of Kitara.
Western Highlands [D60]:	Rwanda, Rundi, Hangaza, Shubi, Ha, Vinza, [Fuliro?]. Very homogeneous large group.
Konjo [D40]:	Konjo, Nande, and others. A homogeneous group (?).

For modern locations of these groups see map 14.

These smaller subgroups can then be arranged into the following broader groups at a deeper level of relationship:

1. Central Kenya.
2. Chaga-Taita (possibly subsumable under 6, following, although Ehret, unpublished *a*, groups it instead with 1 preceding).
3. West Tanzania—Langi.
4. Lacustrine (Luyia, East Nyanza, Suguti, Kitara, North Nyanza, Western Highlands, Konjo). Of the subgroups, the one that is most obviously different today, lexicostatistically and phonologically, is Luyia, but the difference can be attributed to interaction with non-Bantu groups, especially Southern Cushites and South-

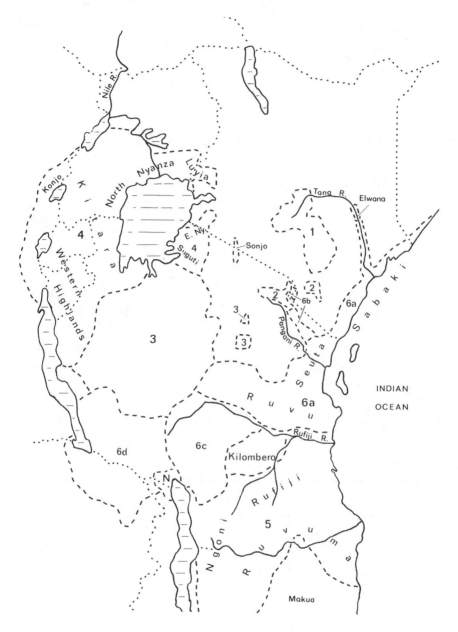

Map 14. Modern national boundaries are shown by dotted lines. Heavier dash lines mark the approximate boundaries of Bantu subgroups, while numbers corresponding to those used in the text identify the six broad groups: 1. Central Kenya; 2. Chaga-Taita; 3. Western Tanzania; 4. Lacustrine; 5. Southern Tanzania; 6. Tanzania-Coastal. Abbreviations: E. Ny., East Nyanza, and N, Nyakyusa.

ern Nilotes (see Ehret 1971, 1976). East Nyanza also scores relatively low with the rest.

5. Southern Tanzania (Tanzanian Ngoni, Rufiji, Ruvuma).
6. Tanzania-Coastal. It seems likely that the remaining subgroups may all be placed together in one large group that would be subdivided thus:
    a. Northeast Coastal Bantu (Sabaki, Seuta, Ruvu)
    b. Pare
    c. Njombe
and possibly
    d. Corridor.

This general grouping ignores certain details. It is not at present clear how exactly to incorporate into the picture Makua, Sonjo, Mwera 2 at Bwamba Bay on eastern Lake Nyasa in Tanzania, and Elwana spoken on the Tana upstream from the Pokomo. Nor is it obvious how Nyakyusa/Ndali and Kilombero are ordered relative to the other groups. It should also be remembered that we have considered only East Africa. Since groups 4, 5, and 6 abut on neighboring areas to the west and south, it is possible they form part of larger groupings, but we cannot presently substantiate this supposition.

It would be helpful if we could further subgroup these six macro-groups so that some would be more closely related to each other than to others. We would then have a simpler historical picture. At present, since it is not obvious how to subgroup them, they are left coordinate.

Finally there is a correlation between the relative homogeneity of a group and time and/or space and/or contact with outsiders. That is, the fact that a group is homogeneous implies that its members derived relatively recently from its historical protocommunity. Conversely, lack of homogeneity implies a split of the protogroup at an earlier period. The speed at which the members of a single group diverge may be accelerated by increasing the physical distance between the members. Surface divergence would be further accelerated if some members were heavily influenced linguistically by neighboring language groups.

3*b*. Interpretations

From the preceding we see at first a large number of relatively discrete language communities. These can be reduced to a smaller number, at which point it becomes difficult to see how exactly to order the members of this smaller number relative to one another. Put in such general terms, this is the kind of picture suggested by other linguists who have considered the situation. Guthrie presents sixteen coordinate zones for the whole Bantu area, which are seen as basically divided into a Western and an Eastern area. Heine typifies the views of a decade of reflection on Guthrie by suggesting that the Western area comprises only a relatively few languages in the northwest of the Bantu-speaking area, while seeing most of the rest of south-central and East Africa as consisting of a large number (26) of coordinate subgroups.

For East Africa, the classification given in section 3a above presents a smaller number of coordinate subgroups than other linguists have done so far, but it does not yet suggest the exact relationship among them. This failing partly reflects the need for further research in Mozambique, Zambia, Zaire, and southern Africa; it partly points to the difficulty encountered by historical linguists at this level of delicacy: Which iso-glosses are most significant? But it also partly corroborates the findings of other linguists that coordination rather than subordination is a prevailing feature of the Bantu linguistic stage in East, central, and southern Africa.

Assuming the six (or five if Chaga-Taita is subsumed into the last group) groups to be valid, we see from a glance at map 14 certain patterns.

Around Lake Victoria and into Rwanda and Burundi, there is one group of language communities. A group of closely linked languages presupposes a single historical ancestral community. Where did this community enter East Africa? It is not likely to have come down from the north. Since it is established that the original Bantu community inhabited the far northwest of the Bantu-speaking area, it is simpler to assume direct entry into East Africa from the west rather than from the south or the east.

A second large group stretches from the Somali coast along eastern Kenya, into eastern Tanzania, diagonally across Tanzania to the south-west; how much farther it goes, we cannot say at present. The members of its ancestral community can hardly have entered from the east or the north. One explanation would be entry into East Africa via the corridor between Lakes Nyasa and Tanganyika and a gradual spread northeast (as Ehret 1973). Another possible scenario would be an original entry from a point somewhere in northwest Tanzania, then a spread east or southeast to central or northeast Tanzania/southeast Kenya, at which point the group would divide, one section going north, the other going southeast (see Phillipson 1977b, d).

When we have established the larger picture with the two groups just treated we are left with a number of standouts: the West Tanzania,

Central Kenya, and Southern Tanzania groups. In the present state of our knowledge, it is premature to speculate on the affiliations of these groups. Linguistically we need more data from Zaire and Mozambique, while southern Tanzania and the region where West Tanzania languages are spoken are obvious areas for archaeological research.

Ultimately even the six (or five) communities we are discussing must have derived from a single still earlier community. Where did the break-up of this earlier society occur? Alternatively, did the ancestors in language of the present Bantu of East Africa enter as one group and then split up, or did they immigrate as small separate groups from a dispersal point farther west? The answers to this question have been various. Oliver (1966), following Guthrie (1962), saw three principal stages of migration from a point in Zaire. Phillipson (1977b) saw an initial movement into the lakes area, with two subsequent principal spreads, one to the east and another south/southwest. Ehret (1973) saw several successive extensions of Bantu population outward from an area just north or northwest of Lake Tanganyika.

Since our evidence for the area to the west of Uganda/Kenya/Tanzania is not complete, any linguistically based answer has to be tentative. However, three of our groups along with the large Tanzania-Coastal group are open to the west. Further, the present linguistic evidence indicates no way of linking them other than ultimately at the Eastern Bantu (Heine's Osthochland) level. These factors indicate support for the hypothesis of multiple rather than single entry. Multiple entry may imply either broadly contemporaneous movements or different times of movement.

4. Other Studies

Previous work may be divided into two types—linguistic (4a) and primarily historical (4b)—although the line between the two is not absolute.

4a. Linguistic Studies

Recent and relevant studies whose brunt is classificatory are those of Ehret (1973, 1974a), Guthrie (1967–1972), Heine (1973, 1974), Henrici (1973), Hinnebusch (1973, 1976a, b), Nurse (1979a), Nurse and Philippson (1980), and Hinnebusch, Nurse, and Mould (forthcoming). Henrici uses lexicostatistics on Guthrie's twenty-eight test languages which are scattered over the whole Bantu area. Since he mentions therefore only

Gikuyu, Kamba, and Swahili in East Africa, we cannot usefully consider his work here.

Heine also covers the whole Bantu area by lexicostatistics. He divides it into eleven coordinate branches, ten of which are in the northwest of the area, mainly in Guthrie's Zone A, with a few from Zones B, C, and D. The eleventh is itself subdivided into nine coordinate subbranches, seven of which are mainly in Guthrie's Zone C, with a few from Zones B, H, K, and L. The eighth is his Western Highlands group, from Guthrie's Zones R and H. The ninth, his Eastern Highlands group containing the rest of Guthrie's zones and groups, is subdivided into twenty-six coordinate divisions, reproduced below. (See Ehret, chap. 4, above, for historical interpretation of Heine). Like Henrici, Heine takes selected, rather than all, languages, and therefore his work is not necessarily comparable to our results, at least for East Africa. Since much material is missing for East Africa, we cannot fully consider the smaller details of the migrations discussed here.

Heine's (1973) Osthochland subbranch of Bantu is divided into the following groups:

1. Lega (D20) (Zaire)
2. Ena (D10) (Zaire)
3. Bemba-Luba (K40, L20−40/M40−60, N40) (Zambia, Zaire)
4. Yeye (R40) (Botswana)
5. Luyana
6. Lacustrine (D40, D60, E10−40) (Rwanda, Burundi, Uganda, Tanzania, Kenya, Zaire)
7. Takama (F10−30)
8. Central Kenya (E50)
9. Chaga (E60)
10. Taita (E74)
11. Taveta (G21)
12. Northeast Coast (Sabaki, Seuta, East Ruvu) (E71−73, G20−40)
13. Langi (F33)
14. Gogo, Njombe (G10, G60)
15. Pogolu (G51)
16. Matumbi (P13)
17. Makonde-Yao (P20)

18. Makua (P31)
19. Corridor (M10−30) (Tanzania, Zambia)
20. (Tanzania, Zambia, Malawi) N10−40
21−26. Southern Africa

Guthrie divided the Bantu area into fifteen zones, numbered A−S, plus a peripheral zone in Nigeria. Neither his methods (typological, geographical) nor his aims (taxonomic) are those of this study.[3] The eastern region, including zones D−G, M, N, P, and S, may be summarized thus:

D30 Western Highlands (Rwanda, Rundi, Fuliro, Shubi, Hangaza, Ha, Vinza)

E10 North Nyanza, Kitara (Nyoro, Tooro, Nyankore, Chiga, Ganda Soga, Gwere, Nyala)

E20 Kitara, Suguti (Nyambo, Haya, Zinza, Kerewe, Jita, Kwaya)

E30 Luyia (Gisu, Kisu, Bukusu, Luyia)

E40 Luyia, East Nyanza (Logooli, Gusii, Kuria, Zanaki, Nata, Sonjo)

E50 Central Kenya (Gikuyu, Embu, Meru, Tharaka, Kamba, Daiso)

E60 Chaga (Chaga, Gweno)

E70 Pokomo, Mijikenda, "Taita"

F10 Tongwe, Bende

F20 Nyamwezi, Sumbwa, Kimbu, Bungu

F30 Nilyamba, Nyaturu, Langi, Mbugwe

G10 West Ruvu (Gogo, Kagulu)

G20 Pare-Seuta (Taveta, Asu, Shambala, Bondei)

G30 Seuta, Ruvu (Zigula, Ngulu, Zalamo, Kwele, Lugulu, Kami, Kutu, Vidunda)

G40 Swahili

G50 Kilombero (Pogolu, Ndamba)

G60 Njombe (Sangu, Hehe, Bena, Wanji, Kisi, Pangwa, Kinga)

M10 Corridor-Fipa (Pimbwe, Rungwa, Fipa, Rungu, Mambwe)

M20 Corridor-Nyiha (Wanda, Namwanga, Nyiha, Malila, Safwa, etc.)

---

[3]Guthrie proposed that all the Bantu languages could be divided into two, Western and Eastern. This division is not widely accepted today.

    M30 Nyakyusa
    N10 Tanzanian Ngoni (Manda, Ngoni, Matengo, Mpoto)
    N20 Rufiji (Ndengeleko, Rufiji, Matumbi, Ngindo, Mbunga)
    P20 Yao, Mwera, Makonde, Ndonde, Maβiha

At the microlevel these subgroups correspond more or less accurately to
ours. At the macrolevel Guthrie's zones do not fit well with our higher-
level groups. Based as they are on a number of shared features, his zones
have been widely criticized in the past decade and are not accepted by
many today (for discussion see Nurse 1979a: chap. 2; Flight 1980).

Hinnebusch's writing before 1979 deals mainly with the Northeast
Coast, and his conclusions may be represented by the accompanying
diagram. This representation is explicitly genetic and is based on use of a
100-word list and on comparative phonology. It corresponds very closely
to the results of this study, except for the position of Saghala.

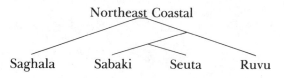

In Hinnebusch, Nurse, and Mould (forthcoming), Hinnebusch combines phonological with lexicostatistical and other considerations. He
posits a number of coordinate groups similar to those given at the end of
section 3a, but he is unwilling to commit himself to any higher-level
ordering at present. The present study takes Hinnebusch's findings into
account.

Ehret has subdivided East, central, and southern African Bantu
languages on the basis of older loanwords from non-Bantu languages.
Although this method of classification is not a conventional one, it leads to
results not dissimilar in certain ways to those of the present survey. Ehret
(1973) looks at the interaction of early Bantu immigrants with speakers of
Central Sudanic languages who are assumed to have spread south into
East and central Africa. He comes to the conclusion that a protocommunity which later gave rise to most of the Bantu languages of East Africa
was established just northwest of Lake Tanganyika around 600−400 B.C.
It split into three, with one branch later subdividing again into two. The
four resulting large groups (which, of course, later split up further) he
calls Lega-Guha, Lacustrine, Pela, and Pembele. Ignoring Lega-Guha

(eastern Zaire), we find the next two corresponding roughly to our Lacustrine and Tanzania-Coastal/Chaga-Taita/Central Kenya/Southern Tanzania groups. Without further data, it is difficult to comment on the southern Africa situation (Pembele). Thus, at this macrolevel, Ehret's groups fit roughly with our groups.

At the microlevel the two views differ. Extrapolating from Ehret (1974*b*:18), in which he looks at Southern Cushitic loanwords in Bantu, we find a number of microgroups that arose after the breakup of the four larger groups just outlined. The microgroups are not spelled out in detail and they tend partly to cut across our subgroups. It seems likely that they may be taken to refer to events that occurred after the breakup of the early community north or northwest of Lake Tanganyika—interactions between migrating Bantu speakers and already established Southern Cushitic groups.

4*b*. Historical Studies

There is such abundance and variety of historical work on this subject that we can comment on only a selection of major proposals: Oliver (1966, based on Guthrie's linguistic work), Soper (1967*b*, 1971*b*), Schmidt (1978), and Phillipson (1977*b*).

The best synopsis of the information available up to the mid-sixties is the article by Oliver, who used both linguistic and archaeological data in an attempt to reconcile the views of Greenberg and Guthrie. He posits a four-stage Bantu expansion of which only the last three stages concern East Africa. Stage 2 is an expansion from a Katanga nuclear area at the beginning of the Christian era, west from Zaire to the Atlantic and eastward to the Indian Ocean at approximately the Ruvuma River. Stage 3, belonging in the second half of the first millennium A.D., was an interlacustrine spread into western Tanzania and Uganda, with a further thin strip of settlement along the Indian Ocean coast. The fourth and final stage took place in the second millennium A.D. and filled the rest of Kenya, Tanzania, and southern Africa.

There are certain objections to this picture. Stage 2, and therefore stages 3 and 4, are based on the notion of a Bantu nuclear area in Zaire. This notion in turn is based on the alleged fact that languages in that area retained a higher proportion of proto-Bantu lexis than all the other languages outside that particular area. That, it seems to me, is like saying, to paraphrase Greenberg, that the center of the Germanic area must have been Iceland because modern Icelandic retains more archaic Germanic vocabulary than other modern Germanic languages. The notion that Zaire is the place whence expansion started must be rejected if it is based only on that kind of linguistic evidence.

Posnansky (1968*b*) opines that the date then set for Bantu genesis—some 2,000 years ago—is too late; he sees a longer time span as necessary. His view is borne out by later studies of specific areas. Soper (1967*a, b*), Odner (1971*a, b*), and also Nurse (1979*a*) indicate that Bantu speakers had probably reached Kilimanjaro, the Pare Mountains, the Usambaras, and the east coast by the early centuries of the Christian era. The work of Schmidt makes it probable that Bantu speakers were already southwest of Lake Victoria even earlier, in the fifth century B.C. If it is correct to ascribe these remains to Bantu-speaking communities, then the original dispersal must precede them and be placed at least as early as the first half of the last millennium B.C.

A third question relates to the nature and the date of Guthrie/ Oliver's stage 3 and particularly to the narrow coastal strip. A date in the second half of the first millennium for the coast settlement of Bantu is too late in the light of the information in the preceding paragraph. Further, since it is likely that the Swahili dialects were in situ at least as early as the end of the first millennium A.D., it would require a period of several centuries for these dialects to have diverged from a single community and again for that community to have diverged from Swahili's neighbors, Pokomo and the Miji-Kenda. An early or mid- first millennium A.D. date for proto-Sabaki speakers on the coast is plausible.

Stage 3 extends Bantu speakers to the Indian Ocean at a point at, or south of, the Ruvuma River. Presumably this narrow strip represents Sabaki speakers. Sabaki languages are now spoken along the Somali, Kenyan, and north and central Tanzanian coasts. There are only minor Swahili dialects as far south as Mozambique. Sabaki languages are part of the Northeast Coast group, which stretches from central Tanzania to northeast Kenya. Hence a much more likely point to strike the Indian Ocean coast would be northern Tanzania or southern Kenya. Oliver is not explicit as to whether the narrow coastal strip is a northern expansion of the stage 2 Indian Ocean area or a leap across from the lacustrine region.

The work of Soper and others, in the late 1960s and early 1970s in northeast Tanzania and southeast Kenya, shows a series of dates for Kwale and Maore wares and related types during virtually the entire first millennium A.D. in the Usambaras, the coastal hinterland, the Taita Hills (no dates), the Pare Mountains, and Kilimanjaro. They assume that these dates can be related to Bantu-speaking groups; hence the latter had reached the whole area early in the first millennium A.D.

Schmidt's work in Buhaya, along southwestern Lake Victoria, reveals Urewe Ware and ironworking in that area as early as the fifth century B.C., based on carbon-14 dating. Other finds in Rwanda point to a date B.C. (Sutton 1972). Schmidt is very cautious about ascribing these finds to any language community: "It is clear that archaeological phenomena cannot be tied to generalized linguistic phenomena" (1978:293). Despite this caveat, most observers feel that the Buhaya collection was the work of some group of Bantu speakers. Given these dates south and west of Lake Victoria, it is clear that Oliver's dates are too late.

The latest attempt at an integrated picture is that of Phillipson (1977*b*), who pulls together archaeological and linguistic data available up to approximatly 1976. Presenting a scenario quite different from that of Oliver, he sees expansion from the lakes region into East, central and southern Africa. His presentation has several stages, of which the relevant ones are:

Stage 3:   Bantu speakers from the Cameroons north of the forest to the interlacustrine area: Urewe Ware, Early Iron Age, 400–300 B.C.

Stage 6:   Move from the interlacustrine area to southeast Kenya and northeast Tanzania: Kwale Ware, Early Iron Age, 100–200 A.D.

Stage 7*b*:   East coast down as far as South Africa: Early Iron Age, 300–400 A.D.

Stage 10:   Spread from Shaba area to the eastern half of subcontinent, including East Africa: Later Iron Age, 1000–1100 A.D.

In other words, Phillipson sees a two-stage Bantu populating of East Africa: an older, Early Iron Age expansion from the lakes region to the east coast and then south, completed in the early centuries A.D., and a second, Later Iron Age expansion from the Shaba area north and east into East Africa. This second wave is identified as the arrival of Heine's Eastern Highlands speakers who, as we have seen, include representatives of every Bantu subgroup now present in East Africa. These two separate movements are seen to be required by the presence of two

---

¹It is not obvious why "Interlacustrine and coastal languages" should be singled out here; for lack of contrary evidence we take it that the statement also includes the large number of non-Lacustrine and noncoastal languages.

supposedly distinct pottery traditions in East Africa. There are said to be apparent survivals of "earlier linguistic forms" in interlacustrine and coastal languages, although these are not discussed, but are said to be supported by an unpublished personal communication.

Two main questions arise from this hypothesis. One concerns the "apparent survival of earlier linguistic forms in Interlacustrine and coastal languages."[4] It is disturbing to find that all the relevant linguistic evidence consists of inaccessible unspecified personal communication, especially when it relates to so important an issue. It is true that no comparative linguistic data come with dates attached. It is also true that all languages retain "some earlier forms," but these "forms" do not necessarily support or contradict the assumption of great age for any language By that argument Icelandic, because of certain archaic lexical elements, would be of greater "age" than German or Scandinavian, which it certainly is not. What presumably is meant is that some Bantu subgroups, whether of lower or higher level, are "older" there than others that arrived in the hypothetical second wave, said to have taken place only 1,000 years ago.

Which might these groups be? If we are correct in attributing the archaeological dates to the linguistic ancestors of the macrogroups in whose area the remains are found, then we have to exclude large numbers of East African subgroups from the category of later arrivals. Within the borders of the areas presently covered by speakers of Lacustrine, some Northeast Coast, and Chaga-Taita, there is archaeological evidence dating from between 2,500 and 1,800 years ago. Areas for which relatively late, or no, dates are available are those of Central Kenya and Western and Southern Tanzania groups and much of Northeast Coast, in part simply because little or no archaeological attention has yet been paid to most of those regions. At least some of these areas are peopled by groups that oral tradition or linguistic evidence indicates have migrated (Central Kenya) or expanded (Central Kenya: Sukuma, Nyamwezi) relatively recently. The immediate linguistic affiliations of the groups concerned are not clear. Thus it is possible that the language groups in those regions formed part of Phillipson's second wave—but not necessarily. The lack of clarity about the immediate linguistic affiliation of the groups concerned is probably the result of the lack of detailed work done on the affiliations. Until concrete proof is produced—and it is not clear to me that it can be produced—we must say that there is no linguistic support for the hypothesis of a second wave only 1,000 years ago.

The second question centers on the nature of the fit between the direction of expansion proposed by Phillipson based, for East Africa, on archaeological, not linguistic, data, and the suggestions of section 3*b* based on linguistic, not archaeological, information.

About the Lacustrine group there is little disagreement. Historians, ethnographers, and others have long felt that all the groups in the inter-lake area had an underlying similarity. The lexicostatistical and other linguistic information supports the idea of an underlying historical unity. The work of Schmidt and others indicates early Bantu settlement in the area during the second half of the last millennium B.C. The only question is the point from which early settlers arrived at Lake Victoria. Phillipson suggests a northerly route via Lake Albert—insupportable, as David (chap. 6, above) argues—and Oliver's suggestion of a much more south-erly route is based on discredited evidence. What seems most probable is entrance directly from the west. Juxtaposition of Schmidt's early dates for Buhaya with the lexicostatistical connection to Rwanda and Burundi suggests the possibility of a route in via Rwanda and the western Rift area.

How and when the linguistic ancestors of the Central Kenya (Thagi-cu) group arrived is not at all clear. Linguistic data suggest that this group is notably different from surrounding groups, and I find at present no unambiguous evidence that it is more closely related to Lacustrine or to Tanzania-Coastal or Chaga-Taita, or indeed that it is closely related to any of them. Phillipson talks of linguistic remnants but does not specifi-cally mention the Central Kenya group. Oral traditions relating to the past 500 years, or perhaps a little longer, are contradictory for the mem-bers of the group. The earliest published archaeological material, prob-ably of Bantu origin, is relatively late, about 1100 A.D. Beyond that we have no concrete evidence for the group at this time.

The three subgroups in the southwest and southeast of Tanzania—Guthrie's N10 (Tanzanian Ngoni), P10 (Rufiji), and P20 (Yao-Makonde)—have an uncertain allegiance. Both lexicostatistically and phonologically these subgroups fit well together (possibly also with Kilom-bero?) and are in some respects dissimilar to other groups to the north of them. Until further archaeological and linguistic work is done, they will have to remain as a separate but coordinate group.

The macrogroup that leaves the largest margin for disagreement is the Tanzania-Coastal, stretching from central and southwest Tanzania up to the coast of Somalia. One mainly linguistic difficulty is its relation-ship to Chaga-Taita, Kilombero, and the Corridor languages. At present one can consider them all as subgroups of one huge branch of East African Bantu or not, depending on what evidence one considers. They are all obviously similar in a number of ways. Until we have considered carefully data from outside East Africa, we will temporarily treat them as possible members of one large group.

Another real difficulty is the historical direction in which the Northeast-Coastal group and its affiliates moved. If we accept the correlation of Bantu speakers and certain pottery types, we are talking of Phillipson's first wave, stage 6, with later movements south and southwestward. Alternative scenarios suggest themselves if we accept a connection between the Northeast Coast languages and the groups in southwest Tanzania and the Corridor area. One would be an initial movement from the southern Lake Victoria region to central Tanzania, with the group splitting, one section, the Northeast-Coastal group proper, going east and northeast, another moving southwest. This would presuppose that the West Tanzania languages (Sukuma, Nyamwezi, etc.) moved into their present area after the group from Lake Victoria had passed through. Another possibility is an initial movement from southern Lake Victoria southward to southwest Tanzania, whence one group went northwest.

All these suggestions presuppose, in Phillipson's first wave, one original group near Lake Victoria, whence all other Bantu-speaking groups derived. There is, however, no linguistic objection to having several groups all entering East Africa between 2,500 and 2,000 years ago: Lacustrine in the immediate Lake Victoria area, Tanzania-Coastal farther south, and Central Kenya, Chaga-Taita, and Southern Tanzania at other points, as yet undetermined. The fragmented linguistic picture presented here would favor this sort of scenario.

In summary, Phillipson's hypothesis fits the linguistic data better than the proposals of the 1960s, but there are two serious doubts about it. There is no linguistic evidence for the idea of a second wave of migration approximately 1,000 years ago. And although the notion of a spread east and/or south from the Lake Victoria region, starting some two millennia ago, is not contradicted by linguistic evidence, the details of this spread are not clear, nor are they likely to be as simple as Phillipson posits.

5. Summary

5a. Linguistic Methodology

The main linguistic evidence produced in the last ten years for Bantu expansion in East Africa has been lexicostatistical (Heine 1973; Henrici 1973; Nurse and Philippson 1980). The exception is Ehret (1973), who used lexical innovation. Lexicostatistics has its strengths and weaknesses.

It will satisfactorily establish language families (Greenberg 1972), and it will fairly satisfactorily isolate microgroups (Heine 1973; Nurse and Philippson 1980).

It is time to supplement what we have with different kinds of linguistic work in order to take us further: phonology, morphology, and lexical isoglosses. As far as phonology is concerned, we know more or less what proto-Bantu looked like, and we can therefore work out for each group what innovations have occurred. This work is already well underway. Having worked out for each group the changes, we can fit them together better than they presently are. Such phonological isoglosses have been widely used in Indo-European studies, but they have not been taken far enough in Bantu work.

Work on morphology is only in its infancy. If we look carefully at the details of nominal and especially verbal systems in Bantu we see much similarity. But we also see that each group is distinguished by certain features, and that juxtaposition of these will further facilitate ordering of the groups.

5b. Linguistic Picture

It is clear that languages in the northwest of the Bantu area in the Cameroons, Gabon, Congo, and northern Zaire (Guthrie's Zones A, B, C, and parts of D) do not form a unity as opposed to the rest of the area. This lack of unity would support the widely accepted notion that an early center of dispersal was in the northwest, probably the Cameroons.

If we turn to East Africa, we are faced with a contrast between a few (two?) large groups and several smaller isolated groups. The fact that some of the latter happen to contain languages with large numbers of speakers (e.g., Gikuyu and Sukuma) is not relevant. Two of the isolates— West Tanzania and Central Kenya—are conservative, in the sense that they have not undergone, or are only starting to undergo, the sound shifts that must have occurred in most other East African languages a millennium or longer ago. This clearly suggests that the linguistic ancestors of these two groups have been linguistically long separated from other East African groups, and it might therefore point to a separate immigration pattern.

The other group distinguished, the Southern Tanzania, shows the opposite kind of development, in that it has taken further the phonological developments marking most other East and southern African languages. Since it must have undergone these common developments historically, it can therefore be seen as a subgroup related to some neighboring group (s?).

5c. Historical Conclusions

The linguistic evidence does not contradict the notion of an initial entry into East Africa of Bantu from west of Lakes Tanganyika and Victoria. The Central Kenya and West Tanzania groups are isolates, and they are also conservative in having each retained certain features that recur in some of the more distantly related languages to the west and north of the forest zone. Their distinctiveness suggests that migration was not a simple movement to the lacustrine region, with two subsequent streams going east and south as Phillipson suggests. The differentness of these two groups from each other and from the Lacustrine, Tanzania-Coastal, and Southern Tanzania groups indicates that several separate communities, as many as five or six, may have emerged into East Africa west of Lake Victoria and then made their way farther east or south. The large Lacustrine division, with its various subgroups, would be the linguistic descendants of the immigrants who moved at first into areas immediately west of Lake Victoria. In the Tanzania-Coastal group, the major split is between the Northeast-Coastal languages coming down as far as Gogo near Dodoma and the languages to the southwest of there. The most economical linguistic statement would be to posit a movement from the lake area, probably south along the east side of Lake Tanganyika to the Rukwa region, and then a split, with the ancestral speakers of Northeast-Coastal going along the Ruaha and Ruvu valleys northeast across Tanzania and the ancestors of the Njombe group spreading a little to the east and those of the Corridor group a little to the south. Others of the early Bantu settlement communities could have passed through the areas in between, more immediately to the south of Lake Victoria.

Finally, there is no obvious linguistic support for any second wave of immigration. There is no reason to think that the ancestors of Lacustrine speakers did not arrive in the Lake Victoria region 2,500—2,000 years ago, and those of the Tanzania-Coastal speakers in their possible western area of initial split just as early. Although we have no clear dates for the isolates in western Tanzania and central Kenya, no basis exists for thinking they arrived as recently as 1,000 years ago. In the light of what we know in general about the rate of linguistic change, 900—1,000 years would not result in wide linguistic differentiation. The West Tanzania group alone would require a lengthier period of internal divergence than that. All Bantu groups in East Africa could be adequately explained, however, by 2,000-plus years of divergent development.

Bantu Expansion into Eastern Africa: Archaeological Evidence

11

ROBERT SOPER

THE TITLE OF THIS paper presupposes the feasibility of correlating archaeological remains with the evidence of historical linguistics and, in particular, the correlation of the archaeological Early Iron Age Complex with early speakers of Bantu languages in eastern Africa. To make socially meaningful and useful reconstructions of prehistoric events it is necessary to establish links with present populations. Present-day communities and ethnic groups are, however, the outcome of complex historical interactions and as currently constituted cannot be traced far into the past. It is therefore better to think in terms of much broader categories, and such categories are conveniently provided by linguistic classification at various levels of subdivision, from major language families down to local groupings of closely related dialects, provided the necessary correlations can be made with a sufficient degree of confidence.

The linguistic affiliations of prehistoric and nonliterate archaeological "cultures" are never directly detectable but have to be deduced by correlations with the reconstructions of historical linguistics, involving parallels in geographical distributions, relative dating, and distinctive cultural items. Even such correlations rest on the a priori assumption that demonstrable archaeological relationships, especially in ceramics, reflect broader cultural and ethnic relationships, including language. Yet there are enough known exceptions to this general rule to enjoin us to regard ceramics, language, race, and economy as independent variables until demonstrated otherwise in individual situations. Still, these exceptions should not prevent us from suggesting provisional correlations on the basis of the evidence available, but let us not lean too heavily on them until they are shored up by sufficient accumulated circumstantial evidence. In view of these reservations, it must be stressed that in the present state of knowledge we are talking in terms more of working hypotheses than of firmly established history, and the following reconstructions must be read in this light.

The correlation of Bantu speakers with the Early Iron Age has been argued by many people, myself included, with no serious dissension, though it is now clear that most of the known distribution of the Early Iron Age can relate to only those stages of secondary Bantu expansion covering the eastern side of the subcontinent (cf. Ehret, chap. 4 above). Since my main purpose, however, is to review the archaeological evidence, I attempt in the first instance to concentrate on the Early Iron Age and to eschew any preconceptions derived from linguistics. Thereafter I turn to the problem of linguistic correlation.

Archaeology of the Early Iron Age

The Early Iron Age is here taken to mean what has been termed in full the Early Iron Age Complex of southern Africa, stretching down the eastern half of the continent from the interlacustrine area of East Africa to the Transvaal and Natal. It is represented by sites dated mainly to the first millennium A.D. and linked by more or less clear typological relationships of styles of pottery, which is either the earliest known pottery where it occurs or contrasts markedly with preexisting or contemporary ceramic industries. The complex also provides the earliest evidence for iron metallurgy over the whole area of its distribution and must on present evidence be assumed to have been responsible for its introduction. How far the archaeological relationship based on pottery reflects linguistic relationship is not of course directly deducible, and human skeletal evidence is as yet too sparse to provide detailed conclusions on race.

Degrees of relationship among the potteries of the different geographical subdivisions of the complex have been explored by Huffman (1970), Soper (1971b), and, on a more general and intuitive level, by Phillipson (e.g., 1977b). Soper (1971b) attempts the most comprehensive analysis but is now somewhat out of date, so that new evidence and more sophisticated methods of analysis would certainly refine and modify his conclusions in detail. Phillipson has attempted the most ambitious historical reconstruction but his methodology, or rather lack of it, has been criticized by Huffman (1979) and Garlake (1979).

In East Africa we are concerned with only part of the complex, and the relevant Early Iron Age regional groupings are Urewe, Lelesu, Kwale, and perhaps Kalambo and Mwabulambo. These are all relatively closely interrelated and all fall within Phillipson's "eastern stream." (He would put Kalambo in an intermediate position between eastern and western streams, but the position of Kalambo is not relevant to the present discussion, and in any event I disagree with him.)

The Urewe group (ex-Dimple Base Ware) is found in the interlacustrine region between eastern Zaire and the northeastern side of Lake Victoria, northward to at least the Victoria Nile in the Murchison Falls area (Chobi). Uvinza in western Tanzania (Sutton and Roberts 1968) probably belongs to it or shows some transition to Kalambo, but the assemblage is very small. Van Noten (1979) has recently suggested that Urewe pottery is not sufficiently homogeneous over its full geographical range to be regarded as a single ware; certainly some regional variation is to be expected, but no comparative analysis has yet been undertaken to define it. Carbon-14 dates in the first few centuries A.D. are fairly well distributed throughout this area, but a group of much earlier dates has been obtained by Schmidt (1978) in the Buhaya area of northwestern Tanzania which, with dendrochronological calibration, would extend back to about the eighth century B.C. This dating, while it appears internally consistent, is distinctly anomalous to the chronology of the rest of the Early Iron Age Complex and difficult to reconcile with what is known of the spread of iron technology in Africa; it thus requires some comment. The dates fall into four groups:

  a) three dates of eleventh to fifteenth century b.c., one stratigraphically preceding the Early Iron Age occupation and two apparently introduced into Early Iron Age features by later disturbance at Katuruka;

  b) four dates around the fifth or sixth century b.c. on charcoal from associated features in a small area of the Katuruka site; these samples could well come from a single batch of charcoal for iron smelting which, if it came from the heartwood of a very old tree, could inflate the apparent antiquity;

  c) three dates in the first or second century a.d. from Katuruka and Makongo; and

  d) two dates in the tenth century a.d. from Makongo.

It seems wise to regard (*b*) with some caution unless and until it is supported from other sites; (*c*) is quite acceptable and provides the earliest dating for Urewe apart from (*b*); (*d*) may relate to a final Urewe phase but again requires confirmation from other sites.

Lelesu pottery comes from only a few sites in Sandaweland and the Lake Eyasi area in north-central Tanzania (Smolla 1956; Sutton 1968) and is as yet undated.

The known distribution of Kwale Ware extends from a little north of

Mombasa through the highlands of northeastern Tanzania from Kilimanjaro to the Usambaras, and at least as far south as the Ngulu Hills. To
the north typical Kwale Ware is found at Kilungu in Kambaland, Ithanga,
and the Tana Valley east of Mount Kenya, and a devolved but readily
recognizable Kwale bowl form persists as a component of Gatung'ang'a
Ware in central Kenya, around Mount Kenya, across to Nyandarua, and
south to the Nairobi area (Siiriäinen 1971). Northeastward up the coast,
some of the early pottery from Manda, dated to about the eighth century
a.d., has some affinities to Kwale but could certainly not be subsumed
within it, while the suggestion that the Early Iron Age may have got as far
as Brava in southern Somalia (Chittick 1969) rests only on one or two
sherds in a very weathered state (identified by myself) and is thus not
conclusive. Dates for Kwale sites range from the first or second century at
Kwale itself to perhaps as late as the ninth or tenth century at Usangi
Hospital in North Pare (Odner 1971c), while those for Gatung'ang'a fall
in the twelfth to fourteenth century with a further date around the
seventh century for Gatare Forest in Nyandarua.

The Kalambo group has so far been found only in northern Zambia,
but Kalambo itself is right on the border so that the group should certainly
extend into Tanzania. Dates span from the fourth to about the twelfth
century.

No Early Iron Age pottery has yet been discovered in the southern
half of Tanzania, but typological comparisons lead me to predict with
some confidence the following occurrences (fig. 9):

1. The presence of pottery closely related to Urewe Ware in western
    and southwestern Tanzania, for example, Ufipa.
2. The extension of Kwale-related wares southward to the Uluguru
    Mountains, to southeastern Tanzania, and through Mozam-
    bique, probably with a progressive loss of decorative elements
    farther south. This judgment is based on close and specific affini-
    ties among Kwale Ware, Nkope Ware around the southern end of
    Lake Nyasa (Malawi) (but cf. views of Collett, chap. 9, above), the
    ware of Matola IV near Maputo (Cruz e Silva 1980) and Silver
    Leaves in the Transvaal. I would, however, consider very tenuous
    Phillipson's suggestion (1977b:110) that the early local pottery at
    Kilwa belongs to the Early Iron Age.

It may be noted that no Early Iron Age pottery has been found in the
main Rift Valley or western highlands of Kenya or north of Lake Eyasi.

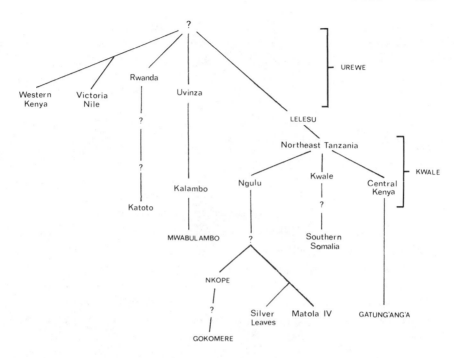

Fig. 9. Tentative tree diagram of the "eastern stream" of the Early Iron Age. The relative vertical position carries some implication of typological distance (judged by personal intuitive assessment) which may be controlled by physical difference, age difference, or other factors. The question marks for Katoto and south Somalia indicate typological distance unknown. Other queries indicate uncertainty about particular proposed points of connection (see Collett, chap. 9, above). Although, for the sake of argument and on grounds of date, Buhaya is taken as a possible starting point in map 15, it is not included here because its detailed typology is unpublished. Names of particular ceramic complexes are capitalized throughout.

The absence of sites in Tanzania is not significant, but it seems to be real in Kenya where more systematic archaeological work has been completed.

The typological relationship between assemblages of pottery from the Urewe type site in western Kenya, Sandaweland, and Mumba-Höhle at Lake Eyasi (Lelesu Ware), and Kwale were examined by Soper (1971a), who concluded that the overall relationship was very close and that Lelesu was intermediate, typologically as well as geographically, between Urewe and Kwale.

What then of the pattern of initial Early Iron Age settlement in East Africa? In considering directions of spread, negative evidence (lack of sites in a given area) is rarely significant unless sufficient archaeological research has been undertaken to show that the absence is real rather than only apparent. In East Africa, only the central Rift Valley fills this requirement and probably also the western highlands of Kenya, although I think that Sutton's (1973) work here was perhaps too problem-oriented to be conclusively negative as far as the Early Iron Age is concerned.

The earliest carbon-14 dates for the Early Iron Age (if we exclude two dates of 1100−1200 b.c. from Ngulu, not too certainly associated) are at the site of Katuruka in Buhaya, mentioned above, on the southwestern side of Lake Victoria, excavated by Schmidt (1978), who incidentally links it indirectly via oral traditions to the present people of the area. A couple of other b.c. dates have been obtained by van Noten (1979) in Rwanda from graves that on traditional grounds should be fairly recent. Other dates for Urewe sites fall in the first few centuries A.D. and are not significantly earlier than the range of Kwale dates, or indeed than other Early Iron Age dates farther south, as far as the Transvaal. Phillipson (1975) has proposed a sequential dating for the southward spread of the Early Iron Age, but again his handling of the radiocarbon determinations and his use of an intersextile method of selection have been criticized by Huffman (1979). Of course where there are only a few dated sites for each area, there is no reason that they should be the earliest sites; indeed, they are more likely to belong to the period of maximum settlement density than to the earliest phases. However, the primacy of Urewe Ware among Early Iron Age pottery was at least supported, though hardly proved, by the typological analysis in Soper (1971b). We may therefore provisionally accept Urewe as the origin of the Early Iron Age for the rest of East Africa and, for the sake of argument and with the reservations expressed above, Buhaya as the nearest thing we have to the "cradle" of Urewe.

I would not at present wish to push the question of ultimate origins beyond this point, except at the level of general affinities without implications of specific areas and routes. Contrary to Posnansky (1968b), there seems to be little close resemblance to pottery of the Nok Culture in Nigeria, though very little Nok pottery has been published and what I have seen, from Taruga, may not be very representative of the whole "culture" or its earliest phases, there being some suggestion of local or chronological variation (Fagg 1970). Also, most Nok sites seem to include important rouletted elements, both twisted and carved, which are conspicuously absent from Early Iron Age pottery. Of more direct significance is the very recent recognition, among pottery excavated by Bassey

Andah and Lawrence Walu from Tse Dura rock shelter near Katsina Ala south of the Benue in Nigeria, of a component with beveled rims (including a multiple beveled overhanging rim), fine diagonal hatching, and coarser cross-hatching, which is distinctly reminiscent of Urewe. As the pottery is unfortunately very weathered, I would not wish to make too much of it as yet; but it is certainly in the right place, and quite probably at something approaching the right time, to fit in with the linguistic proposals as to Bantu origins (see also David, chap. 6, above).

If Buhaya is taken provisionally as the starting point for the spread of the Early Iron Age Complex across the eastern part of Africa, the following pattern of spread may be postulated (map 15):

a) north and east around Lake Victoria, to the Victoria Nile at Chobi and east to the Wami Gulf and northern islands of the lake, but not, apparently, as far as Kisii and the Mount Elgon area (Bower 1973*b*) or farther north or east;

b) southward to the east of Lake Tanganyika, via Uvinza to the Kalambo group of northern Zambia and the Mwabulambo group of northern Malawi; probably some movement also west of Lake Tanganyika to account for the occurrence of related sherds at the Katoto cemetery in southeastern Zaire (Hiernaux et al. 1973);

c) eastward to Sandaweland (Lelesu variant) and thence to Kilimanjaro and the highlands of northeastern Tanzania; whence

i) southward to Ngulu (or more directly here from Lelesu) and far south to Mozambique, southern Malawi, and the Transvaal; a direct sequence of derivation for Nkope and thence to the Gokomere complex of Zimbabwe can also be tentatively postulated;

ii) northward, probably from Kilimanjaro or the Pare Mountains to Kambaland (Kilungu) and the upper Tana, with a probably later devolved form as an element of Gatung'ang'a Ware in central Kenya; and

iii) possibly northeastward from Kwale along the coastal hinterland, perhaps as far as southern Somalia.

These movements are shown schematically in map 15. I have also tried in figure 9 to express the same information in the form of a tree diagram to indicate how I see the stages and levels of relationship within this part of the Early Iron Age Complex. The scheme is put forward in the hope that it may strike some positive chord (or discord) in the linguistic evidence and help to show whether or not the present Bantu languages in the relevant areas preserve anything of the pattern of their original expansion (now assuming that the Early Iron Age peoples were the original Bantu speakers of the particular settlement areas).

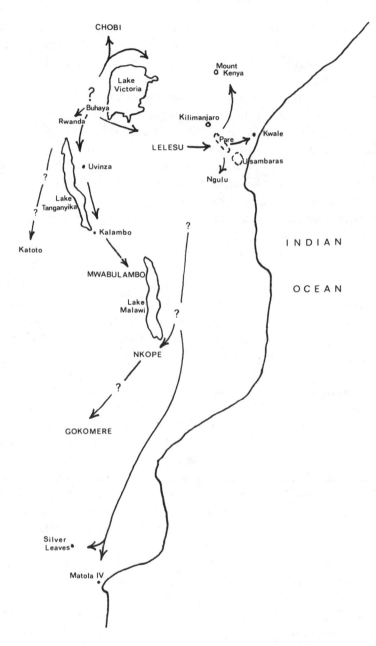

Map 15. Spread of the "eastern stream" of the Early Iron Age. Archaeo-logical sites and geographical locations are given in lowercase letters; ceramic traditions, in capital letters.

All the'se movements had probably reached the limits of their primary expansion at least by around 400 A.D., if not earlier, except perhaps for the penetration of central Kenya. There followed presumably a period of development as the Early Iron Age communities grew and interacted with preexisting populations or further arrivals, speaking related or unrelated languages. The pottery by which we recognize the Early Iron Age would have been progressively modified or superseded until at some point it would no longer be recognized as such. When this point was—that is, how long the Early Iron Age lasted—is not yet very clearly defined but would seem in most areas to have been reached around the end of the first millennium A.D., apparently later in the case of the rather restricted Kwale elements in Gatung'ang'a Ware.

Early Iron Age Linguistic Correlations

To what extent does this pattern coincide with the historical linguistic evidence?

Nurse's paper (chap. 10, above) gives us the most detailed comprehensive classification of the East African Bantu languages thus far available and attempts some historical interpretation which may now be compared with the archaeological picture. He proposes six linguistic groups: (1) Central Kenya; (2) Chaga-Taita; (3) West Tanzania; (4) Lacustrine; (5) Southern Tanzania; and (6) Tanzania-Coastal, extending across Tanzania from southwest to northeast and up the Kenya coast into Somalia. Nurse stresses the apparent coordinate nature of these groups and of Bantu subdivisions in general and the difficulties of establishing the exact relationships among them which might have elucidated the original pattern of spread. This coordinate status would seem to carry the implication that the groups are the descendants of the original Bantu inhabitants in their respective areas and also disposes Nurse to accept the possibility of a series of migrations, perhaps from the west, as the origins of the different groups, rather than a single migration with internal ramifications. One wonders, however, whether the production of coordinate groups at this level is not an artifact of the lexicostatistical method.

Ehret (1973) gives us a broader classification encompassing all the Eastern Bantu. He makes Lacustrine (partly but not completely congruent with Nurse's group 4 one branch of Eastern Bantu coordinate with a second branch, Tuli, containing Nurse's other five subgroups along with the languages of Mozambique, Malawi, Zimbabwe, and South Africa. The Bemba and Ila-Tonga groups of Zambia, formerly included by him in Tuli (Ehret 1973), are now considered to be more distantly related, probably forming (with Luba) an earlier-branching coordinate with the combined Tuli and Lacustrine group (Ehret, personal communication).

The two classifications are not fundamentally at variance. Ehret's lower-level subgrouping for East Africa in general matches Nurse's, except that it combines Nurse's groups 1 and 2 at a higher level (as Upland Bantu) and it separates the East Lake Victoria languages from the rest of Nurse's group 4. Nurse's West Tanzania group 3 is Ehret's West Pela; his group 5, Southern Tanzania, is Ehret's South Pela; and his group 6 is Ehret's Central Pela. They disagree, other than about the full composition of the Lacustrine group, only in the levels of grouping they are willing to attempt. Nurse feels that the evidence he has for East Africa does not yet justify the establishment of intermediate groups between the overall Eastern Bantu level and the six divisions he has identified. Thus he leaves the East African languages in six provisionally coordinate subgroups. Ehret, from mapping of lexical innovations coming into early Eastern Bantu from non-Bantu languages, feels able to propose some possible intermediate levels of relationship.

Whereas in both systems all the linguistic groupings concerned fall within the actual or anticipated distribution of the Early Iron Age eastern stream, the internal features or proposed directions of spread are in several areas at variance with the pattern of archaeological spread outlined above. In Nurse's case, the basic difference is the contrast of his discontinuous coordinate groups with my conception of a more or less continuous spread in which typological variation is mainly a function of distance along general lines of advance. Ehret is prepared to hypothesize a pattern of spread but here again it hardly coincides with my view of the archaeological picture.

If we examine the fit of the evidence for East Africa we see that the Urewe distribution fits quite well with Nurse's Lacustrine group. Kwale distribution covers the eastern part of Central Kenya group 1 and Chaga-Taita group 2 (linked in one Upland group by Ehret) but also a large chunk of the area presently occupied by the northeastern end of group 6, while its southward extension must at least pass through the area of Southern Tanzania group 5. Nurse's group 6 (Ehret's Central Pela) fits none of the Early Iron Age variants so far defined. In the case of Ehret, the coordinate status of Lacustrine and Tuli contradicts Urewe as a direct source of the rest of the eastern stream, while the northeastward spread of the Pela division of Tuli from the Lake Tanganyika/Nyasa corridor area cannot be accommodated by the archaeological evidence any more than Nurse's group 6 can.

In view of these discrepancies it is worth considering whether alternative interpretations of the archaeological evidence are possible which might more comfortably accommodate the linguistic scenario, given that the large gaps in this evidence and the lack of exhaustive coverage of even local areas leave us some room for maneuver.

First we may consider the possibility of the main Early Iron Age variants—Urewe, Kwale, Lelesu, and Kalambo—being coordinate, rather than partly sequential. This hypothesis is rather less economical than the one already outlined, but it does perhaps find a few suggestive hints of support which, however, can hardly be considered as hard evidence at present. [It is also supported by the discontinuous spread model of Collett, chap. 9 above.] A hypothetical common source would have to be typologically very closely related to Urewe, with some local or chronological variation to account for the antecedents of the different variants. Since there are no suggestions of a possible source for coordinate branches in the known areas, one may look elsewhere, either west of Lake Tanganyika or northwest to the northeastern corner of the Congo forests. A hint here lies in some modern pottery from the latter area discussed in Soper (1971*d*) which has Early Iron Age affinities relating as much to Kwale as to Urewe in spite of the much greater distance.

Multiple origins in the northwest would entail two or more parallel or possibly successive movements through part of the Urewe area or very near it (see Nurse, chap. 10, above). The only explicit suggestion of successive phases within Urewe which could represent such repeated movements comes from Schmidt's work in Buhaya discussed above; his radiocarbon dates could imply successive phases or be attributed to long-term occupation by a single community. Unfortunately, Schmidt does not discuss or even illustrate any of the pottery in this publication or mention any correlation of typological variation with date, so it is not possible to pursue this point further at present. [Editors' note: If, however, the widespread Urewe pottery can be separated, as van Noten (1979) thinks, into more than one regional ware, such different wares might then possibly reflect parallel movements of early Bantu communities into the larger lake region. Historically linked and roughly contemporaneous movements are linguistically much more probable than successive ones in the early Eastern Bantu case.]

At a lower level, the possibility of coordinate branches within Kwale appears unlikely on geographical and typological grounds. The central

Kenya Early Iron Age is best explained as typologically derived from northeastern Tanzania or southeastern Kenya, whereas the latter areas show no more typological variation than could be explained by local or chronological factors. The relationship of the Ngulu material to the rest of Kwale has not yet been submitted to comparative analysis.

As to more specific geographical linguistic correlation, there is as noted no evidence for any southwest/northeast continuum within the Early Iron Age corresponding to Nurse's group 6. Any direct relationship between Kalambo and Kwale at the extremes of this span must, on the basis of present data, be rejected on typological grounds. These data of course have a very large distributional gap in central and southwestern Tanzania which might allow for extension from one or both ends or for a separate Early Iron Age variant to have existed still undetected. But as yet group 6 as a whole cannot be seen to coincide with any Early Iron Age grouping. The Lelesu Early Iron Age Ware falls within or next to the present-day territory of Nurse's West Tanzania languages, but at present this territory extends much farther to the west and southwest. Whether the makers of Lelesu Ware were ancestral to the West Tanzania peoples or were a more ephemeral settlement in marginal lands remains to be seen. Thus a straight one-for-one correlation of Early Iron Age variants with modern Bantu subgroupings does not seem to be tenable, and perhaps it should never have been expected, implying as it does a sort of "columnar" development through all the vicissitudes of history for nearly 2,000 years.

The possibility of undetected levels in the linguistic data was the basis of Phillipson's attempt (1977b and elsewhere) to reconcile the archaeological evidence with Ehret's (1973) and Heine's (1973) hypotheses of Bantu expansion. He argues that the present distribution of Bantu languages is mainly the result of a secondary major Bantu spread originating in the Shaba area of southeastern Zaire, dating from around 1000 A.D. and correlated with the Later Iron Age, effectively obscuring the linguistic evidence of a primary Bantu expansion in the Early Iron Age. This hypothesis does not seem to have found favor among linguists and in my own view is not supported, at least in its full ramifications, by the archaeological evidence, though the latter is too incomplete for any firm conclusions as far as East Africa is concerned. For southern Africa Huffman (1978) has proposed a south-to-north movement bringing the Later Iron Age with Shona speakers into Zimbabwe after a transitional phase from the Early Iron Age in the Transvaal; this suggestion is, of course, completely at variance with Phillipson. Even if we reject the full scale of

Phillipson's ideas, however, we may still ask if and how closely the linguistic picture expressed in Nurse's paper (chap. 10, above) necessarily reflects the primary Early Iron Age Bantu spread and how much it may have been distorted by subsequent developments.

An alternative hypothesis that might better fit Nurse's data (as well as Ehret's) is that Lacustrine and Central Kenya plus Chaga-Taita could represent survivals of an original Early Bantu/Early Iron Age spread, with the remainder of Kwale and Kalambo overlain by later expansions of group 6 peoples. The present state of knowledge of the Later Iron Age in most of the group 6 area precludes archaeological judgment on this matter. The status of group 5, Southern Tanzania, remains uncertain in the absence of archaeological evidence, as does that of group 3 unless it derives from Lelesu.

A final point which may or may not be relevant is the apparent coincidence of Lacustrine with Later Iron Age roulette-decorated pottery south of the "Bantu line." Rouletting is foreign to the Early Iron Age and modern savanna Bantu speakers. It is postulated elsewhere (Soper 1979*a*) that rouletting was borrowed from probably Nilotic sources. I had previously considered that the technique diffused through the interlacustrine Bantu area without significant population movements, but that did not necessarily happen. (See also David and Ambrose, chaps. 6 and 7, above, for further discussion of rouletting and its historical significance.)

Later Iron Age Correlations

Later developments in the Iron Age should parallel the historical processes that led to the emergence of the present Bantu languages of East Africa. Both language and material culture, though perhaps influenced by different factors, may be expected to reflect the broader cultural trends and continuities of basic populations, where oral traditions may be distorted or manipulated to suit the interests of dominant minorities. They may thus provide us with a truer historical picture so far as the majority of the population is concerned.

To provide a basis for comparison between Later Iron Age archaeology and linguistic reconstructions of the development of present northeastern Bantu languages, I give a somewhat impressionistic account of what I can deduce or guess about the later prehistory of the area from central Kenya to northeastern Tanzania. It should be emphasized that this account is based upon scattered and fragmentary evidence, often unstratified and undated, which has been presented in very summary form in Soper (1980). Again, the account is a considerable oversimplification even of this incomplete evidence, emphasizing those elements of ceramic typology which link larger areas and underplaying or ignoring apparently more localized styles.

In South Pare two different styles of pottery, both distinct from Early Iron Age Kwale Ware, have been dated by single radiocarbon determinations to around the ninth century a.d. (Soper 1976b). The only dated Early Iron Age site in South Pare, Bombe Kaburi, has been given a date around the third century, and the relationship of this site to the later wares is uncertain. One of these later types, Maore Ware, has a wider distribution; it is found in the Taita Hills and extends into North Pare and Kilimanjaro where it occurs on a number of sites together with Kwale Ware. Although the stratigraphical evidence does not prove their contemporaneity, Odner (1971b, c) regards their consistent association on a number of sites as a strong indication that they were made and used by the same communities. Dates from Usangi Hospital in North Pare would put this proposed association at about the sixth to the ninth or tenth century a.d. There is no evidence as yet for the antecedents of Maore Ware or the other Later Iron Age wares in northeastern Tanzania.

In central Kenya, rather roughly made but easily recognizable Kwale-type bowls are consistently found in association with necked pots, also rather roughly made, whose most characteristic decoration is rocked zigzag impression (rocker stamping). This association is best seen at the site of Gatung'ang'a (Siiriäinen 1971) where carbon-14 dates range from the twelfth to the fourteenth century a.d., but the same association seems to extend at least from the eastern slopes of Mount Kenya, to Nyandarua, to Ngong, and to the Kulungu area of southern Kambaland. A case could be made, but it is yet to be argued in detail, for the origin of the necked pots in Kwale Ware also, but in any event the bowls give firm evidence for the ceramic continuity from Kwale to Gatung'ang'a, suggesting, though not of course proving, continuity of population and language.

There are sufficient aspects in common between Maore and Gatung'ang'a wares for them to constitute a single related continuum, and both follow the trend toward simplification of shapes and decoration which seems to be a frequent characteristic of Later Iron Age pottery in much of Bantu Africa. In this instance the trend would seem to culminate in the present pottery of the Kamba and surrounding peoples as far as North Pare and Taita. This pottery has virtually no decoration and a very restricted range of vessel shapes, generally lacking in bowl forms.

It is not yet clear when Gatung'ang'a Ware emerged or how long it and Maore Ware continued to be made. One would suggest sometime in the second half of the first millennium A.D. for the beginning, and sites in the Chyulu Hills have given a couple of dates in the sixteenth century associated with pottery in the Maore Tradition without Kwale elements.

Unfortunately no direct continuity has as yet been traced from this Later Iron Age continuum to any present peoples. The Chyulu Hills sites (Soper 1976) were tentatively ascribed to ancestral Kamba groups in the course of their northward migrations from the Kilimanjaro area, but this supposition rests more on grounds of oral tradition than on archaeological continuity. My investigations in the Embu area (Soper 1979*b*) again failed to show continuity to the present peoples of the Mount Kenya area, though they did not exclude the possibility. Traditions of migration, if taken literally, would suggest that the transition from Later Iron Age took place in the area on the east of Mount Kenya from which the Gikuyu, Embu, and their congeners claim to have come, but this area has yet to be examined archaeologically.

No coherent information is yet available for the coastal hinterland occupied by the Mijikenda or the Saghala people of the Taita Hills.

To sum up, there is evidence for a general widespread continuum represented by Gatung'ang'a and Maore wares, emerging by the end of the first millennium A.D. and either stemming directly from the Kwale Early Iron Age variant or having had direct relationships with its makers. It is a reasonable inference that the makers of this later continuum were Bantu speakers, on the basis of distribution, probable origins in Kwale, and the general trend of the ceramic style toward present-day pottery of current Bantu speakers. The area covered by the two parts of the continuum include at least those areas now occupied by the following peoples:

Gatung'ang'a—Meru, Embu, Chuka, Mbeere, Gikuyu, Southern Kamba (all belonging linguistically to Nurse's Central Kenya group); Maore—Chaga, Gweno, Daβida (and some Asu who have moved in recent centuries from South Pare into formerly Gweno parts of North Pare).

The distribution does not appear to extend to Usambara or Ngulu or into the central Rift Valley or north of Mount Kenya, but its extent in other directions is unknown. The correlation of archaeology and language may support the alternative hypothesis suggested above, that the Central Kenya and Chaga-Taita peoples represent linguistic descendants of the original Early Iron Age Bantu settlement of Kwale Ware makers in Tanzania and eastern Kenya, but this hypothesis would be more convincing if direct continuity of ceramic traditions could be fully demonstrated down to the present.

It is clear that the linguists are thinking in terms of a much more detailed definition than archaeologists, who have yet to undertake the sort of detailed studies of recent periods which could define the processes of diversification within closely related clusters of peoples. At the moment archaeology unfortunately cannot help in the area of differentiation and the later movements of the Northeast Coastal Bantu or in most other aspects of Later Iron Age history in East Africa.

In general it seems as if correlations between Bantu linguistics and archaeology on a local scale should be sought within the Later Iron Age, while the Early Iron Age is likely to provide parallel data only on a much wider regional or continental scale. This is not a failing of archaeological methods, which are potentially capable of providing an equal standard of definition of culture areas, whether 200 or 2,000 years ago, but the linguistic data must necessarily lose definition the farther into the past they are extrapolated.

I have not attempted to cover later periods in other parts of Bantu East Africa, partly through lack of time and partly because coherent information is rarely available. For the interlacustrine region, the predominance of roulette-decorated pottery in the Later Iron Age and its probable introduction by Nilotic speakers have been mentioned above. Elsewhere a number of different pottery wares have been described, for instance in Kisii by Bower (1973*b*) and various parts of Tanzania by Sutton (e.g., 1968), Fagan and Yellen (1968), and Soper and Golden (1969), but these descriptions have yet to be fitted together into any kind of regional picture.

In this paper the archaeological approach has been via the single avenue of ceramics, because pottery provides the only common culturally diagnostic factor. The interpretation is explicitly migrationary, and thus I have in effect been discussing the migration of pots—or at least of pottery styles—rather than of people. My excuse for this approach is the belief that in this instance pots mean people, and that pottery styles could not have moved so far so fast, with such typological continuity, unless carried by significant numbers of people.

Part IV

West Africa

OVERVIEW

Although the study of West African languages has a more respectable antiquity than language study in a number of other parts of sub-Saharan Africa, there has been very little attempt by archaeologists, historians, and linguists to work together or even to make use of each other's findings to reconstruct early history. This failing is partly attributable to the fact that archaeology did not really get underway until the postwar period and partly to the presence of sublimely beautiful art objects in Nigeria, which focused archaeological attention on their date, origin, technology, social context, and artistic and historical significance. Only in the past fifteen years have archaeologists and historians turned their attention to some of the wider and more fundamental issues of Nigeria's past, such as the transition to an agricultural way of life, early ironworking, urban origins, and town and country interrelationships. There was nothing so obvious as the problem of the Bantu to attract archaeologists and linguists in West Africa to work together and to encourage archaeology into more wide-ranging investigations and efforts at synthesis.

Gross misuse of linguistic data by several scholars may have helped to set back the clock for constructive cooperation. E. Meyerowitz, in a string of books from 1951 to 1974 which dealt with the Akan-speaking peoples, attempted to link modern Ghanaians to ancient Egypt. Oluminde Lucas, in his work on the Yoruba (Lucas 1948), resurrected the lost tribes of Israel as well as the Nile Valley connection. Both these misconnections have been adequately dismissed by later writers (Westcott 1961). Of a more serious nature, because of his following in the Francophone African world, are the writings of Cheikh Anta Diop (1967, 1981), who attempted to redress the Eurocentric biases of Western historians and archaeologists. Diop tries to establish a common linguistic and physical ancestry for his own people, the Wolof of Senegal, and the ancient Egyptians. He avoids the issue of sound shifts because he has no idea of the exact sound correspondences of the long-extinct language. Although Diop's appeal for reevaluation of the African physical character of the ancient Egyptian population and for recognition of the indigenous African sources of much of early Egyptian culture was timely, his linguistic arguments have deservedly received little attention and no strong body of support. Far longer lasting were the claims made by Meinhof (1912) and others that Fulani was a Hamitic language. These claims have been laid to rest by

Greenberg (1963), among others, but they indicate the former pervasiveness of the Hamitic myth of African history which derived most elements of "civilization" from northeast Africa.

An adequately grounded use of linguistic correlation with archaeology in West Africa must begin with the fundamental fact that most of the languages of West Africa belong to a single language family, Niger-Congo. The precise subgrouping of the family at the deepest levels of relationship remains a problem for future research, but the most distant subgroups within Niger-Congo surely reflect a history of linguistic and therefore ethnic diversification extending back more than 8,000 years and probably as much as 10,000 to 12,000 years (Greenberg 1964; Ehret, forthcoming *a*). If Welmers's (1958) argument, that the first split within Niger-Congo was between the Mande branch and all the rest, holds up, then the earliest spread of Niger-Congo peoples, at some point between 8,000 and 12,000 years ago, is likely to have emanated from parts of the woodland savanna zone of West Africa, perhaps in the upper Niger Basin or somewhere nearby. The reconstructibility of a proto-Niger Congo root word for "yam" (Wrigley 1960; Williamson 1970) makes it attractive to speculate that a particular style of intensive food collecting, emphasizing the yam, may have provided the crucial subsistence advantage of such early Niger-Congo communities. That kind of adaptation would make perfect sense as a subsistence response of West Africans to the replacement of a previously open savanna environment by woodlands, a shift that followed on the spread of wetter conditions in tropical Africa beginning shortly before 12,000 years ago.

The establishment of Niger-Congo societies through the zone of the West African rain forest cannot be pushed back to so early a date. The degree of linguistic differentiation among southern Nigerian languages suggests a dating of Niger-Congo spread there roughly in the range of about 4000 B.C. (Armstrong 1964). In areas to the west of southern Nigeria, Niger-Congo settlement would seem to date no later than about 3000 B.C. (Wilson 1980). For these areas a possible archaeological correlation can be proposed, namely the linking of the spread of cultures using ground-stone axes (Shaw 1978–79) with the linguistically required Niger-Congo expansion in the forest zone. It seems probable that the users of the ground-stone axes were food producers rather than just hunters and collectors. The shift to cultivating such plants as the yam, at a date therefore preceding 4000 B.C., could have helped engender the movement of Niger-Congo peoples into the forest, an environment where natural clearings required by yams were few and where stone axes would have been important supplements to fire in the clearing of land for planting.

For the periods of West African history between the fourth millennium B.C. and the second half of the first millennium A.D., at which point written records begin to be available, little in the way of correlating archaeology and linguistics can yet be proposed. The Bantu and Ubangian expansions out of eastern West Africa into the equatorial regions of the continent have been dealt with in previous sections of this volume. In West Africa proper only the broadest and most general level of historical inference from Niger-Congo linguistic evidence has yet been attempted (e.g., Mauny 1952). As yet the results of such efforts usually have no comparable archaeology with which to seek correlation. Mande expansion may be proposed, for instance, to have begun in or about the region of the inland delta of the Niger just over 4,000 years ago (Bimson 1978). The latest stages, including among other developments the territorial expansion of the Mandinka-Bambara dialect cluster and the divergence of southeastern Mande, correlate very nicely with relatively well-documented directions of change of the past thousand years. And that is all the correlation that can yet be made. Murdock's (1959) proposal of a Mande role as early inventors of agriculture in West Africa is clearly wrong on botanical as well as chronological grounds (Baker 1962). But what then set off Mande expansion? Was it the climatic shift of the third millennium B.C.? Might Mande development of an important new food crop, African rice, have been a contributing factor? Beyond excavations at insufficiently early sites, Jenne and Kumbi, and at Dar Tichitt (see Munson 1980), the relevant archaeology is almost unknown.

Two other families of languages impinge on West Africa. The connection of Nilo-Saharans, represented in the West African Sahel by Songhai and Kanuri-Kanembu, to the Aquatic tradition is discussed earlier (see overview to Part I). The Chadic languages of northern Nigeria, Cameroon, and Chad are an offshoot of the Afroasiatic family. The early Chadic societies of the fourth or fifth millennium B.C. appear to have had the same role in the establishment of an agricultural way of life in the central Sudan region as the contemporary Eastern Sudanic-speakers can be argued to have had in the middle Nile Basin to the east (see overview, Part I, above). The archaeology of early Chadic expansion, probably most often at the expense of previously established Nilo-Saharan communities (Saxon 1975), remains to be identified. A possible area to look for the still earlier Proto-Chadic origins may be among the Sahara "Neolithic" populations of the sixth millennium. At the other

extreme of the time scale, one good effort to correlate linguistic, archaeological, and other sources for the history of a particular Chadic society
does exist, and that is J. E. G. Sutton's (1979) examination of early Hausa
history.

In the two chapters that follow, Ghana has been chosen for intensive
review because of the significant dialogue already taking place between
historians and linguists. Only a few tentative correlations emerge as yet,
but the framework for an eventual wide-ranging matching up of linguistics and archaeology has been constructed.

12 | The Peopling of Southern Ghana: A Linguistic Viewpoint

M. E. KROPP DAKUBU

A FEW YEARS AGO THERE WAS considerable discussion of the way in which the peoples of southern Ghana came to be where they are now, and particularly of the historical relationship between the peoples and their cultures and languages. Since recent research, from the point of view at least of the linguist, has made much of the discussion of the mid-1960s seem unsatisfactory, the time is opportune to revive the subject.

Southern Ghana west of the Volta is inhabited almost entirely by people speaking one or another of the Volta-Comoe group of languages. The only exceptions are the speakers of Ga and Dangme and a few speakers of Ewe. On the eastern side of the Volta are more speakers of Volta-Comoe languages, but these are probably outnumbered by speakers of Ewe and of Togo languages (map 16).

Most of the discussion has been concerned with the arrival and subsequent expansion of people who now speak Volta-Comoe languages, but not because other people are not thought ever to have moved. Among many of the Ewe of Ghana there are strong traditions of migration from the east, especially from the area of the Togo-Benin border (see, e.g., Cornevin 1959). The Ga and Dangme also have migration traditions, from the east and also from the north (Kropp Dakubu 1972). The speakers of the various Togo languages apparently have traditions of migration, but the migrations seem to have been more or less within the area they now occupy; there is no tradition of the entire group having arrived from anywhere (Heine 1968).

It seems fairly certain that many of the Ewe, including the carriers of the language, arrived from an easterly direction, beyond the borders of modern Ghana, possibly in the not so distant past, and today most of the speakers of the Ewe-Fon dialect cluster reside east of Ghana.

The Volta-Comoe group of languages has far wider ramifications, both geographically and linguistically, than either the Ga-Dangme or the Togo group. It has three major branches: (1) the Ono or Western branch,

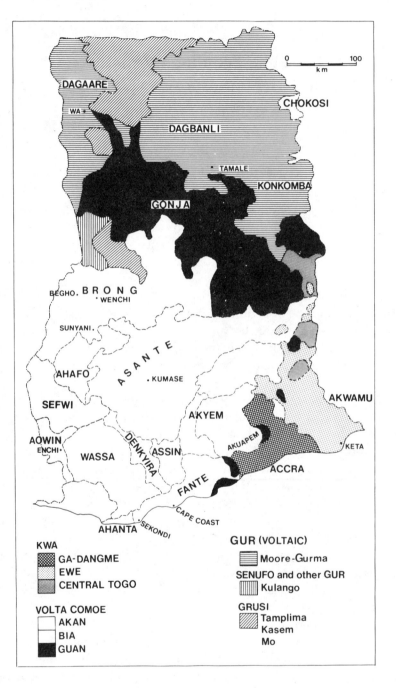

Map 16. Languages and dialects of Ghana.

consisting of two small languages, Abouré and Betibé, which are spoken only near the Ono Lagoon in the Ivory Coast; (2) the Tano or Central branch, which in turn has two branches, Bia, consisting of Nzema-Ahanta and Anyi-Bawule, and Akan; and (3) the Guang branch. Of the Bia languages, Nzema-Ahanta is spoken mainly in Ghana, but also in the Ivory Coast, and Anyi-Bawule (or Agni-Baoulé) is spoken in the Ivory Coast and in Ghana as Aowin, Sehwi, and Chakosi in the north. Akan, the Volta-Comoe language with the most speakers, is spoken mainly in Ghana, but also in the Ivory Coast. The Guang languages are mainly in Ghana, spreading into Togo and also into the Republic of Benin. Thus the geographical focus of the Tano branch seems to be east of the Ghana–Ivory Coast border, and, of the Guang branch, just west of the border with the Republic of Togo. If one branch is associated with the Tano River, the other may be associated with the Volta.

As I see it, the historical problems are essentially three. First, from what direction did the speakers of Volta-Comoe languages arrive at the point where they dispersed into different cultural communities? Or, in linguistic terms, where was the proto-Volta-Comoe language spoken, and from what direction did its speakers arrive at that location? Second, where was the cradle of the Akans? Linguistically, this question implies an intermediate question: Given the location of the proto-Volta-Comoe-speaking community, after the people dispersed into three communities speaking respectively proto-Ono, proto-Tano, and proto-Guang, where was the proto-Tano community just before it divided into communities speaking proto-Bia and proto-Akan? And after that, where was proto-Akan spoken before it dispersed and the three major dialects (or perhaps dialect groups)—Brong, Asante, and Fante—arose? The third question concerns movements after or perhaps in the course of the dispersal of Akan. Is it true that the Fante arrived in their present location from the area of Takyiman in Brong-Ahafo and, if so, were they preceded on the coast by other Akan speakers or by speakers of Guang languages or by both? Considering this question from a linguistic point of view requires considering the probable course of the dispersal of proto-Guang. Another question in the relatively recent history of the Akan is the validity of the tradition, found in many communities speaking one of the Asante group of dialects, that they migrated from the Adanse-Denkyira area.

In connection with each of these questions we must keep in mind that migration traditions may reflect movements of large numbers of people, or at any rate of the original population of a locality on which its later population is largely based genetically, or they may reflect the arrival of a group that founded the community as a political entity without necessarily constituting the majority of its population. Languages disperse in both ways. In a migration of the base population, we expect that the migrating population spoke an antecedent form of the language now spoken in the locality. We know, however, that communities sometimes do change their languages; examples that come immediately to mind are the formerly Guang-speaking towns of Akwapim, such as Mamfe, which are now Akan-speaking, and the town of Kpone, once Dangme- but now Ga-speaking, on the coast. This change may come about through conquest, when a state-forming group imposes its language on the population already present, even though its numbers may be smaller, but it seems that such an event must be accompanied by strong social and economic motivation for change, and perhaps by a high degree of intermarriage, since in some places the chief's court is conducted in a different language from that of most people's everyday life. It may also come about peacefully, when the linguistic community is assimilated into another that is expanding economically and perhaps politically. I stress this point because it implies, I think, that the question of the relationship between the Fante and the Guang, to which I later return, may not be solvable.

We now consider the three major points in turn, historically and linguistically. Concerning the origin and point of dispersal of the proto-Volta-Comoe community, there seem today to be two major competing theories, one essentially historical and the other purely linguistic. The former has been summarized by Boahen (1966). The discussion had previously been dressed as an argument about the origin of the Akan: Did they come from ancient Ghana, from Arabia and Iraq, or did they originate nearer home? There seems to have been considerable confusion as to whether the entire population or the ruling aristocracy, with or without the language, was involved.

Boahen points out that among the Akan as a whole no ruling aristocracy can be isolated, and that the general Akan-speaking population and the founders of the state organization are not separable, at least in principle or for the whole community. He proposed that the Dahomey Gap was the cradle of Kwa dispersion, and that afterward the "ancestors of the speakers of the Akan-Guang languages [i.e., of proto-Volta-Comoe] skirted the forest regions westwards into the region of the Comoe River and the Black Volta" (1966:3). In this region, he suggests, contacts with peoples from the north had important social and cultural implications, before the ancestors of the Akan speakers moved south into the forest.

John Stewart (1966*a*:57), on the other hand, comes to almost the opposite conclusion, that proto-Volta-Comoe was spoken within its present area. He also claims that the closest known relatives of the Volta-Comoe languages are the Potou Lagoon languages, spoken in the Ivory Coast not far from where the Volta-Comoe Ono languages are spoken. Therefore, proto-Potou-Volta-Comoe must have been spoken near the Ebrié and Potou lagoons. The speakers of proto-Volta-Comoe then moved east before dispersing north, east, and eventually west.

As Stewart admits, this model rests on the assumption that the closest relative of proto-Volta-Comoe was proto-Potou, but he gives no evidence of this relationship. Apparently he bases his claim on the fact that he was able to find regularly corresponding cognate forms between Potou and Volta-Comoe more easily than between Volta-Comoe and other groups, such as Ga-Dangme, the Ewe-Fon group, or the Togo group. Although a larger number of apparent cognates may naturally lead us to expect a closer relationship, it certainly does not demonstrate it. In a recent paper I proposed a number of correspondences and sound changes which seem to indicate that Volta-Comoe may in fact be more closely related to Ga-Dangme and to Ewe than it is to Potou (Kropp Dakubu 1977). The innovation on which this grouping is based is admittedly not a very well-defined one, and it might be said to constitute an innovative trend rather than a single change. Nowhere, however, does Stewart (as far as I know) give even this much evidence. If my grouping is correct, it completely undermines Stewart's theory of a southwestern origin for proto-Volta-Comoe and makes an ancient migration from the east seem quite plausible. It does not, however, provide an obvious answer to the question of where proto-Volta-Comoe was last spoken before its dispersal.

This question is best postponed until after consideration of the location of the proto-Akan-speaking community. As noted above, geographically the Tano branch is more or less centered on the Ghana–Ivory Coast border. The Anyi-Bawule branch of Bia is spoken along that border, and Nzema-Ahanta is also spoken on the border south of Anyi-Bawule and especially east, in Ghana. The Akan dialects border the Bia languages, and the Brong dialect of Akan extends farther north. Clearly, the proto-Tano language must have been spoken somewhere in this area. The simplest model, I suggest, is that proto-Tano was spoken in the western Brong region, and that the Bia languages derived from proto-Tano as it came to be spoken by a section of the community that moved south along the Bia River. This argument is not entirely linguistic, for it takes into account the fact that the Sehwi-Aowin-Nzema area of western

Ghana seems not to have been consistently inhabited until relatively recently (van Dantzig 1977), making it unlikely that proto-Tano formed within the forest area.

We now return to the question of whether Boahen's proposal of the region between the Comoe and Black Volta rivers is a reasonable one for the location of proto-Volta-Comoe. From this time distance, the best we can do is to consider whether it is the point from which the Ono, Tano, and Guang were most likely to have dispersed, that is, the point requiring the least traveling for all concerned. We must therefore consider the geographical relationship between the proposed proto-Tano homeland and the area from which the Guang languages dispersed.

It is a widely held conjecture that the Guang achieved their present distribution, scattered along the Black Volta, the Volta, and near the coast in the southeast, via migration from north to south (Goody 1963:185). Goody also believes that this movement emanated from the "main area of concentration" between Krachi and Salaga. He sees little support for the theory that the Guang were once distributed throughout most of southern Ghana, although in pre-Ashanti days Guang as well as Gur speakers were found scattered along the northern margin of the forest, and the Gonja state moved north under Akan pressure (1966:21).

Concerning the coast, Fynn (1975) considers the question of whether or not the western Fante were of Guang origin. His discussion is somewhat marred by the fact that he seems to accept a tradition from a town or state as always applying to the entire population of that town or state. For example, he lists Efutu as an eastern Fante state without comment, even though a Guang language (Awutu/Afutu) is spoken there today. He comes to the conclusion that the populations of the western and central Fante states have no Guang component, but whether or not he is correct, the arguments he produces are less than compelling. He cites the fact that linguistic specimens collected on the coast from the seventeenth century onward are Akan, not Guang (1975:23), but this demonstrates only what we already know, that Fante became a lingua franca of the coast. That fact does not preclude the presence of communities using a Guang language for internal purposes, then or earlier. Fynn also quotes Painter to the effect that if Guang was ever spoken in Cape Coast and to the west, it has disappeared without known traces. He considers such a disappearance unlikely, but in fact things like that do happen. A third argument, that the Fante-speaking peoples say they inherited their language from their ancestors, is extremely unreliable, since that kind of memory is much affected by politics and the passage of time; in any event, we cannot be sure that it was the only language of the ancestors.

The arguments of nonlinguists concerning Guang movements and distribution seem to have been very largely linguistic. Painter (1966) and Stewart (1966*a*), who are linguists, both seem inclined to a southerly origin, which conflicts with the conclusions of both Goody and Fynn. Painter (1966:62) claims that the Guang moved north from the mouth of the Tano, which he calls the cradle of Western Kwa (he means Volta-Comoe), to the Afram-Volta-Kintampo region, somewhat south and west of Goody's proposed location, from which they dispersed.

Stewart's hypothesis of a southeastern home area for proto-Volta-Comoe also seems to imply that the Guang moved from south to north, either before they divided or in the course of doing so, even though he claims it does not. I consider this hypothesis ill-founded. Stewart (1966*a*) explicitly disagrees with Goody's north-to-south theory, apparently because the largest number of speakers of Guang languages are now and have long been in the south. It seems to me that this argument is quite irrelevant. What matters is the location of the greatest linguistic diversity. The Guang languages spoken in the south belong to a single subgroup, coordinate with at least three subgroups spoken no farther south than Nkonya: Nkonya-Nawuri-Krachi-Nchumuru, Acode-Anyanga, Gonja. The little-known Dumpo and Semere languages, farther west near the Black Volta, also seem to constitute subbranches (Cleal 1974:244–245). In the absence of any knowledge of what the supposed vanished Guang languages of Fanteland might have been like, this evidence strongly favors a northern center for dispersal, more or less as suggested by Goody.

Stewart elsewhere (1972:82) suggests that speakers of a language ancestral to Akan (i.e., proto-Tano or proto-Akan) "broke through" a once continuous Guang crescent at a number of points. Evidence from place-names suggests several formerly Guang-speaking places along the Volta had already disappeared before the recent flooding of the Volta Lake (Kropp Dakubu 1972:103–104). There are also Akwapim-Guang traditions of previous settlements on the Accra Plain in the general area of modern (Akan-speaking) Nsawam (Kwamena-Poh 1973: App. I), but these settlements seem to have been of rather short duration. On balance, the notion that the Guang area may once have held no Akan speakers need not be taken to imply that Guang speakers were once more numerous than they are now, or that Akan speakers have frequently pushed Guang speakers out of land they once occupied.

The problem of whether the present non-Guang Fante areas once held Guang-speaking communities, however, is still not solved, and I do not think that it can be solved by the means we have been using thus far.

There may be a clue in ethnic names, however. The names Oguaa, "Cape Coast," and Eguafo, "Cape Coast people" (-fo is an Akan suffix meaning "people"), are extremely suggestive of the name Gwa which, according to Painter (1972), the Anum-Boso use as the name of their language (a southern Guang language). It may be, however, that Gwa is a name that has migrated, undoubtedly with a group or groups of people who have been assimilated into more than one linguistic group, so that the name cannot now be firmly attributed. This suggestion is based on van Dantzig's report (1977:55) that the Abouré around Grand Bassam, who speak one of the two Ono languages, are also known as Agoua; according to Stewart, however, Gwa is another name for Mbato, a non-Volta-Comoe Potou Lagoon language (Stewart 1966a:55).

Another suggestive name is Abora, the name of a central Fante state, the pre-Akan Kyerepong (Guang) name for the Akwapim town now called Akropong, and also, as Abola, the name of the quarter of Accra which provides the chief of Accra. No further progress can be made in this direction without a great deal of research into the development of the Fante dialects. Similarities between Akan and Guang have generally been attributed to the influence of Akan on Guang, owing to its status as a widely known second language, and not vice versa (e.g., Stewart 1966a:56).

If proto-Tano was spoken between the sources of the Tano and the Bia, and proto-Guang around the Volta where it bends south (or used to), the most likely homeland for proto-Volta-Comoe is present-day Brong-Ahafo. Since the Ono branch is west of the others, we may weight it in that direction in favor of western Brong-Ahafo, not far indeed from the area suggested for proto-Tano. Since that area is Akan-speaking today, it is entirely likely that neither proto-Tano nor proto-Akan resulted from a migration but rather developed as the speech of the population that remained settled when others left, and that the western Brong-speaking communities are the direct linguistic descendants of communities that have occupied parts of that land since proto-Volta-Comoe times.

This hypothesis is at variance with the proposals of historians. Boahen (1966:8) proposes that proto-Volta-Comoe was spoken in "the region of modern Takyiman, Banda and Gyaman," with which I agree, but he goes on to say that "it was the branch that hived off from this group and moved south to settle in the area of the confluence of the Pra and the Ofin that developed into the Akan of today." Fynn (1975:29) believes that the cradle of Akan culture extended farther south to include the Etsi area of Fanteland. Their arguments are nonlinguistic, based on such facts as that the Brong do not share the matrilineal clan system common to the

Asante, Fante, Akwapim, and others, and that many Akan states have traditions of origin from the Adanse/Denkyira, or Ofin-Pra, area.

We must here dissociate sociocultural development from linguistic descent. If the Brong are as culturally different as claimed, Boahen's proposal of a movement south before the development of certain characteristic cultural traits seems reasonable. Linguistically, however, these people formed an entity with those who stayed behind to become the Brong of today. If it is true that we are still talking of migrations of peoples, this means that after part of the proto-Tano-speaking community departed to become the community speaking what became proto-Bia, enough time elapsed for several characteristically Akan linguistic innovations to occur, in other words, the emergence of the proto-Akan language, before part of the community speaking that language moved south.

Within the Akan-speaking area today, migration traditions seem to be inextricably tied to state formation. They point in two directions: to the Ofin-Pra area, where the first Akan forest states arose, and to Takyiman, the capital of Bono, a Brong state that preceded the Akan forest states. The movement of peoples out of that region seems to have followed or become most intense after the defeat of Adanse by the Denkyira (Daaku 1966:11). The Denkyira themselves claim to have migrated from Brong-Ahafo and to include an element of northern, possibly Mande, origin (Anquandah 1975:53, after Daaku; also Kumah 1966:33). Kwahu is said to have been founded by settlers from Brong together with other Akans from the west (Ameyaw 1966:39). The Akwamu also are thought to have started from the Denkyira area (Kwamena-Poh 1973), and the Asante states were founded by immigrants from Adanse (Fynn 1966:24; Agyeman-Duah 1960:21). On the other hand, it is claimed that the Elmina, or at least the founders of the Elmina state, originated from Takyiman (Feinberg 1970:20), as did several of the Fante groups (Fynn 1975).

Linguistically, we can look at these migration stories in several ways. First, does the dialect picture support or at least not conflict with a trend of migration from the north, followed by another series of movements fanning out from a point intermediate between the Brong area and the coast, that is, Adanse/Denkyira?

Here we base our arguments on the Akan dialect studies of F. Dolphyne.[1] First, the Brong dialects are in many ways the most conservative of the Akan dialects (Dolphyne 1979, 1976*b*). Although the conserva-

---

[1]A paper by Dolphyne, to appear in *Tarikh*, and to which I had access only after my paper had been completed, interprets the same data and comes to much the same conclusions.

tism of the Brong does not necessarily mean that they have not moved, it is at least consistent with such a situation. Second, the major isogloss bundles quite clearly separate Asante and related dialects, such as Kwahu and Akyem, from Brong on the one hand and Fante-Agona-Akwapim on the other (Dolphyne 1979). There is a secondary division in the south between Fante-Gomua on the one hand and Akwapim on the other, with Agona sharing innovations with each but more with Akwapim. The difference between Akwapim and Fante seems to be due partly to Akwapim innovations but more to Akwapim adoption of Asante innovations, which we may presume has followed on the conquest of the Akwapim by Akyem in the eighteenth century.

It might be objected that if Asante is equidistant from Brong and Fante, it would be simplest to postulate that the Brong moved north, the Fante south, and the Asante stayed put or moved east. The dialect divisions, however, are of a different nature. Although Brong has made a few innovations (Dolphyne 1976a), most of the differences with Asante are the result of Asante innovations. The difference between Asante and Fante, on the other hand, is due to a great deal of innovation in Fante. Much of this innovation has occurred since the first specimens of the language were written down, and some have spread to Asante (Stewart 1966b; Boadi 1975:13).

It seems that all the dialects other than Brong share the innovation of regressive nasalization, although it is more extensive in Fante-Gomua (Dolphyne 1976b), as well as a general loss of nasal stem-final syllables. On the other hand, Brong and Asante (excluding Fante) do not seem to share any innovation that cannot be attributed to Asante influence on Brong. The primary split therefore seems to be between Brong and the others. This supposition is consonant with a general movement south, not necessarily all at once, in which the present-day major division between Fante-Akwapim and Asante did not develop until after the coastal region had been settled by most of its current occupants. It is interesting that the Akan speakers of Akwapim are mainly of Akwamu origin, claiming to have come from the Denkyira area (Kwamena-Poh 1973:129). That the Akwapim dialect seems to have been virtually identical with Fante before the nineteenth century may be further evidence that the Fante-Asante split is much more recent than the Brong split with other Akan dialects. That the Asante migrations from Adanse/Denkyira are thought to have occurred within the last 400 years is consistent with the relatively uniform nature of the speech of Asante-Kwahu-Akyem, which indicates that Akan has expanded fairly recently in the area.

We have then a pattern of several waves of linguistic dispersal from the Brong-Ahafo area: first, Ono went southwest and Guang went east, then Bia went south, and finally Akan went south except for what became the Brong dialect, which stayed put. I think we may assume, until contrary evidence is presented, that the dispersal was a consequence of the movements of the people who introduced the language into the country as they arrived. It is impossible, however, to be certain that no other language was ever spoken in any part of the area.

It must be stressed that the comparative linguistics on which classification is based reconstructs only the skeleton of the history of a language group, the thread of continuity, and there is much in any language that has come into it at different times from outside. The same is true of the migration history we have reconstructed by applying the historical linguistic classification. It provides only a thread of continuity underlying linguistic communities. We suppose that it is matched by a thread of genetic continuity between generations of speakers, but even if this is so, the migration histories themselves indicate that many of the biological ancestors of the speakers of various languages were originally members of other language communities. For example, the statement that the Baoulé are of Ashanti (Asante) origin (van Dantzig 1977:78) can mean only that the ancestors of some of today's Baoulé speakers came from Asanteland and were linguistically assimilated into the Baoulé-speaking community, since Baoulé is a Bia language. Often indeed there is linguistic evidence that many of the speakers of a given language are probably descended from people who spoke another. Retord (1971) shows that there has been strong Akan influence on Agni-Sanvi, which supports the tradition that the speakers of this dialect of Anyi originated from Asante and were absorbed into an Anyi-speaking community.

13 | Archaeological and Linguistic Reconstruction in Ghana

MERRICK POSNANSKY

GHANA HAS A RELATIVELY well-established tradition of historical studies, thanks in part to its long period of educational development. Its oral literature, particularly in those societies with chiefs or kings, is a rich one. The intensive study of local tradition, researched independently by local scholars, has tended, however, to complicate the historical literature. The dangers of feedback from amateur scholars, often with an inadequate and unbalanced knowledge of African history, to the societies they are studying are very high. This caveat applies particularly to the plethora of conflicting tales of origin and migration. The migration myths as recorded by local scholars tended to look outside Ghana for origins, as far afield as Mesopotamia for the Akan, studied by J. B. Danquah (1957), Egypt for the societies investigated by Eva Meyerowitz (1960), and Benin City for many of the Ga (Reindorf 1898). There was a need for historical validation, for a pedigreed connection to a well-known ancient group. Unfortunately this quest for outside origins has died hard, and a tendency has appeared to ignore what clues there are to movements in the oral traditions because of a fear of being tainted with the diffusionist brush. It is particularly to provide a balance to the discredited interpretations based on oral traditions that archaeology and linguistics are so useful to the historian, for both disciplines can effectively deal with wider geographical relationships.

In contrast with the situation in eastern and central African historiography, there has been until recently a certain caution in integrating West African archaeological evidence into a linguistic framework. The only scholar who has attempted to provide a chronological and comprehensive framework for Ghana is Painter (1966). Using glottochronology, Painter postulated a division of the Niger-Congo languages around 5000–4000 B.C. leading to a divergence of Mande from Kwa, then a split of Voltaic from Kwa about 1800 B.C., with slightly later splits of Ewe and Ga off the line of descent leading to the Volta-Comoe group to which the Akan and Guang languages of Ghana belong. This provocative scheme was linked to a rather inadequately known archaeological framework. At the time only three radiocarbon dates were available for Ghana, compared with nearly a hundred at present (Posnansky 1976). The scheme was postulated before two major research endeavors had been carried out, the Volta Basin Research Project and the West African Trade Project, which added information on at least sixty sites to the previous meager archaeological data base.

Painter was probably not far wrong in dating the breakup of Proto-Volta-Comoe to the last millennium B.C., but his earlier dates were much too recent. The Ga/Ewe/Volta-Comoe split falls probably in the range of 3000 B.C. (Wilson 1980), and the initial Niger-Congo split, in the area of 8,000 to 10,000 years ago (Greenberg 1969; Ehret, forthcoming *a*) at the minimum. Kropp Dakubu's companion paper (chap. 12, above) brings the linguistic classification for central and southern Ghana and adjoining regions up to date, and it offers a broad overview of Volta-Comoe population movements implied by the classification. In this paper I review the archaeological discoveries of the past fifteen years and assess their significance for an integrated approach to Ghana's early history (map 17).

It is becoming evident that Ghana's earliest population dates back to later Pleistocene times and possibly to the mid-Pleistocene. No diagnostic evidence is yet available to establish the later Pleistocene occupation claimed by Davies (1967). The work of Nygaard and Talbot (1976) along the Ghana coast to the east of Accra firmly indicates a Stone Age settlement along the drier coastal plain; at present the date is uncertain, but morphologically the artifacts have affinities to those rather loosely defined "Sangoan" industries of eastern and central Africa. It is argued by Davies (1967), probably correctly, that the Stone Age settlers along the coast came there through the Dahomey Gap. On a recent visit to Togo I was impressed by the presence of Acheulean hand axes and other material in central Togo which suggest an earlier settlement, or at least a more noticeable presence, than in Ghana.

The strands of continuity are unfortunately difficult to trace, but there is a strong presence of Late Stone Age societies in southern Ghana, particularly in the Kwahu Escarpment area where Shaw (1944) and later Smith (1975) found at Bosumpra rock shelter a fourth millennium B.C. occupation with pottery. Dombrowski (1977) has more recently found evidence of coastal societies with a dependence on shell food at Goa Lagoon east of Tema and with pottery at a similar time or even earlier (also Nygaard and Talbot 1977). What all this adds up to is that Ghana, like Nigeria, Sierra Leone, and several other West African countries, had

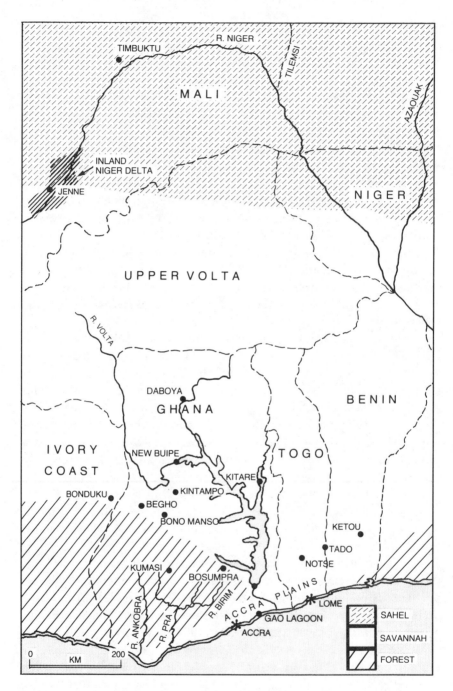

Map 17. Archaeological sites in Ghana.

a continued human presence from Stone Age times. The linguistic affiliation of these peoples is, as yet, beyond our reach, but what is likely is that this ceramic tradition from the north reached them presumably in the fourth millennium B.C. or earlier.

Sometime after this event we find the first widely dispersed and reasonably well-described industry (Flight 1976) in Ghana, known from its first find spot, Kintampo. Characterized by an artifact unique to Ghana, the soft-stone rasp ("terracotta cigar") or, more probably, general-purpose potting tool (Anguandah 1965), the Kintampo Industry exhibits the first evidence of livestock raising and possibly cultivation. The sites, dated from the middle of the second millennium B.C., provide the first evidence also of villages with wattle-and-daub houses; of plastic art in the form of terra-cotta figures of probable domestic animals; and of stone beads and stone walls. Davies (1966), in a paper with a typically provocative title, "The Invasion of Ghana from the Sahara in the Early Iron Age," postulates a movement from the Sahel to account for the Kintampo "Neolithic" features, particularly the lithic material at Ntereso, the impressed pottery, and the stone bracelets with triangular cross section. The cattle were certainly brought from the north, at least. Smith (1975) has suggested that around 2000 B.C. pastoralists moved south down the Azouack and Tilemsi valleys because of increasing desiccation and possibly overintensive land use.

A big problem, however, is to know whether the Kintampo people, whose sites are largely found in the Volta Basin, in Brong-Ahafo and Gonja as well as on the Accra plains, were the first to settle in the forest. Several Kintampo sites are found in the forest in patches of savanna like that at Boyasi (Newton and Woodell 1976). Are these savanna patches man-induced or man-maintained? One possibility is that during the drier conditions before 9000 B.C., evidenced at Lake Bosumtwi (Talbot and Delibrias 1977),[1] these areas were already settled. Possibly the areas nearby were exploited for such oleaginous trees as oil palm, borassus palm, and *Canarium schweinfurthii*, which grow best in forest ecotone areas. As the climate became more humid, the savanna patches were maintained by continuous settlement and consolidated once an agricultural mode had been adopted. The nature of the avian fauna as well as flora has suggested that such patches were maintained throughout the wetter phase which followed the dry (Woodell and Newton 1975). If the maintenance was

---

[1]A further possibility is to link these relict savanna patches to a dry phase of small proportions about 3500–1000 B.C.

supplied by a human agency, it means that certain elements of the Kintampo Industry hark back to the Stone Age populations that preexisted in
southern Ghana; we also have evidence that these people exploited the
oleaginous plants (Posnansky, forthcoming).

In location the spread of Kintampo includes the positions postulated
linguistically for proto-Volta-Comoe speakers (see chap. 12, above). On
the other hand, the Volta-Comoe expansion may better fit chronologi-
cally—if Painter's dating is to be believed—into the as yet archaeologically
little-known period of 2,500 years between the mid-second millennium
B.C. and the present millennium. Until the end of the first millennium A.D.
or the early second millennium we have no evidence of further movements from the north or from any other direction, but this deficiency may
be attributable to the lack of excavation of any evidence for the period,
rather than to the lack of evidence itself.

The earliest date so far for ironworking is in the second century A.D.
from near the later important trade center of Begho in Brong-Ahafo.
One assumes that iron came from the east. The rich Togolese ironworking
sites may provide clues as to origins. The analysis of the terms used in
ironworking in West Africa should also ultimately throw light on its
origins. There is a dearth of Early Iron Age sites in Ghana. One possible
such site recently discovered at Begho seems to exhibit a ceramic tradition
which has some resemblance to the Kintampo which preceded it and to
the Begho Tradition which followed. Unfortunately the site was one that
could not be adequately dated. Otherwise there is as yet no evidence of
continuity between the Kintampo material of before 1000 B.C. and the
Begho material of A.D. 1000 and later.

From the elements of ceramic continuity within the Begho materials,
and from the wealth of oral data, we have no hesitation in thinking of
Begho as a predominantly Brong and thus an Akan settlement. Examination of the oral traditions of the villages whose inhabitants claim to have
lived at Begho during its heyday reveals that they have a uniform tale of
origin: they came from a hole in the ground at Nsesrekeseso. A similar
hole nearby turned out to be a man-made water cistern similar to the
bílegas of northern Ghana and the Sudanic belt. Relatively close to the hole
were a large series of grinding hollows where the ancestors ground grain,[2]
and all around are sites of the Kintampo Industry. One is tempted to

---

[2]The oral traditions abound with tales of the earliest Akan peoples using millets (or
sorghums?), thus indicating Akan ancestry in nonforest milieus.

suggest that we have here a case of improperly remembered history. The water hole was important in the past, and its importance was remembered; after it had silted up and the community had moved to a better-watered area, however, its original function was forgotten.

What the tradition of the hole does clearly illustrate, however, is that the Akan population of the area has an autochthonous origin. When one examines the holes of origin of the people of Takyiman, Bono Manso, Wankyi, and several other Brong communities, a similar situation is found. The Bonoso hole from which the Wankyi people emerged has been dated to A.D. 750 and 900 (N-2343) (Posnansky, forthcoming), and that of the people of Takyiman at Amouwi has been dated to the fifth century A.D. (Posnansky 1976). Both of these latter holes produced evidence to indicate ceramic continuity with the later states founded by people reputed to have emerged from them (Effah-Gyamfi 1975). It is this kind of evidence which reinforces the linguistic evidence that points to Brong as the earliest Akan-speaking area (see chap. 12, above).

Both the archaeology and the linguistic maps (maps 16, 17) provide clear evidence of a Mande intrusion into Ghana. How to date the invasion is another matter. Goody (1964) suggests that the forest blacksmiths were "proto"-Mande. It is certainly true that in the Begho area today the remaining blacksmiths are predominantly Ligbi or Numu. The Brong ironworkers have disappeared, but there is no evidence in the past that the smiths were not Brong. Mande influence can also be seen in items of regalia, mud architectural traditions, brass casting, musical instruments, textile technology, and the language of the gold trade (Posnansky 1976; Wilks 1962).

Until 1977 it was assumed that the Mande trade south from Jenne postdated A.D. 1200, as it was assumed that Jenne itself had been founded only in the twelfth or thirteenth century. The new date for old Jenne (Jenne-Jeno), which places its foundation up to two millennia ago (Keech McIntosh and McIntosh 1980), causes one to reexamine the Mande-Akan relations. It is probable that as Jenne developed as a market town its influence stretched farther and farther south. The gold and the forest crops like kola, and possibly shea butter, were probably traded well before the establishment of Begho as a town early in the second millennium A.D. Looking at the linguistic map (Map 16) of the Begho area, one sees a mosaic: hardly two adjacent villages speak the same language. It is an area of dynamic developments, presumably with the Akan moving north to seize the opportunities of trade, with the Mande moving south, whilst many Voltaic groups were also represented in the loosely structured towns. Both the Voltaic Dunso of Bondoukou and the Pantera of Debibi, for example, claim a Begho ancestry.

The technological debt of Asante to the Brong area is clearly admitted in their traditions (Arhin 1979) and, with other lines of evidence, indicates the Brong area as ancestral to many of the complex societies of the forest area. Do we, however, have any idea of the societies that preceded the forest states? The research of Kiyaga-Mulindwa (1976, 1980) on the Birim Valley earthworks has provided a picture of a stable population which, around the fifteenth or sixteenth century A.D., was building a series of earthworks, some as thick as 400 to 500 meters. The nineteen earthworks that have been recorded so far seem to have been built slowly (at least some were never finished), and each possibly served a local group. They often required a great deal of labor, for some have banks that rise up to 6 meters above the bottom of the associated ditches. They are characterized by a pottery unlike that of the present-day societies in the area.

The earthworks pottery is succeeded by pottery attributed to the Atweafo. The Atweafo's descendants have no idea who built the earthworks; they say they "met" them on arrival. Though only 80 kilometers from the coast, they were unknown to the coastal peoples. The Atwea pottery is similar to that in other areas of the forest, and the Atwea are evidently an Akan group. The earthworks people who either fled or were absorbed or destroyed could have been the descendants either of the original inhabitants or conceivably of the Guan, who are usually thought to have preceded the Akan. Kropp Dakubu (chap. 12, above), however, warns against such assumptions about the Guan. If the Kintampo Industry is regarded as the work of the proto-Volta-Comoe, then one perhaps expects some links between the two populations. But the passage of 2,000 years could have been sufficient to erase overt evidence of ceramic affinities.

What the earthworks-Atwea sequence clearly illustrates, however, is that the forest had been settled for some considerable time by agriculturalists presumably growing forest crops. No ceramic affinities are apparent between the earthworks people and the Kintampo, and so far no Kintampo artifacts have been found in the forest section of the general area of Kumasi. Why the earthworks were built is again difficult to answer. Kiyaga-Mulindwa (1976) suggests they were for occasional defense, presumably against the early Atwea movements.

On the coast the work started by James Anquandah (1978–79) on the past settlements of the Ga and Dangme peoples should eventually provide chronological data on the movements of these groups from the Togo/Benin areas. Traditions claim that the Dangme met the Ga peoples. The Dangme are very closely related in language to the Ga, however, so that neither need have settled the area much more than a thousand years ago (see esp. Wilson 1980). Archaeological evidence from Ladoku and other sites indicates a long pre-European phase of settlement, termed Cherekecherete by Anquandah, indicating that the coastal settlements are not just another example of a "frontier of opportunity." Like the Akan, the Ga and Dangme had a local tradition of terra-cotta figures, an indication of the widespread presence of the plastic arts in clay. Unfortunately, as no work has been undertaken in Togo, we cannot find out anything about the antecedents of the coastal populations east of Accra.

A folk movement rather more amenable to study may be that of the Ewe people. Their ancestral sites in Togo, at Tado near the Benin border and Notse some 110 kilometers north of Lomé, the capital, have impressive banks and ditches. The abundance of pottery should make a seriation study from the Ewe sites on the western migration route into Ghana a worthwhile exercise. As there has been continuous occupation at the Togo sites, the pottery should be found in a stratigraphic sequence, and the differences between the Ghanaian sites and the parent sites will provide a measure of the cultural divergence that has taken place during the migrations period.

The flooding of the Volta Basin in order to create the Akosombo Dam and Volta Lake provided an opportunity for an intensive rescue campaign of fieldwork in the Gonja area. Although not fully published as yet, the data so far made available indicate the changes brought about by the arrival of Ngbanya and the creation of the Gonja state. These took the form at New Buipe of ceramic changes (York 1973), the building of trade houses, and expanded trade. At Kitaare, Mathewson (1972) excavated a multiditched enclosure that pointed to a northeast trade with the Hausa, possibly in slaves but certainly in kola nuts, a trade that was already well established before the Ngbanya burst upon the scene in the late sixteenth century. The linguistic impact of the Ngbanya was slight, as the area is Guang-speaking.

New research by Shinnie at Daboya (personal communication), where he is excavating a town site with at least 3.6 meters of deposit, has indicated that the pottery is very different from that of New Buipe. Whereas more than 85 percent of the pottery at New Buipe comes under the painted classification, less than 5 percent does at Daboya. The burials have the same orientation as the Akan graves of the Brong area. This is all very suggestive of the relatively slight cultural, as opposed to political, influence that the Ngbanya really exerted (Kense 1979). Their cultural impact was possibly very closely confined to the Volta Valley.

It must be noted that archaeologists, in discussing the problems of the peopling of Ghana, have had to rely very heavily on ceramic evidence, largely because of its abundance and because of the lack of other artifacts or of architectural data. Ethnographic fieldwork is, however, indicating the dangers implicit in trying to adduce culture or even linguistic group from ceramic evidence alone. At the potting village of Bonakyere near Begho, Mo potters, who belong to a Voltaic group, produce pots for both Akan- and Mande-speaking groups within a radius of 30 to 40 kilometers. There is evidence of continuity between the pots of Begho and those that the Mo presently make, suggesting either that the Mo made the pots for the large trade town of Begho and lived there, of which the traditions give no evidence, or that the trade is of some antiquity. Many villages regularly obtain pots from two or more sources. Unless we can prove that pots are made in a given center, it is impossible to state, as has been done for sites like New Buipe (York 1973:176), that two different communities were in residence or that one group of people succeeded another on the basis only of ceramics. Reliance on a single category of evidence proves in this part of Africa to be unsatisfactory.

Further points to be borne in mind in any discussion linking archaeological and linguistic data must be the demographic and environmental conditions. The population of Ghana in 1000 A.D. must have been very small. Taking the early twentieth-century census figures as a standard, we deduce a population of possibly no more than 1.25 million in 1900. Calculating back, allowing for a minimal annual increase of perhaps 0.5 percent, we arrive at a population of less than 50,000 by A.D. 1000. Even if we allow a larger medieval population, which was significantly reduced by the slave trade, we may still be dealing with a relatively small population which was nowhere highly concentrated before the rise of the first city-states, like Begho on the forest-savanna ecotone. The fairly thick vegetation of at least three-fourths of the area of present Ghana would have inhibited movement and presumably encouraged linguistic diversity. A model based on such ground rules would presume relative ease and rapidity of movement from the Sahel belt to the savanna and along the Dahomey Gap and coastal plain, and conversely, stability, slow movement, and considerable linguistic divergence in the area between, which became the Akan heartland. It may have been only with the stimulus of long-distance trade that wealth and ultimately population increased. It would thus be reasonable to think of the Akan as developing in situ during the first millennium A.D. with very little movement taking place. Once the economic stimuli had had a chance to exert themselves, major movements such as the divergence of the Fante and Asante took place, but certainly not until the second millennium A.D.

In Ghanaian history there is still a wide scope for the study of loanwords relating to agricultural activities and to crafts like potting and ironworking, as well as to economic, social, and ritual organization. The arrival of the Portuguese on the coast in 1471 was a watershed in cultural development. Societies began looking seaward as well as into the interior for trade. Had this shift left its impact on the vocabularies of the coastal peoples, it would have provided yet one more clue for dating their movements. Their later town formations are well documented, but not their origins.

Does the schema so prematurely presented by Painter (1966) still have any validity? In detail no, but in concept yes. If we are to move ahead in Ghanaian historiography, it is perhaps necessary to erect "aunt Sallies to Shie at." As they fall we reerect them with a little bit more circumstantial knowledge. Once the protolanguages have been distinguished, they can be examined for circumstantial knowledge of economic practice or environment, which can then be matched against the archaeological evidence. The archeology suggests that a major change took place in Ghana about 35 or 40 centuries ago when the Kintampo Industry appeared; it must surely have had some linguistic impact. Later population movements occurred only in the past ten centuries. The twenty-five or thirty centuries in between were probably marked by the establishment of Volta-Comoe populations across a wide area of Ghana, and the latter part of the period, by emergence of Akan as a separate division of the group. The Akan migrations were not great north-south movements but small regional ones that took place probably in response to the evolving economic environment. In all our speculations it is apparent that archaeologically many of our answers lie to the north of Ghana and to the east in the Dahomey Gap and along the coastal plain. With expanded linguistic analysis and an accelerating rate of archaeological research, the next fifteen years should prove even more fruitful than the last.

References

References

Adams, W. Y.
   1964a.   An introductory classification of Meroitic pottery. *Kush* 12:126–173.
   1964b.   Post-Pharaonic Nubia in the light of archaeology, I. *Journal of Egyptian Archaeology* 50:102–120.
   1966.   Post-Pharaonic Nubia in the light of archaeology, III. *Journal of Egyptian Archaeology* 52:147–162.
   1968.   Invasion, diffusion, evolution? *Antiquity* 42:194–215.
   1976a.   Correspondence. *Geographical Journal* 142:381–384.
   1976b.   *Meroitic North and South: A Study in Cultural Contrast.* Meroitica 2.
   1977.   *Nubia: Corridor to Africa.* Princeton: Princeton University Press.
   1978.   On migration and diffusion as rival paradigms. In P. G. Duke, J. Ebert, G. Langemann, and A. P. Buchner, eds., *Diffusion and Migration: Their Role in Cultural Development.* Pp. 1–5.
   Forthcoming. Meroitic textual material from Qasr Ibrim. In *Proceedings of the Third International Meroitic Conference* (Toronto, 1977).
Adams, W. Y., D. P. Van Gerven, and R. S. Levy
   1978.   The retreat from migrationism. *Annual Review of Anthropology* 1978:438–532.
Addison, F.
   1949.   *Jebel Moya.* London: Oxford University Press.
Agyeman-Duah, J.
   1960.   Mampong, Ashanti: a traditional history of the reign of Nana Safo Kantinka. *Transactions of the Historical Society of Ghana* 4(2):21–25.
Ali Osman
   1973.   Christian Nubia: the contribution of archeology to its understanding. M.A. thesis, University of Calgary.
Ambrose, S. H.
   1977.   Masai Gorge rock shelter: the significance for central Kenya prehistory. B.A. thesis, Department of Anthropology, University of Massachusetts, Boston.
   1980.   Elmenteitan and other Late Pastoral Neolithic adaptations in the central highlands of East Africa. In *Proceedings of the Eighth Panafrican Congress of Prehistory and Quaternary Studies* (Nairobi, 1977).
   Forthcoming. The introduction of pastoral adaptations to the central highlands of East Africa. In J. D. Clark and S. A. Brandt, eds., *From Hunters to Farmers.*
Ambrose, S. H., F. Hivernel, and C. M. Nelson
   1980.   The taxonomic status of the Kenya Capsian. In *Proceedings of the Eighth Panafrican Congress of Prehistory and Quaternary Studies* (Nairobi, 1977).

Ameyaw, Kwabena
1966.   Kwahu: an early forest state. *Ghana Notes and Queries* 9:39−45.
Ammerman, A., and L. Cavalli-Sforza
1973.   A population model for the diffusion of early farming in Europe.
           In Renfrew, C., ed., *The Explanation of Culture Change*. London:
           Duckworth.
Andah, B. W., and F. Anozie
1976.   Preliminary report on the prehistoric site of Afikpo (Nigeria).
           Paper presented at the Inaugural Session of the West African
           Archaeological Association (Enugu).
Andrzejewski, J.
1968.   *The Study of the Bedauye Language: The Present Position and Prospects*.
           Khartoum: Sudan Research Unit.
Anquandah, J.
1965.   Ghana's terracotta cigars. *Ghana Notes and Queries* 7:25.
1975.   State formation among the Akan of Ghana. *Sankofa* 1:47−59.
1978−79.   The Accra plains archaeological and historical project: report on
           1977/76 fieldwork. *Nyame Akuma* 12:24−27; 15:14−18.
Anthony, B.
1973.   The Stillbay question. In *Sixième Congrès Panafricain de préhistoire*
           (Dakar, 1967).
Antilla, R.
1972.   *An Introduction to Historical and Comparative Linguistics*. New York:
           Macmillan.
Arhin, K.
1979.   *Brong Kyempim*. Accra: Afram.
Arkell, A. J.
1951.   An Old Nubian inscription from Kordofan. *American Journal of
           Archaeology* 55:353−354.
1961.   *A History of the Sudan from Earliest Times to 1821*. Rev. ed. London:
           Athlone.
Armstrong, R. G.
1964.   *The Study of West African Languages*. Ibadan: Ibadan University
           Press.
Baker, H. G.
1962.   Comments on the thesis that there was a major centre of plant
           domestication near the headwaters of the river Niger. *Journal of
           African History* 3:229−233.
Barth, F.
1969.   *Ethnic Groups and Boundaries*. Boston: Little, Brown.
Barthelme, J.
1977.   Holocene sites north-east of Lake Turkana: a preliminary report.
           Azania 21:33−41.
Forthcoming. Holocene land-use patterns to the east of Lake Turkana, Kenya.
              In J. D. Clark and S. A. Brandt, eds., *From Hunters to Farmers*.
Baucom, K. L.
1974.   Proto-Central Khoisan. In E. Voeltz, ed., *Third Annual Conference on*

African Linguistics. Bloomington: Indiana University Research Center for the Language Sciences.

Beach, D. M.
1938.   *The Phonetics of the Hottentot Language.* London: Cambridge University Press.

Behrens, P.
1981.   C-Group Sprache—Nubisch—Tu Bedawiye. *Sprache und Geschichte in Afrika 3.*

Bender, M. L.
1969.   Chance CVC correspondence in unrelated languages. *Language* 45:519–531.
1971.   The languages of Ethiopia. *Anthropological Linguistics* 13:165–288.

Bender, M. L., ed.
1976.   *The Non-Semitic Languages of Ethiopia.* East Lansing: Michigan State University.
Forthcoming. *Eastern Sudanic Studies II: Linguistics.* Carbondale: University of Southern Illinois.

Bender, M. L., J. D. Bowen, R. L. Cooper, and C. A. Ferguson, eds.
1976.   *Language in Ethiopia.* London: Oxford University Press.

Bernal, M. G.
1980.   Speculations on the disintegration of Afroasiatic. North American Conference on Afroasiatic Linguistics (San Francisco).

Bimson, K.
1978.   Comparative reconstruction of Proto-Northern-Western Mande. Ph.D. thesis, University of California, Los Angeles.

Bird, C. S.
1971.   The development of Mandekan (Manding): a study of the role of extra-linguistic factors in linguistic change. In D. Dalby, etc., *Language and History in Africa.* New York: Africana. Pp. 146–159.

Birdsell, J. B.
1957.   Some population problems involving Pleistocene man. *Cold Spring Harbor Symposium in Quantitative Biology* 22:47–69.

Blackburn, R. H.
1973.   Okiek ceramics: evidence for central Kenya prehistory. *Azania* 8:55–70.
1974.   The Okiek and their history. *Azania* 9:139–158.
1976.   Okiek history. In B. A. Ogot, ed., *Kenya before 1900.* Nairobi: East African Publishing House. Pp. 53–83.

Blankoff, B.
1969.   L'état des recherches préhistoriques au Gabon. *Études et Documents Tchadiens,* mémoire 1:62–80.

Boadi, L. A.
1975.   Nzema-Ahanta medial [k] and its reflexes in other central Volta-Comoe languages. *Archivum Linguisticum* 5:1–13.

Boahen, Adu
1966.   The Akan of Ghana. *Ghana Notes and Queries* 9:3–10.

Bower, J. R. F.
1973*a*.   Seronera: excavations at a stone bowl site in the Serengeti National Park, Tanzania. *Azania* 8:71−104.

1973*b*.   Early pottery and other finds from Kisii district, western Kenya. *Azania* 8:131−140.

1976.   Notes on the rock art, and cord rouletted pottery at the Seronera stone bowl site, Serengeti National Park, Tanzania, *Azania* 11: 176−179.

Bower, J. R. F., and C. M. Nelson
1979.   Early pottery and pastoral cultures of the central Rift Valley, Kenya. *Man* 13:554−566.

Bower, J. R. F., C. M. Nelson, A. F. Waibel, and S. Wandibba
1977.   The University of Massachusetts' Later Stone Age/Pastoral Neolithic comparative study in central Kenya. *Azania* 12:119−146.

Brandt, S. A.
Forthcoming. New perspectives on the origins of food production in Ethiopia. In J. D. Clark and S. A. Brandt, eds., *From Hunters to Farmers*.

Brown, J.
1966.   The excavation of a group of burial mounds at Ilkek, near Gilgil, Kenya. *Azania* 1:59−78.

Burckhardt, J. L.
1819.   *Travels in Nubia*. London: John Murray.

Butzer, K. W.
1971.   The significance of agricultural dispersal into Europe and northern Africa. In S. Struever, ed., *Prehistoric Agriculture*. Garden City, NY: Natural History Press. Pp. 313−334.

Butzer, K. W., G. L. Isaac, J. L. Richardson, and C. Washbourn-Kamau
1972.   Radiocarbon dating of East African lake levels. *Science* 175: 1069−1076.

Cahen, D.
1976.   Nouvelles fouilles à la pointe de la Gombe (ex-pointe de Kalina), Kinshasa, Zaïre. *L'anthropologie* 80:573−602.

Calvocoressi, D., and N. David
1979.   A new survey of radiocarbon and thermoluminescence dates for West Africa. *Journal of African History* 20:1−29.

Campbell, J., M. Baxter, and L. Alcock
1979.   Radiocarbon dates for the Cadbury massacre. *Antiquity* 53:31−38.

Chapman, S.
1966.   A Sirikwa hole on Mt. Elgon. *Azania* 1:139−148.

1967.   Kansyore Island. *Azania* 2:165−208.

Chittick, H. N.
1969.   An archaeological reconnaissance of the southern Somali coast. *Azania* 4:199−232.

1978.   British Institute in Eastern Africa report of fieldwork. *Nyame Akuma* 12:8.

Chittick, H. N., and S. Ambrose
    In preparation. Report on 1978 excavations at Deloraine Farm, Rongai. *Azania*
            16.
Chitty, D.
    1960.   Population processes in the vole and the relevance to general
                  theory. *Canadian Journal of Zoology* 35:19–113.
Clark, D. L.
    1968.   *Analytical Archaeology*. London: Methuen.
Clark, J. D.
    1954.   *The Prehistoric Cultures of the Horn of Africa*. London: Cambridge
                  University Press.
    1977.   The domestication process in sub-Saharan Africa with special ref-
                  erence to Ethiopia. Paper presented at IX Congrès, Union Inter-
                  nationale des Sciences Préhistoriques et Protohistoriques (Nice,
                  1976), colloque XX:56–115 (preprint).
Clark, J. D., and S. A. Brandt, eds.
    Forthcoming. *From Hunters to Farmers*. Berkeley, Los Angeles, London: Univer-
                  sity of California Press.
Clark, J. D., and A. B. L. Stemler
    1975.   Early domesticated sorghum from central Sudan. *Nature* 254:
                  588–591.
Cleal, A. M.
    1974.   A comparative study of three Guan languages: Ncumuru, Acode
                  and Anyanga. M.A. thesis, Legon, Institute of African Studies.
Coetzee, J. A.
    1964.   Evidence for a considerable depression of the vegetation belts
                  during the Upper Pleistocene on the East African mountains.
                  Nature 204:564–566.
    1967.   Pollen analytical studies in eastern and southern Africa. In E. M.
                  van Zinderen Bakker, ed., *Paleoecology of Africa* 3.
Cohen, D. W.
    1974.   The River-Lake Nilotes from the fifteenth to the nineteenth
                  century. In B. A. Ogot, ed., *Zamani: A Survey of East African History*.
                  Nairobi: Longmans and East African Publishing House.
                  Pp. 135–149.
Cohen, M.
    1970.   A reassessment of the stone bowl cultures of the Rift Valley, Kenya,
                  Azania 5:27–38.
    1972.   Deloraine Farm, a new type of pottery. *Azania* 7:161–166.
Cole, S.
    1963.   *The Prehistory of East Africa*. New York: Macmillan.
Cornevin, R.
    1959.   *Histoire du Togo*. Paris: Berger-Levrault.
Crawford, O. G. S.
    1951.   *The Fung Kingdom of Sennar*. Gloucester: John Bellows.

Crossland, L. B., and M. Posnansky
1978.   Pottery, people and trade at Begho, Ghana. In I. Hodder, ed., *The Spacial Organization of Culture*. London: Duckworth.
Crowfoot, J. W.
1925.   Further notes on pottery. *Sudan Notes and Records* 8:125–136.
Cruz e Silva, T.
1980.   First indications of the Early Iron Age in southern Mozambique: Amatola IV 1/68. In *Proceedings of the Eighth Panafrican Congress of Prehistory and Quaternary Studies* (Nairobi, 1977).
Daaku, K. Y.
1966.   Pre-Ashanti states. *Ghana Notes and Queries* 9:10–13.
Dalby, D.
1975.   The prehistorical implications of Guthrie's comparative Bantu: problems of internal relationship. *Journal of African History* 16: 481–501.
1977.   *Language Map of Africa and Adjacent Islands*. London: International African Institute.
Danquah, J. B.
1957.   *The Quest for Ghana*. Accra.
David, N.
1976.   History of crops and peoples in north Cameroun to A.D. 1900. In J. R. Harlan, J. M. J. de Wet, and A. B. L. Stember, eds., *Origins of Africa Plant Domestication*. The Hague: Mouton. Pp. 223–267.
N.d.   Tazunu: megalithic monuments of central Africa.
Forthcoming. Early Bantu expansion in the context of central African prehistory: 4000–I B.C. In L. Bouquiaux, ed., *Expansion bantoue*. Paris: CNRS.
David, N., P. Harvey, and C. J. Goudie
In press.   Excavations in the southern Sudan, 1979. *Azania* 16.
David, N., and P. Vidal
1977.   The Nana-Modé village site (Sous-Préfecture de Bouar, Central African Republic) and the prehistory of the Ubangian-speaking peoples. *West African Journal of Archaeology* 7:17–56.
Davies, O.
1966.   The invasion of Ghana from the Sahara in the Early Iron Age. In *Proceedings of the Fifth Panafrican Congress of Prehistory and Quaternary Studies* (Tenerife, 1963).
1967.   *West Africa before the Europeans*. London: Methuen.
de Bayle des Hermans, R.
1975.   *Recherches préhistoriques en République Centrafricaine*, Paris: Klincksieck.
de Maret, P.
1976.   Premières datations des hâches polies associées à de la céramique au Bas-Zaïre. Paper presented at IX Congrès, Union Internationale des Sciences Préhistorique et Protohistorique (Nice).
1980.   *Mission archéologique belge au Cameroun: Rapport sur la première cam-*

pagne (janvier–février 1980). Tervuren: Musée Royale de l'Afrique Centrale.

de Maret, P., and F. Nsuka

1977.   History of Bantu metallurgy: some linguistic aspects. *History in Africa* 4:43–56.

Diop, Cheikh Anta

1967.   *Anteriorité des Civilisations nègres: Mythe du venté historique.* Paris: Présence Africaine.

1981.   Origin of the ancient Egyptians. In G. Mokhtar, ed., *General History of Africa.* UNESCO. Berkeley, Los Angeles, London: University of California Press.

Dolphyne, F. A.

1976a.   Delafosse's Abron wordlist in the light of a Brong dialect survey. *Communications from the Basel Africa Bibliography*, 14.

1976b.   Dialect differences and historical process in Akan. *Legon Journal of the Humanities* 2:15–27.

1979.   The Brong (Bono) dialect of Akan. In K. Arhin, ed., *Brong Kyempim.* Accra: Afram. Pp. 88–118.

Dombrowski, J.

1976.   Mumute and Bonoasé: two sites of the Kintampo Industry. *Sankofa* 2:64–71.

1977.   Preliminary note on excavations at a shell midden near Tema, Ghana. *Nyame Akuma* 10:31–34.

Dumont, H. J.

1978.   Neolithic hyperarid period preceded the present climate of the central Sahel. *Nature* 274:356–358.

Dyen, I.

1965.   *A Lexicostatistical Classification of the Austronesian Languages. International Jounral of American Linguistics,* memoir 19.

Dyson-Hudson, R., and E. A. Smith

1978.   Human territoriality: an ecological reassessment. *American Anthropologist* 80:21–41.

Effah-Gyamfi, E.

1975.   Aspects of the archaeology and oral traditions of the Bono state. *Transactions of the Historical Society of Ghana* 15:217–227.

Ehret, C.

1964.   A lexicostatistical classification of Bantu, using Guthrie's test languages. Unpublished.

1967.   Cattle-keeping and milking in eastern and southern African history; the linguistic evidence. *Journal of African history* 8:1–17.

1968.   Sheep and Central Sudanic peoples in southern Africa. *Journal of African History* 9:213–221.

1971.   *Southern Nilotic History: Linguistic Approaches to the Study of the Past.* Evanston: Northwestern University Press.

1972.   Bantu origins and history: critique and interpretation. *Transafrican Journal of History* 2:1–9.

1973. Patterns of Bantu and Central Sudanic settlement in central and southern Africa (ca. 1000 BC–500 AD). *Transafrican Journal of History* 3:1–71.

1974a. Agricultural history in central and southern Africa, c. 1000 BC to AD. 500. *Transafrican Journal of History* 4:1–25.

1974b. *Ethiopians and East Africans: The Problem of Contacts.* Nairobi: East African Publishing House.

1976. Aspects of social and economic change in western Kenya, c. A.D. 500–1800. In B. A. Ogot, ed., *Kenya before 1900.* Nairobi: East African Publishing House. Pp. 1–20.

1979. On the antiquity of agriculture in Ethiopia. *Journal of African History* 20:161–177.

Forthcoming a. Historical linguistic evidence on early African agriculture. In J. D. Clark and S. A. Brandt, eds., *From Hunters to Farmers.*

Forthcoming b. East Africa: the interior. In D. T. Niane, ed., *Africa: Twelfth to Sixteenth Centuries.* Vol. 4: *General History of Africa.* UNESCO.

Unpublished a. The invention of highland planting agriculture in northeastern Tanzania: cultural and linguistic background.

Unpublished b. Technological change in central and southern Africa, ca. 1000 B.C. to A.D. 500.

Ehret, C., M. Bink, T. Ginindza, E. Gotschall, B. Hall, M. Hlatshwayo, D. Johnson, and R. L. Pouwels
1972. Outlining southern African history: a re-evaluation, A.D. 100–1500. *Ufahamu* 3(1):9–27.

Ehret, C., T. Coffman, L. Fliegelman, A. Gold, M. Hubbard, D. Johnson, and D. Saxon
1974. Some thoughts on the early history of the Nile-Congo watershed. *Ufahamu* 5(2):85–112.

Ehret, C., and M. Kinsman
1981. Shona dialect classification and its implications for Iron Age history in southern Africa. *International Journal of African Historical Studies* 14.

Ehret, C., and D. Nurse
1981. The Taita Cushites. *Sprache und Geschichte in Afrika* 3.
In press. History in the Taita hills: a provisional synthesis. *Kenya Historical Review.*

Elliott Smith, G., and D. E. Derry
1910. Anatomical report. *Archaeological Survey of Nubia*, Bulletin 5:11–25.

Elphick, R.
1977. *Kraal and Castle.* New Haven: Yale University Press.

Emlen, J. M.
1973. *Ecology: An Evolutionary Approach.* New York: Addison-Wesley.

Epstein, E.
1971. *The Origin of the Domestic Animals of Africa.* 2 vols. New York: Africana Publishing House.

Fagan, B. M.
1965.   *Southern Africa in the Iron Age*. London: Thames and Hudson.
Fagan, B. M., and J. Yellen
1968.   Ivuna: ancient salt-working in southern Tanzania. *Azania* 3:1−43.
Fagg, A.
1970.   Aspects of the Nok culture. *West African Archaeological Newsletter* 12:80−81.
Farrand, W. R., R. W. Redding, M. H. Wolpoff, and H. T. Wright III
1976.   *An Archaeological Investigation of the Loboi Plain, Baringo District, Kenya.* University of Michigan, Museum of Archaeology, Technical Report #4, Research Reports in Archaeology Contribution no. 1.
Faugust, P. M., and J. E. G. Sutton
1966.   The Egerton Cave on the Njoro River. *Azania* 1:149−175.
Feierman, S.
1974.   *The Shambaa Kingdom*. Madison: University of Wisconsin Press.
Feinberg, H. M.
1970.   Who were the Elmina? *Ghana Notes and Queries* 11:20−26.
Fernea, R. A.
1979.   Tradition and change in Egyptian Nubia. In *Africa in Antiquity*. Berlin: Akademie Verlag.
Fleming, H. C.
1964.   Baiso and Rendille: Somali outliers. *Rassegna di Studi etiopici* 20: 35−96.
1969.   Asa and Aramanik: Cushitic hunters in Masailand. *Ethnology* 8:1−36.
1976.   Sociology, ethnology and history in Ethiopia. *International Journal of African Historical Studies* 9:248−278.
Flight, C.
1976.   The Kintampo Culture and its place in the economic prehistory of West Africa. In J. Harlan, J. M. J. de Wet, and A. B. L. Stemler, eds., *Origins of African Plant Domestication*. The Hague: Mouton. Pp. 211−221.
1980.   Malcolm Guthrie and the reconstruction of Bantu prehistory. *History in Africa* 7:81−118.
Frend, W. H. C.
1972.   Coptic, Greek, and Nubian at Q'asr Ibrim. *Byzantinoslavica* 33: 224−229.
Fynn, J. K.
1966.   The rise of Ashanti. *Ghana Notes and Queries* 9:24−30.
1975.   The pre-Bɔrbɔr Fante states. *Sankofa* 1:22−31.
Gabel, C.
1969.   Six rock shelters on the northern Kavirondo shore of Lake Victoria. *International Journal of African Historical Studies* 2: 205−254.

Garlake, P.
1979.   Review of D. W. Phillipson, *The Later Prehistory of Eastern and South-ern Africa. Journal of African History* 20:457–459.
Gifford, D. P.
1978.   Ethnoarchaeological observations of natural processes affecting cultural materials. In R. Gould, ed., *Explorations in Ethnoarchaeology.* Albuquerque: University of New Mexico Press. Pp. 77–101.
Gifford, D. P., G. L. Isaac, and C. M. Nelson
In press.   Prolonged drift. *Azania* 15.
Gleason, H. A.
1959.   Counting and calculating for historical reconstruction. *Anthropological Linguistics* 1:22–32.
Goodman, M.
1971.   The strange case of the Mbugu (Tanzania). In D. Hymes, ed., *Pidginization and Creolization of Languages.* London: Cambridge University Press.
Goody, J.
1963.   Ethnological notes on the distribution of the Guang languages. *Journal of African Languages* 2:178–189.
1964.   The Mande and the Akan hinterland. In J. Vansina, R. Mauny, and R. V. Thomas, eds., *The Historian in Tropical Africa.* London: Oxford University Press for International African Institute. Pp. 193–218.
1966.   The Akan and the north. *Ghana Notes and Queries* 9:18–24.
Gramly, R. M.
1972.   Report on the teeth from Narosura. *Azania* 7:87–91.
1975*a*.   Pastoralists and hunters: recent prehistory in southern Kenya and northern Tanzania. Ph.D. thesis, Harvard University.
1975*b*.   Meat feasting and cattle brands; pattern of rock shelter utilization in East Africa. *Azania* 10:107–122.
1976.   Upper Pleistocene archaeological occurrences at site GvJm/22, Lukenya Hill, Kenya. *Man* (n.s.) 11:468–474.
1978.   Expansion of Bantu-speakers *versus* development of Bantu language *in situ*: an archaeologist's perspective. *South African Archaeological Bulletin* 33:107–112.
Greenberg, J. H.
1955.   *Studies in African Linguistic Classification.* New Haven: Compass Press.
1963.   *The Languages of Africa.* The Hague: Mouton.
1964.   Historical inferences from linguistic research in sub-Saharan Africa. In J. Butler, ed., *Boston University Papers in African History.* New York: Praeger. I:1–15.
1972.   Linguistic evidence regarding Bantu origins. *Journal of African History* 13:189–216.
1973.   Nilo-Saharan and Meroitic. In T. Sebeok, ed., *Current Trends in Linguistics* 7. The Hague: Mouton.

Griffith, F. Ll.
1911.   *Karanog: The Meroitic Inscriptions of Shablul and Karanog.* Phila-
             delphia: University of Pennsylvania Museum. Eckley B. Coxe
             Junior Expedition to Nubia. Vol. VI.
1913.   *The Nubian Texts of the Christian Period.* Abhandlung der
             königlichen preussischen Akademie der Wissenschaften, Philo-
             sophisch-Historische Klasse, no. 8.
1925.   Pakhoras-Bakharas-Faras in geography and history. *Journal of
             Egyptian Archaeology* 11:259–268.
Gudschinsky, S.
1964.   The ABC's of lexicostatistics. In D. Hymes, ed., *Language in Culture
             and Society.* New York: Harper and Row.
Guthrie, M.
1962.   Some developments in the pre-history of the Bantu languages.
             Journal of African History 3:273–302.
1967.   *The Classification of the Bantu Languages.* London: International
             African Institute.
1967–1972. *Comparative Bantu.* 4 vols. Farnsborough: Gregg International
             Publishers.
Haaland, R.
1977.   Archaeological classification and ethnic groups: a case study from
             Sudanese Nubia. *Norwegian Archaeological Review* 10:1–31.
1978.   The seasonal interconnection between Zakiab and Kadero, two
             Neolithic sites in the central Sudan. *Nyame Akuma* 13:32–35.
1979.   Some new C-14 dates from central Sudan. *Nyame Akuma* 15:56–58.
Harinck, G.
1969.   Interaction between Xhosa and Khoi: emphasis on the period
             1620–1750. In L. Thompson, ed., *African Societies in Southern
             Africa.* London: Heinemann. Pp. 145–169.
Harlan, J. R.
1971.   Agricultural origins: centers and noncenters. *Science* 174:
             468–474.
Harlan, J. R., J. M. J. de Wet, and A. B. L. Stemler, eds.
1976.   *Origins of African Plant Domestication.* The Hague: Mouton.
Harris, D. R.
1973.   The prehistory of tropical agriculture: an ethno-ecological model.
             In C. Renfrew, ed., *The Explanation of Culture Change: Models in
             Prehistory.* London: Duckworth. Pp. 391–417.
1976.   Traditional systems of plant food production and the origins of
             agriculture in West Africa. In J. R. Harlan, J. M. J. de Wet, and
             A. B. L. Stember, eds., *Origins of African Plant Domestication.* The
             Hague: Mouton. Pp. 311–356.
Hartle, D. D.
1966.   Archaeology in eastern Nigeria. *West African Archaeological News-
             letter* 5:13–17.
1967.   Archaeology in eastern Nigeria. *Nigeria Magazine* 93:134–143.

1972.   Archaeology east of the Niger: a review of culture-historical developments. Nsukka. Mimeographed. 14 + vi pp.

Hasan, Y. F.
1967*a*.   *The Arabs and the Sudan.* Edinburgh: Edinburgh University Press.
1967*b*.   Main aspects of the Arab migration to the Sudan. *Arabica* 14: 14−31.

Haycock, B. G.
1965.   The kingship of Cush in the Sudan. *Comparative Studies in Society and History* 7:461−480.
1968.   Towards a better understanding of the kingdom of Kush. *Sudan Notes and Records* 49:1−16.
1972.   The History Department study tours in the area from Abidya to Mograt, 1969−1971. *Adab* 1 (Khartoum).

Heine, B.
1968.   *Die Verbreitung und Gliederung der Togorestsprachen.* Kölner Beiträge zur Afrikanistik, 1. Berlin: Dietrich Reimer.
1973.   Zur genetischen Gliederung der Bantu-Sprachen. *Afrika und Übersee* 56:164−184.
1974.   Historical linguistics and lexicostatistics. *Journal of African Languages* 11(3):7−20.

Heine, B., H. Hoff, and R. Vossen
1975.   Neuere Ergebnisse zur Territorialgeschichte der Bantu. Cologne. Mimeographed. 13 pp.

Heine, B., F. Rottland, and R. Vossen
1979.   Proto-Baz: some aspects of early Nilotic-Cushitic contacts. *Sprache und Geschichte in Afrika* 1:75−90.

Henrici, A.
1973.   Numerical classification of Bantu languages. *African Language Studies* 14:82−104.

Hiernaux, J., E. Maquet, and J. de Buyat
1973.   Le cimetière protohistorique de Katoto, vallée de Lualaba, Congo-Kinshasa. In *Sixième Congrès Panafricain de préhistoire* (Dakar, 1967).

Higgs, E., and C. Vita-Finzi
1972.   Prehistoric economies: a territorial approach. In E. Higgs, ed., *Papers in Economic Prehistory.* London: Cambridge University Press.

Hinnebusch, T. J.
1973.   Prefixes, sound changes, and subgrouping in the Kenya coastal languages. Ph.D. thesis, University of California, Los Angeles.
1976*a*.   The Shungwaya hypothesis: a linguistic reappraisal. In J. T. Gallagher, ed., *East African Culture History.* Syracuse University, Foreign and Comparative Studies, Eastern Africa, 25. Pp. 1−41.
1976*b*.   Swahili: genetic affiliations and evidence. *Studies in African Linguistics*, supp. 6:95−108.

Hinnebusch, T. J., D. Nurse, and M. Mould
Forthcoming.   *Studies in the Classification of Eastern Bantu Languages.* Beiheft 3, *Sprache und Geschichte in Afrika.* Hamburg: Buske.

Hintze, F.
1959.   *Studien zur Meroitischen Chronologie und zu den Opfertafeln aus den Pyramiden von Meroe.* Abhandlungen der Deutschen Akademie der Wissenschaften zu Berlin, Klasse für Sprachen, Literatur, und Kunst, no. 2.
1967.   Meroe und die Noba. *Zeitschrift für Ägyptische Sprache und Altertumskunde* 94:79−86.

Hivernel, F.
1975.   Preliminary report on excavations at Ngenyn, Kenya. *Azania* 10: 140−144.
1978.   An ethnoarchaeological study of environmental use in the Kenya highlands. Ph.D. thesis, Institute of Archaeology, London.

Hodder, I.
1977.   The distribution of material culture items in the Baringo district, western Kenya. *Man* (n.s.) 12:239−269.
1978.   The maintenance of group identities in the Baringo district, western Kenya. In D. Green, C. Haselgrove, and M. Spriggs, eds., *Social Organization and Settlement.* British Archaeological Reports International Series 47:47−74.
1979.   Economic and social stress and material culture patterning. *American Antiquity* 44:446−454.

Hodge, C. T.
1976.   Lisramic (Afroasiatic): an overview. In M. L. Bender, ed., *The Non-Semitic Languages of Ethiopia.* East Lansing: Michigan State University. Pp. 43−65.

Hombert, J.-M.
1979.   Early Bantu population movements and iron metallurgy: the linguistic evidence. Proceedings of the Fifth Annual Meeting, Berkeley Linguistic Society.

Honken, H. D.
1977.   Submerged features and Proto-Khoisan. In A. Traill, ed., *Khoisan Studies* 3:145−169. Johannesburg: University of Witwatersrand.

Hrbek, I.
1977.   Egypt, Nubia and the eastern deserts. In J. D. Fage and R. Oliver, eds., *The Cambridge History of Africa,* 3:10−97. London: Cambridge University Press.

Huffman, T. N.
1970.   The Early Iron Age and the spread of the Bantu. *South African Archaeological Bulletin* 25:3−21.
1977.   The interpretation of Iron Age radiocarbon dates. *Arnoldia* 8(17): 1−5.
1978.   The origins of Leopards Kopje: an 11th century difaquane. *Arnoldia* 8(23):1−23.
1979.   African origins. Review of D. W. Phillipson, *The Later Prehistory of Eastern and Southern Africa. South African Journal of Science* 75: 232−237.
1980.   Ceramics: classification and Iron Age entities. *African Studies,* 39: 123−174.

Hymes, D.
1959.   Genetic classification: retrospect and prospect. *Anthropological Linguistics* 1:50–66.
1960.   Lexicostatistics so far. *Current Anthropology* 1:3–44.
Inskeep, R. R.
1962.   The age of the Kondoa rock paintings in the light of recent excavations at the Kisese II rock shelter. In *Actes du IV Congrès Panafricain de préhistoire et de l'étude du Quaternaire.* Pp. 249–254.
1979.   *The Peopling of Southern Africa.* New York: Barnes and Noble.
Jacobs, A. H.
1975.   Maasai pastoralism in historical perspective. In T. Monod, ed., *Pastoralism in Tropical Africa.* London: International African Institute. Pp. 406–425.
Jauze, J. B.
1944.   Contribution à l'étude de l'archéologie du Cameroun. *Bulletin de la Société d'Études Camerounaises* 8:105–123.
Jeffreys, M. D. W.
1948.   Stone-age smiths. *Archiv für Völkerkunde* 3:1–8.
John of Biclarum
1894.   *Chronicle.* Trans. Th. Mommsen. *Monumenta Germaniae Historica, Auctores Antiquissimi,* 40:207–220.
John of Ephesus
1860.   *Ecclesiastical History.* Trans. R. Payne-Smith. London: Oxford University Press.
Keech McIntosh, S., and R. J. McIntosh
1980.   Jenne-Jeno: an ancient African city. *Archaeology* 33(1):8–14.
Kendall, R. L.
1969.   An ecological history of the Lake Victoria Basin. *Ecological Monographs* 39:121–175.
Kense, F. J.
1979.   Daboya: report on the 1979 season. *Nyame Akuma* 15:20–22.
Kimambo, I. N.
1969.   *A Political History of the Pare of Tanzania.* Nairobi: East African Publishing House.
1974.   The Eastern Bantu people. In B. A. Ogot, ed., *Zamani: A Survey of East African History.* Nairobi: Longmans and East African Publishing House. Pp. 195–209.
King, K. Jr., and J. L. Bada
1979.   Effects of in-situ leaching on amino acid racemization rates in fossil bone. *Nature* 281:135–137.
Kirwan, L. P.
1935.   Notes on the topography of the Christian Nubian kingdoms. *Journal of Egyptian Archaeology* 21:57–62.
1937a.   Studies in the later history of Nubia. *University of Liverpool Annals of Archaeology and Anthropology* 24:69–105.
1937b.   A survey of Nubian origins. *Sudan Notes and Records* 20:47–62.
1939.   *The Oxford University Excavations at Firka.* London: Oxford University Press.

1958.   Comments on the origins and history of the Nobatae of Procopius. *Kush* 6:69–73.

1960.   The decline and fall of Meroe. *Kush* 8:163–173.

Kiyaga-Mulindwa, D.

1976.   Archaeological and historical research in the Birim Valley. *Sankofa* 2:90–91.

1980.   The Akan problem. *Current Anthropology* 21:503–506.

Klichowska, M.

1978.   Preliminary results of palaeoethnobotanical studies on plant impressions on potsherds from the Neolithic settlement at Kadero. *Nyame Akuma* 12:42–43.

Klima, G.

1970.   *The Barabaig: East African Cattle Herders*. New York: Holt, Reinhart and Winston.

Kroeber, A. L.

1927.   Disposal of the dead. *American Anthropologist* 29:308–315.

Kropp Dakubu, M. E.

1972.   Linguistic pre-history and historical reconstructions: the Ga-Adangme migrations. *Transactions of the Historical Society of Ghana* 13:87–111.

1977.   The Potou lenis stops and Western Kwa. *Anthropological Linguistics* 19:431–435.

Krzyaniak, L.

1976.   Note on the 5th season of fieldwork at Kadero. *Nyame Akuma* 9:41.

1977.   Polish excavations at Kadero. *Nyame Akuma* 10:45–46.

1978.   New light on early food production in the central Sudan. *Journal of African History* 19:159–172.

1979.   Polish excavations at Kadero. *Nyame Akuma* 15:67–69.

Kumah, J. K.

1966.   The rise and fall of the kingdom of Denkyira. *Ghana Notes and Queries* 9:33–35.

Kwamena-Poh, M. A.

1973.   *Government and Politics in the Akuapem State, 1730–1850*. London: Longmans.

Lack, D.

1954.   *The Natural Regulation of Animal Numbers*. London: Oxford University Press.

Ladefoged, P., R. Glick, and C. Criper

1971.   *Language in Uganda*. London: Oxford University Press.

Lathrap, D. W.

1970.   *The Upper Amazon*. London: Thames and Hudson.

Lawton, A. C.

1967.   Bantu pottery in southern Africa. *Annals of the South African Museum* 49:1–440.

Leakey, L. S. B.

1931.   *The Stone Age Cultures of Kenya Colony*. London: Cambridge University press.

1935.   *The Stone Age Races of Kenya*. London: Oxford University Press.

1942.   The Naivasha fossil skull and skeleton. *Journal of the East African Natural History Society* 16:169–177.
1952.   Capsian or Aurignacian: which terms should be used in Africa? In *Proceedings of the First Panafrican Congress of Prehistory* (Nairobi, 1947).
Leakey, L. S. B., and M. D. Leakey
1950.   *Excavations at the Njoro River Cave.* Oxford: Clarendon Press.
Leakey, M. D.
1945.   Report on the excavations at Hyrax Hill, Nakuru, Kenya Colony, 1937–38. *Transactions of the Royal Society of South Africa* 30(4).
1966.   Excavation of burial mounds in Ngorongoro Crater. *Tanzania Notes and Records* 66:123–125.
Leakey, M. D., R. L. Hay, D. L. Thurber, R. Protsch, and R. Berger
1972.   Stratigraphy, archaeology and age of the Ndutu and Naisiusiu beds, Olduvai Gorge, Tanzania. *World Archaeology* 3:328–341.
Legassick, M.
1969.   The Sotho-Tswana before 1800. In L. Thompson, ed., *African Societies in Southern Africa.* London: Heinemann. Pp. 86–124.
Livingston, D. A.
1976.   Late Quaternary climate change in Africa. *Annual Review of Ecology and Systematics* 6:249–280.
Lucas, J. O.
1948.   *The Religion of the Yorubas in Relation to the Religion of Ancient Egypt.* Lagos: C.M.S. Bookshop.
Lynch, B. M., and L. H. Robbins
1978.   Namoratunga: the first archaeoastronomic evidence in sub-Saharan Africa. *Science* 200:766–768.
1979.   Cushitic and Nilotic prehistory: new archaeological evidence from north-west Kenya. *Journal of African History* 20:319–328.
McBurney, C. B. M.
1975.   The archaeological context of the Hamitic languages in northern Africa. In J. and T. Bynon, eds., *Hamito-Semitica.* The Hague: Mouton.
MacDiarmid, P. A. and N.
1931.   The languages of the Nuba mountains. *Sudan Notes and Records* 14:149–162.
McGaffey, W.
1961.   The history of Negro migrations in the Sudan. *Southwestern Journal of Anthropology* 17:178–197.
1966.   Concepts of race in the historiography of northeast Africa. *Journal of African History* 7:1–17.
McMaster, M.
1977.   The Bua of northern Zaire: an approach to cultural history. Seminar paper. University of California, Los Angeles.
1978.   Linguistic evidence for the history of Bua/Mangbetu interactions. Seminar paper. University of California, Los Angeles.
MacMichael, H. A.
1920.   Darfur linguistics. *Sudan Notes and Records* 3:197–216.

1922.   *A History of the Arabs in the Sudan.* London: Macmillan.
Maggs, T. O.
1977.   Some recent radiocarbon dates from eastern and southern Africa.
               Journal of African History 18:161–197.
Marliac, M.
1973.   L'état des connaissances sur le paléolithique et le néolithique du
               Cameroun. Yaounde: Organisation de la Recherche Scientifique et
               Technique d'Outre-Mer.
Masao, F. T.
1979.   *The Later Stone Age and Rock Paintings of Central Tanzania.* Studien
               zur Kultur 48. Weisbaden: Steiner.
Mathewson, R. D.
1972.   Kitare: an early trading center in the Volta Basin. In *Sixième Congrès
               Panafricain de préhistoire* (Dakar, 1967).
Mauny, R.
1952.   Essai sur l'histoire des metaux en Afrique occidentale. *Bulletin
               d'Ifan* 15:545–595.
Meeussen, A. E.
1956.   Statistique lexicographique en Bantu: Bobangi et Zulu. *Kongo-
               Overzee* 22:86–89.
Mehlman, M. J.
1977.   Excavations at Nasera Rock. *Azania* 12:111—118.
1979.   Mumba-Höhle revisited: the relevance of a forgotten excavation to
               some current issues in East African prehistory. *World Archaeology*
               11:80–94.
Meinhof, C.
1912.   *Die Sprachen der Hamiten.* Hamburg: Friederichsen.
Merrick, H. V.
1975.   Change in Later Pleistocene lithic industries in eastern Africa.
               Ph.D. thesis, University of California, Berkeley.
Meyerowitz, E. L. R.
1960.   *The Divine Kingship in Ghana and Ancient Egypt.* London: Faber.
Miller, S. F.
1969.   Contacts between the Later Stone Age and the Early Iron Age in
               southern and central Africa. *Azania* 4:81–90.
1979.   Lukenya Hill: GvJm46 excavation report. *Nyame Akuma* 14:31–
               34.
Millet, N.
1964.   Some notes on the linguistic background of modern Nubia. Aswan,
               Symposium on Contemporary Nubia.
Miracle, M.
1967.   *Agriculture in the Congo Basin.* Madison: University of Wisconsin
               Press.
Monneret de Villard, U.
1938.   *Storia della Nubia Cristiana.* Pontificio Institutum Orientalium
               Studium, Orientalia Christiana Analecta, 118.
Monnig. H. O.
1967.   *The Pedi.* Pretoria: Van Schaik.

Mortelmans, G.
1962*a*.　Vue d'ensemble sur la préhistoire du Congo occidental. In *Actes du IV Congrès Panafricain de préhistoire et de l'étude du Quaternaire.* Pp. 129–164.
1962*b*.　Archéologie des grottes Dimba et Ngovo (Région de Thysville, Bas-Congo). In *Actes du IV Congrès Panafricain de préhistoire et de l'étude du Quaternaire.* Pp. 407–425.

Munson, P. J.
1976.　Archaeological data on the origins of cultivation in the southwestern Sahara and its implications for West Africa. In J. R. Harlan, J. M. J. de Wet, and A. B. L. Stemler, eds., *Origins of African Plant Domestication.* The Hague: Mouton. Pp. 187–209.
1978.　Africa's prehistoric past. In P. M. Martin and P. O'Meara, *Africa.* Bloomington: Indiana University Press. Pp. 62–82.
1980.　Archaeology and the prehistoric origins of the Ghana empire. *Journal of African history* 21:457–466.

Murdock. G. P.
1959.　*Africa: Its Peoples and Their Culture History.* New York: McGraw-Hill.

Nelson, C. M.
1973.　A comparative analysis of 29 Later Stone Age occurrences from East Africa. Ph.D. thesis, University of California, Berkeley.
1980.　The Elmenteitan lithic industry. In *Proceedings of the Eighth Panafrican Congress of Prehistory and Quaternary Studies* (Nairobi, 1977).

Nelson, C. M., and M. Posnansky
1970.　The stone tools from the excavation of Nsongezi rock shelter. *Azania* 5:119–172.

Newton, L. E., and S. R. J. Woodell
1976.　A newly discovered site for the Kintampo "Neolithic" cultural tradition near Kumasi. *Sankofa* 2:19–22.

Nurse, D.
1979*a*.　*Classification of the Chaga Dialects.* Hamburg: Buske.
1979*b*.　Description of sample Bantu languages of Tanzania. *African Languages/Langues Africaines* 5:1–150.
Forthcoming.　Segeju and Daiso: an essay in methodology. In J. Allen and D. Wilson, eds., *Pwani: Essays Presented to James Kirkman.*

Nurse, D., and G. Philippson
1975.　The north-eastern Bantu languages of Tanzania and Kenya: a classification. *Kiswahili* 45(2):1–28.
1980.　The Bantu languages of northern and central Tanzania, Kenya and Uganda: a lexicostatistical survey. In E. Polomé, ed., *Language in Tanzania.* London: International African Institute.

Nygaard, S., and M. Talbot
1976.　Interim report on excavations at Aoskrochona, Ghana. *West African Journal of Archaeology* 6:13–19.
1977.　First dates from the coastal sites near Kpone, Ghana. *Nyame Akuma* 11:29–30.

Oakley, K. P.
1961.   Bone harpoon from Gamble's Cave, Kenya. *Antiquaries Journal*
               41:86–87.
Odner, K.
1971*a*.   An archaeological survey of the Iramba Plateau, Tanzania. *Azania*
               6:151–198.
1971*b*.   Preliminary report on an archaeological survey on the slopes of
               Kilimanjaro. *Azania* 6:131–149.
1971*c*.   Usangi Hospital and other archaeological sites in the North Pare
               Mountains, north-eastern Tanzania. *Azania* 6:89–130.
1972.   Excavations at Narosura, a stone bowl site in the southern Kenya
               highlands. *Azania* 6:25–92.
Ogot, B. A., ed.
1974.   *Zamani: A Survey of East African History*. Nairobi: Longmans and
               East African Publishing House.
1976.   *Kenya before 1900*. Nairobi: East African Publishing House.
Ohannessian, S., and M. E. Kashoki
1978.   *Language in Zambia*. London: International African Institute.
Oliver, R.
1966.   The problem of the Bantu expansion. *Journal of African History*
               7:361–376.
1978.   The emergence of Bantu Africa. In J. D. Fage and R. Oliver, eds.,
               The Cambridge History of Africa, 2:342–409. London: Cambridge
               University Press.
1979.   Cameroun: the Bantu cradleland? *Sprache und Geschichte in Afrika*
               1:7–20.
Onyango-Abuje, J. C.
1977*a*.   Crescent Island. *Azania* 12:147–160.
1977*b*.   A contribution to the study of the Neolithic in East Africa with
               particular reference to Naivasha-Nakuru basins. Ph.D. thesis, Uni-
               versity of California, Berkeley.
Painter, C.
1966.   The Guang and West African historical reconstruction. *Ghana
               Notes and Queries* 9:58–66.
1972.   *Collected Language Notes no. 12: 14 Papers on Gwa and 52 Texts in Gwa*.
               Legon: Institute of African Studies.
Papstein, R.
1979.   The upper Zambezi: a history of the Luvale people, 1000–1900.
               Ph.D. thesis, University of California, Los Angeles.
Phillipson, D. W.
1975.   The chronology of the Iron Age in Bantu Africa. *Journal of African
               History* 16:321–342.
1976*a*.   The Early Iron Age in eastern and southern Africa: critical re-
               appraisal. *Azania* 11:1–23.
1976*b*.   Fishermen and the beginnings of East African farming: new light
               from northern Kenya. *Kenya Past and Present* 7:2–9.
1977*a*.   The excavation of Gobedra rock shelter, Axum. *Azania* 12:53–82.

1977*b*.   *The Later Prehistory of Eastern and Southern Africa.* London: Heinemann.
1977*c*.   Lowasera. *Azania* 12:1−32.
1977*d*.   The spread of the Bantu language. *Scientific American* 236(4): 106−114.

Plumley, J. M.
1975.   Qasr Ibrim 1974. *Journal of Egyptian Archaeology* 61:5−27.

Plumley, J. M., and W. Y. Adams
1974.   Qasr Ibrim 1972. *Journal of Egyptian Archaeology* 60:212−238.

Plumley, J. M., W. Y. Adams, and E. Crowfoot
1977.   Qasr Ibrim 1976. *Journal of Egyptian Archaeology* 63:29−47.

Posnansky, M.
1967*a*.   The Iron Age in East Africa. In W. W. Bishop and J. D. Clark, eds., *Background to Evolution in Africa.* Chicago: University of Chicago Press. Pp. 629−650.
1967*b*.   Excavations at Lanet, Kenya, 1957. *Azania* 1:89−114.
1968*a*.   Cairns in the southern part of the Kenya Rift Valley. *Azania* 3: 181−187.
1968*b*.   Bantu genesis: archaeological reflexions. *Journal of African History* 9:11−22.
1976.   New radiocarbon dates from Ghana. *Sankofa* 2:60−63.
1977.   The archaeological foundations of the history of Ghana. In J. O. Hunwick, ed., *Proceedings of the Seminar on Ghanaian Historiography and Historical Research* (Legon). Pp. 1−25.
Forthcoming. Early agricultural societies in Ghana. In J. D. Clark and S. A. Brandt, eds., *From Hunters to Farmers.*

Posnansky, M., and C. M. Nelson
1968.   Rock paintings and excavations at Nyero, Uganda. *Azania* 3:47−66.

Priese, K.-H.
1968.   Nichtägyptischen Namen und Worter in den ägyptischen Inschriften der Könige von Kusch. *Mitteilungen des Instituts für Orientforschung der Deutschen Akademie der Wissenschaften zu Berlin* 14: 165−191.
1973*a*.   Articula. *Travaux du Centre d'Archéologie Mediterranéenne de l'Académie Polonaise des Sciences* 14 (*Études et Travaux* 7):156−162.
1973*b*.   Zur Ortsliste des römischen Meroe-Expeditionen unter Nero. In Fritz Hintze, ed., *Sudan in Altertum* (*Meroitica* 1). Pp. 123−126.
1975.   Das "äthiopische" Niltal bei Bion und Juba (Arbeitsbericht). In K. Michalowski, ed., *Nubia: Récentes Recherches.* Warsaw: Musée National. Pp. 108−110.

Protsch, R.
1975.   The Naivasha hominid and its confirmed late Upper Pleistocene age. *Anthropologischer Anzeiger* 35:97−102.
1978.   The chronological position of Gamble's Cave II and Bromhead's

site (Elmenteita) of the Rift Valley, Kenya. *Journal of Human Evolution* 7(2):101–109.

Reindorf, C. C.
1898.   *The History of the Gold Coast and Asante.* Basel: Basel Mission Book Depot.

Retord, G.
1971.   Les differents parlers Anyi et le Baoulé. In M. Houis, ed., *Acts de la Huitième Congrès de la Société Linguistique de l'Afrique Occidentale.* Abidjan. Pp. 293–310.

Richardson, J. L.
1966.   Changes in the level of Lake Naivasha, Kenya, during post-glacial times. *Nature* 209:290–291.

Richardson, J. L., and A. E. Richardson
1972.   The history of an East African rift lake and its climatic implications. *Ecological Monographs* 42:499–534.

Rightmire, G. P.
1975.   New studies of post-Pleistocene human skeletal remains from the Rift Valley, Kenya. *American Journal of Physical Anthropology* 42: 351–370.
1977.   Notes on the human burials from Lowasera. *Azania* 12:30–32.

Robbins, L. H.
1972.   Archaeology in the Turkana district, Kenya. *Science* 176:359–366.

Robbins, L. H., and B. M. Lynch
1978.   New evidence on the use of microliths from the Lake Turkana Basin, East Africa. *Current Anthropology* 19:619–620.

Robbins, L. H., S. McFarlin, J. T. Brower, and A. E. Hoffman
1977.   Rangi, a Late Stone Age site in Karimoja district, Uganda. *Azania* 12:209–233.

Robertshaw, P., and J. Mack
1980.   Preliminary report on the 1980 B.I.E.A. expedition to the southern Sudan. *Nyame Akuma* 16:37–40.

Robins, R. H.
1973.   The history of language classification. In T. Sebeok, ed., *Current Trends in Linguistics II.* The Hague: Mouton.

Robinson, K. R.
1970.   The Iron Age in the southern lake area, Malawi. Malawi Antiquities Department Publication 8.
1973.   The Iron Age of the upper and lower Shire, Malawi. Malawi Antiquities Department Publication 13.
1976.   A note on the spread of the Early Iron ceramics in Malawi: tentative suggestions based on recent evidence. *South African Archaeological Bulletin* 31:163–175.

Sandelowsky. B. H.
1973.   Kapako, an Early Iron Age site on the Okavango River, Southwest Africa. *South African Journal of Science* 65:325.

1974.   Archaeological investigations at Mirabib Hill Rock Shelter. *South African Archaeological Society, Goodwin Series* 2:65–72.

Sandelowsky, B. H., J. H. van Rooyen, and J. C. Vogel
1979.   Early evidence for herders in the Namib. *South African Archaeological Bulletin* 34:50–51.

Sassoon, H.
1966.   Engaruka: excavations during 1964. *Azania* 1:79–99.
1968.   Excavation of a burial mound in Ngorongoro crater. *Tanzania Notes and Records* 69:15–32.

Säve-Söderburgh, T.
1941.   *Ägypten und Nubien*. Lund: Holsan Ohlssons.

Saxon, D. E.
1975.   A lexicostatistical classification of the Chadic languages. Unpublished.
1980.   The history of the Shari River Basin, ca. 500 B.C.–1000 A.D. Ph.D. thesis, University of California, Los Angeles.

Schadeberg, T. C.
1980.   *A Survey of Kordofanian*. Vol. 1: *The Heiban Group*. Beiheft zu *Sprache und Geschichte in Afrika* 1. Hamburg: Buske.

Schmidt, P. R.
1975.   A new look at interpretations of the Early Iron Age in East Africa. *History in Africa* 2:127–136.
1978.   *Historical Archaeology: A Structural Approach to an African Culture*. Westport, CT: Greenwood Press.

Schofield, J. F.
1948.   Primitive pottery. Southern African Archaeological Handbook Series, 3.

Shaw, C. T.
1944.   Report on excavations carried out in the cave known as Bosumpra at Abetifi, Kwahu, Gold Coast Colony. *Proceedings of the Prehistoric Society* 10:1–67.
1978–1979   Holocene adaptations in West Africa: the Late Stone Age. *Early Man News* 3/4:51–82.

Shinnie, P. L.
1955.   The fall of Meroe. *Kush* 3:82–85.
1967.   *Meroe*. New York: Praeger.
1974.   Multilingualism in medieval Nubia. In A. M. Abdulla, ed., *Studies in Ancient Languages of the Sudan*. University of Khartoum, Institute of African and Asian Studies, Sudan Studies Library, 3. Pp. 41–47.

Siiriäinen, A.
1971.   The Iron Age site at Gatung'ang'a, central Kenya. *Azania* 6:199–232.
1977.   Later Stone Age investigation in the Laikipia highlands, Kenya: a preliminary report. *Azania* 12:161–186.

Skeat, T. C.
1977.   A letter from the king of the Blemmyes to the king of the Noubades. *Journal of Egyptian Archaeology* 63:159–170.

Smith, A. B.
1975.   Radiocarbon dates from Bosumpra Cave, Abetifi, Ghana. *Proceedings of the Prehistoric Society* 41:179–182.
Smolla, G.
1956.   Prähistorische Keramik aus Ostafrika. *Tribus* 6:35–64.
Snedecor, G., and W. Cochran
1967.   *Statistical Methods*. Ames: Iowa State University Press.
Snyder, R.
1968.   Reproduction and population pressure. In E. Stellar and J. Sprague, eds., *Progress in Physiological Psychology*. New York: Academic Press. Vol. 2.
Soper, R. C.
1967a.   Kwale: an Early Iron Age site in south-eastern Kenya. *Azania* 2:1–17.
1967b.   Iron Age sites in north-eastern Tanzania. *Azania* 2:19–36.
1969.   Radiocarbon dating of "Dimple-Based Ware" in western Kenya. *Azania* 4:148–153.
1971a.   Early Iron Age pottery types from East Africa: comparative analysis. *Azania* 6:39–52.
1971b.   A general review of the Early Iron Age sites in the southern half of Africa. *Azania* 6:5–37.
1971c.   Iron Age archaeological sites in the Chobi sector of Murchison Falls National Park, Uganda. *Azania* 6:53–87.
1971d.   Resemblances between East African Early Iron Age pottery and recent vessels from the northeastern Congo. *Azania* 6:233–241.
1976.   Archaeological sites in the Chyulu Hills, Kenya. *Azania* 11:83–116.
1979a.   Cord rouletted pottery. *Nyame Akuma* 15:9–12.
1979b.   Iron Age archaeology and traditional history in Embu, Mbeere and Chuka areas of central Kenya. *Azania* 14:31–59.
1980.   Iron Age pottery assemblages from central Kenya. In *Proceedings of the Eighth Panafrican Congress of Prehistory and Quaternary Studies* (Nairobi, 1977).
Soper, R. C., and B. Golden
1969.   An archaeological survey of Mwanza Region, Tanzania. *Azania* 4:15–79.
Spencer, P.
1973.   *Nomads in Alliance: Symbiosis and Growth among the Rendille and Samburu of Kenya*. London: Oxford University Press.
Spiss, C.
1904.   Kingoni and Kisutu. *Mitteilungen des Seminars für orientalische Sprachen* 7(3):270–414.
Stevenson, R. C.
1956.   A survey of the phonetics and grammatical structure of the Nuba Mountain languages. *Afrika und Übersee* 40:73–84.
Stewart, J. M.
1966a.   Akan history: some linguistic evidence. *Ghana Notes and Queries* 9:54–57.

| 1966*b*. | Asante Twi in the Polyglotta Africana. *Sierra Leone Language Review* 5:111–115. |
| 1972. | The languages. In D. Brokensha, ed., *Akwapim Handbook*. Accra: Tema. Pp. 80–90. |

Street, F. A., and A. T. Grove
| 1976. | Environmental and climatic implications of late Quaternary lake-level fluctuations in Africa. *Nature* 261:385–390. |

Strouhal, E.
| 1971. | A contribution to the anthropology of the Nubian X-Group. In *Anthropological Congress Dedicated to Aleš Hrdlicka, Prague, 30th August–5th September, 1969*. Pp. 541–547. |

Sutton, J. E. G.
1964.	A review of the pottery from the Kenya highlands. *South African Archaeological Bulletin* 19:27–35.
1966.	The archaeology and early peoples of the highlands of Kenya and northern Tanzania. *Azania* 1:37–58.
1968.	Archaeological sites in Usandawe. *Azania* 3:167–174.
1971.	The interior of East Africa. In P. L. Shinnie, ed., *The Iron Age in Africa*. Oxford: Clarendon Press. Pp. 142–182.
1972.	New radiocarbon dates for eastern and southern Africa, *Journal of African History* 13:1–24.
1973.	*The Archaeology of the Western Highlands of Kenya*. Nairobi: British Institute in Eastern Africa. Memoir 3.
1974.	The Aquatic civilization of middle Africa. *Journal of African History* 15:527–546.
1978.	Engaruka and its waters. *Azania* 13:37–70.
1979.	Toward a less orthodox history of Hausaland. *Journal of African History* 20:179–201.

Sutton, J. E. G., and A. D. Roberts
| 1968. | Uvinza and its salt industry. *Azania* 3:45–86. |

Talbot, M. R., and G. Delibrias
| 1977. | Holocene variations in the level of Lake Bosumtwi, Ghana. *Nature* 268:722. |

Tew, M.
| 1950. | *Peoples of the Lake Nyasa Region*. London: Oxford University Press. |

Thelwall, R. E. W.
1977.	A note on the Nubian homeland. Unpublished.
1978.	Lexical links between Nubian, Daju and Dinka. In *Études nubiennes*. Cairo: IFAO.
1981.	Lexicostatistical subgrouping and lexical reconstruction of the Daju group. In T. Schadeberg and M. L. Bender, eds., *Nilo-Saharan*. Dordrecht: Foris Publications. Pp. 167–184.

Tigani el Mahi, A.
| 1979. | The influence of man on the ecosystem: a case study, El Kadero and El Zakyab sites, central Sudan. *Nyame Akuma* 14:60–62. |

Titherington, G. W.
  1923.   City mounds in Bahr-el-Ghazal province. *Sudan Notes and Records*
               6:111–112.
Trigger, B. G.
  1964.   Meroitic and Eastern Sudanic: a relationship? *Kush*, 12:188–194.
  1966.   The languages of the northern Sudan: an historical perspective.
               Journal of African History 7:19–25.
  1969.   The social significance of the diadems in the royal tombs at Ballana.
               Journal of Near Eastern Studies 28:255–261.
  1970a.   The cultural ecology of Christian Nubia. In Erich Dinkler, ed.,
               Kunst und Geschichte Nubiens in Christlicher Zeit. Recklinghausen:
               Aurel Bongers. Pp. 347–386.
  1970b.   *The Meroitic Funerary Inscriptions from Arminna West*. Publications of
               the Pennsylvania-Yale Expedition to Egypt, 4.
  1977.   The classification of Meroitic: geographical considerations. In
               Erika Endesfelder, ed., *Ägypten und Kusch*. Akadamie der Wissen-
               schaften der Deutsche Demokratische Republik, Zentralinstitut für
               Alte Geschichte und Archäologie, Schriften zur Geschichte und
               Kultur des Alten Orients, 13. Pp. 421–436.
  1978.   Nubian, Negro, Black, Nilotic? New York: Brooklyn Museum,
               Brooklyn Symposium.
Trimingham, J. S.
  1949.   *Islam in the Sudan*. London: Oxford University Press.
Tucker, A. N.
  1940.   *The Eastern Sudanic Languages*. Vol. 1. London: Oxford University
               Press.
Tucker, A. N., and M. A. Bryan
  1957.   *Linguistic Survey of the Northern Bantu Borderland*. Vol. 4. London:
               International African Institute.
  1966.   *Linguistic Analyses of the Non-Bantu Languages of North-Eastern Africa*.
               London: International African Institute and Oxford University
               Press.
Turner, V. W.
  1954.   *Schism and Continuity in an African Society*. Manchester: Manchester
               University Press.
Twaddle, M.
  1975.   Towards an early history of the East African interior. *History in
               Africa* 2:147–184.
van Dantzig, A.
  1977.   South-western Ghana and the Akan-speaking areas of the Ivory
               Coast: a survey of the historical evidence. In J. Hunwick, ed.,
               *Proceedings of the Seminar on Ghanaian Historiography and Historical
               Research*. Legon Pp. 72–82.
van Noten, F.
  1971.   Excavations at Munyama Cave. *Antiquity* 45-56–58.

1979.   The Early Iron Age in the interlacustrine region: the diffusion of iron technology. *Azania* 14:61–80.

van Zinderen Bakker, E. M., Sr.
1976.   Paleoecological background in connection with the origin of agriculture in Africa. In J. R. Harlan, J. M. J. de Wet, and A. B. L. Stember, eds. *Origins of African Plant Domestication.* The Hague: Mouton. Pp. 43–63.

Vedder, H.
1934.   *Das alte Südwestafrika.* Berlin: Warneck.

Vidal, P.
1969.   *La Civilisation mégalithique de Bouar: Prospections et Fouilles, 1962–1966.* Paris: Firman-Didot Études.

Vossen, R.
1978.   Notes on the territorial history of the Maa-speaking peoples. *Kenya Historical Review* 6.

Wandibba, S.
1980.   The application of attribute analysis to the study of Later Stone Age/Neolithic ceramics in Kenya [summary]. *Proceedings of the Eighth Panafrican Congress of Prehistory and Quaternary Studies* (Nairobi, 1977).

Welmers, W. E.
1958.   The Mande languages. *Georgetown University Monograph Series in Languages and Linguistics* 11. Washington: Georgetown University Press. Pp. 9–24.

Were, G. S.
1974.   The Western Bantu peoples from 1300 to 1800. In B. A. Ogot, ed., *Zamani: A Survey of East African History.* Nairobi: Longmans and East African Publishing House.

Westcott, R. W.
1961.   Ancient Egypt and modern Africa. *Journal of African History* 2:311–321.

Westermann, D.
1911.   *Die Sudansprachen: eine sprachvergleichende Studie.* Hamburg: L. Friederichsen.

1927.   Die westlichen Sudansprachen und ihre Beziehungen zum Bantu. *Mitteilungen des Seminars für Orientalische Sprachen* 30: Beiheft.

Westphal, E. O. J.
1965.   Linguistic research in S. W. A. In *Die ethnischen Gruppen in Südwestafrika.* Windhoek: South West Africa Scientific Society. Pp. 125–144.

Whiteley, W. H.
1974.   *Language in Kenya.* London: Oxford University Press.

Wickens, G. L.
1975.   Changes in the climate and vegetation of the Sudan since 20,000 B.P. *Boisseria* 24:43–65.

Wilks, I.
1962.   The Mande loan element in Twi. *Ghana Notes and Queries* 4:26–28.

Williamson, K.
1970.   Some food plant names in the Niger Delta. *International Journal of American Linguistics* 33:156–167.
Wilson, L. E.
1980.   The evolution of Krobo society: a history from c. 1400–1892. Ph.D. thesis, University of California, Los Angeles.
Woodell, S. R. J., and L. E. Newton
1975.   A standard-winged night-jar breeding in the forest zone of Ghana. *Nigeria Field* 40:169–171.
Wrigley, C. C.
1960.   Speculations on the economic prehistory of Africa. *Journal of African History* 1:189–203.
1962.   Linguistic clues to African history. *Journal of African History* 3:269–272.
York, R. N.
1973.   Excavations at New Buipe. *West African Journal of Archaeology* 3:1–189.
Zyhlarz, E.
1928.   Zur Stellung des Dārfūr-Nubischen. *Wiener Zeitschrift für die Kunde des Morgenlandes* 35:84–123.

Index

Note: Index prepared by Candice L. Goucher